When I Was a Child

When I Was a Child

Children's Interpretations of First Communion

SUSAN RIDGELY BALES

The University of North Carolina Press   Chapel Hill

© 2005 The University of North Carolina Press
All rights reserved
Manufactured in the United States of America
Set in Arnhem and Quadraat Sans
by Tseng Information Systems, Inc.
The paper in this book meets the guidelines for
permanence and durability of the Committee on
Production Guidelines for Book Longevity of the
Council on Library Resources.

Library of Congress
Cataloging-in-Publication Data
Bales, Susan Ridgely.
When I was a child : children's interpretations of
First Communion / Susan Ridgely Bales.
   p. cm.
Includes bibliographical references and index.
ISBN 0-8078-2971-4 (cloth : alk. paper) —
ISBN 0-8078-5633-9 (pbk. : alk. paper)
1. First communion. 2. Lord's Supper—Child
participation. I. Title.
BX2237.B34 2005
264'.02036—dc22   2005008000

cloth   09 08 07 06 05   5 4 3 2 1
paper   09 08 07 06 05   5 4 3 2 1

To my teachers young and old,

especially my parents,

Jane Black Bales and John F. Bales III

When I was a child, I spoke like a child,

I thought like a child, I reasoned like a child;

when I became an adult, I put an end to

childish ways.

—*1 Corinthians 13:11*

contents

figures

acknowledgments

Throughout the course of this project I have received more help and support than I ever thought possible. First and foremost, I thank the communicants, catechists, parents, and priests at Holy Cross and Blessed Sacrament for allowing me to share their First Communion with them. Their friendliness, honesty, and sincerity helped me immensely. Although I cannot thank everyone by name, I would like to express my deepest gratitude to Father David Barry, Ms. Carla Wright-Jukes, and Mr. Cedric Thomas, who welcomed me (and my green notebook) each Sunday at Holy Cross with humor and smiles. Father Briant Cullinane, Mr. John Dwyer, Ms. Ann Fabuel, Ms. Anne Fister, Ms. Minerva Jeffries, Ms. Mary Key, and Ms. Donna Richardson truly made Blessed Sacrament feel like home. I thank them for their openness and their kindness throughout the project. I am especially grateful to Ms. Patricia Matterson for her tireless efforts to help me stay connected to the Latino community at Blessed Sacrament. I greatly appreciate the generosity of both the children and the parents who offered me glimpses of how they understood the Sacrament. I am tremendously grateful to everyone, at both parishes, who read this manuscript in various forms. To participants who may read this in the future, I hope you find yourselves fairly represented in these pages.

Many scholars have assisted me in this study, which emerged during Ann Braude's Women and American Religion senior seminar at Princeton University and took shape in conversations with Leigh Eric Schmidt. First, my adviser, Thomas A. Tweed, helped me see this project through from an idea I had during our first cup of coffee together. Whether over coffee or at a seminar table, he nurtured my ideas, championed my creativity, eased my anxiety, and taught me what it meant to be a mentor. I am indebted to my dissertation committee: Jackson Carroll, Glenn Hinson, Kathleen M.

Joyce, and Laurie F. Maffly-Kipp. Robert A. Orsi pushed me to re-imagine the shape of this project as it developed from an early conference paper into a manuscript. Sarah M. Pike's careful reading and insightful suggestions improved the book immeasurably.

My colleagues at Carleton College, where I enjoyed an Andrew W. Mellon Postdoctoral Fellowship, provided me with a tremendously nurturing environment in which to work through the final revisions. Discussions with the students in my Children and American Religion seminar helped me to refine many of the arguments I present here. I am in awe of the care with which Elaine Maisner, my editor at the University of North Carolina Press, and Nancy Raynor, the copy editor, read and commented on this work. Thank you also to Ruth Homrighaus, who guided me expertly as I struggled to transform the dissertation into a book.

I am grateful for the Jessie B. Dupont Royster Fellowship I received through the Graduate School at the University of North Carolina. It enabled me to have a year to focus solely on writing. A research travel grant from the Cushwa Center for the Study of American Catholicism allowed me to use the vast archives of Notre Dame University to study what catechists hoped to teach First Communicants at various points in American history.

I also want to express my heartfelt gratitude to my friends and colleagues who supported and sustained me from Monday through Saturday, when I was not at Mass or Faith Formation class. L. Stephanie Cobb, Jessica Leiman, and Lynn Neal somehow managed to find a way to mix scholarly critique and friendship in a manner that will forever leave me in awe. My sisters, Patricia Bales Van Buskirk and Elizabeth Bales, and my grandparents, John F. Bales II, Jean Torrence Bales, Branscomb Thomas Black, and Belva McHaney Black, championed all my ideas and kept me going with their tremendous love. Thank you to my running group, particularly Julie Morris and Sallie Whitmore, who listened to every tedious step I took in graduate school as we logged our miles each morning. Their company has meant more to me than they can know. I thank Rachel Baden Herman, Katherine Lonsdale, Bradford Prinzhorn, and Pamela Ryckman for their unwavering support. And I can never express my gratitude enough to my greatest teachers, my parents, John F. Bales III and Jane Black Bales, but this book is a step in that direction.

introduction

Katie sat on the top step of the back staircase at Blessed Sacrament Catholic School, a few feet away from her Faith Formation classroom, talking with me about church, First Communion, and art projects.[1] She chatted with me as easily now as she did when we walked to the Spanish tutorial class each Sunday morning forty-five minutes before the bilingual class began. As we talked, eight-year-old Katie worked diligently on a drawing of her upcoming First Communion. While she colored I asked: "What's your favorite part of Mass?" She leaned over a piece of paper, took a pink crayon from the tattered box next to her, and replied, "When the priest gives out those things." She put her hands to her mouth in a little circle. "I wonder how it will taste. Will it taste like a real body?" As she articulated her interpretation of transubstantiation, her wide eyes and halting style betrayed both her excitement and her concern. This brief conversation with Katie about First Communion illustrates two major themes of this book: first, that children have their own revealing interpretations of the rituals in which they participate which differ from those of adults and, second, that much of the information that they use to develop these understandings comes through their senses—taste, sound, and movement—rather than through classroom lectures and workbook exercises alone.

When I began my research for this book, I never expected to be talking to children about the taste of Jesus' body; I thought our conversations would center on white dresses and parties, as so many adult memories of First Communion do. And, after all, it was seeing my neighbor Natalie's First Communion picture, not the desire to understand the Eucharist, that drew me to this project. Looking at Natalie sitting in her white dress and veil in front of a stained glass window with her white-gloved hands, palms together, in front of her chest, led me to wonder how the little girl frozen in that picture felt about receiving the Sacrament and being posed in such a pious position. To answer the many questions that came to mind when I saw Natalie's picture, I visited libraries and archives. My search through Catholic periodicals and ecclesiastical pronouncements, however, uncovered only unsatisfying official church statements about how the reception of the Eucharist shapes a young Catholic's faith development, as well as a few scholarly studies on the role of the Eucharist as a rite of initiation.

Each year across the United States and around the world, First Communion Masses introduce second-graders such as Katie to the primary ritual of the Roman Catholic Church. According to a Center of Applied Research in the Apostate poll, in 1998 over 14.7 million children, 67 percent of Catholic children in the United States, attended some form of religious education classes.[2] Fifty-two percent of that 67 percent, like Katie, attended parish-based religious development programs. Yet there is almost no record of what these students are actually learning through such lessons. Why, I wondered, were the voices of the primary participants in First Communion, the children, not included in the scholarship? What did this omission say about the academics' understanding of children and the value of children's experiences? Finally, what could scholars learn about the functions and failures of ritual if we allowed the youngest of its participants to speak for themselves?

This last question seemed to visit me daily as I was drinking my coffee, running a trail, or preparing for class. What would children say? Would they, as many of those with whom I shared my interest assumed, simply parrot their instructors' or parents' teachings? Or would their statements reveal that they created their own unique meanings out of their participation in religious rituals, and if so, what would those meanings reveal? To answer these nagging questions of how children interpreted First Communion, I joined the First Communion Faith Formation classes at Holy Cross Catholic Church, an African American Catholic parish in Durham, North Carolina, and at Blessed Sacrament Catholic Church, an Anglo and Latino parish in Burlington, North Carolina.[3] Throughout the course of my ethnographic research, I participated in the

Faith Formation classes each Sunday for the four months leading up to the celebration of the Sacrament at Holy Cross, and I spent eight months at Blessed Sacrament with the children in their joint Anglo and Latino First Communion class. At both parishes I attended rehearsals, retreats, and, of course, the First Communion Masses themselves.

We began from vastly different perspectives: the children as seven- and eight-year-old Catholic boys and girls, and I as a Protestant graduate student. Understandably, each of us interpreted what we heard and saw in different ways. They learned from their teachers, parents, priests, and even me; I learned from everyone. As I participated with the children, my presence also affected what the children learned in ways that I cannot fully know. I asked the children questions that their teachers did not, and I answered their questions as best I could, as we cut out yellow Christmas stars, practiced prescribed ritual gestures, and learned about the transformation of the bread and wine into the body and blood of Christ. As I listened to the children and the adults discuss their understanding of and aims for the celebration, I also realized that for both groups, First Communion consisted of more than the reception of the Sacrament. It included every element of the Faith Development program for First Communion that I attended as well as what the children and parents told me about the many preparations that they did at home. The priest, therefore, did not hand them *the* meaning of First Communion when he put the consecrated Host in their hands for the first time. Rather, throughout the year, the children continued to develop their understanding of the ritual from the material that the adults made available to them through Faith Formation lessons, discussions with parents and friends, television shows, shopping trips, and many other events often too small to notice. Of course, the children's interpretations of this event continue to change — even today after their first participation in the Eucharist, as they are given more information to add to their understanding of this ritual, the Catholic Church, and themselves. In this book, however, I offer a slice of their young religious lives that centers on this rite of initiation. I begin with them as the children receive their first formal introduction to the Church, move through their reception of the Eucharist, and end with their reflections on the event a few months afterward.

Rites of Passage

Immersing myself in this lengthy First Communion process and talking to the many participants—communicants, catechists, parents, and priests—quickly forced me to realize that this rite of initiation was much more complicated than the straightforward pronouncements I had found during my earlier library trips. As anthropologist Arnold Van Gennep explained, rites of passage (of which rites of initiation are one example) "are ceremonies whose essential purpose is to enable the individual to pass from one defined position to another which is equally well defined."[4] While the Church clearly defines the spiritual effects of First Communion, it is less clear how ritual participants comprehend this event and its consequences. If initiation into the Catholic Church is the goal, as the Church states, then this ritual failed for many of the children to varying degrees. On the whole, the children's words and actions demonstrated that they may not have felt connected to the larger Catholic Church after receiving the Sacrament. Most of the children did not return to Faith Formation the next year, nor did they discuss Confirmation, the final rite of initiation. As I listened to the participants I discovered that many of them, both the children and the adults, had other expectations for this rite. Some of these expectations reflected aspects of the Church's objectives, and some did not. Belonging to the Church was not part of what the children counted as important; rather, they constructed their interpretations of the Sacrament around belonging to their parish and coming to know Jesus. Finally, most of the children focused more of their energy on enacting the ritual than on considering their spiritual standing within the universal Catholic Church. This is what one might expect of participants of any age who are faced with performing complicated gestures before an audience.

Analyzing ritual from the participants' perspective places me in conversation with many scholars, beginning with Victor Turner in the 1960s, who developed a theory of performance that sought to shift attention away from textual descriptions of ritual and toward how practitioners perform rituals.[5] By concentrating on ritual as it is practiced, rather than as it is prescribed in texts, scholars from Turner to Ronald L. Grimes have "attempt[ed] to grasp more of the distinctive physical reality of ritual so easily overlooked by more intellectual approaches."[6] These intellectual approaches tended to cause scholars to build their studies of initiation rituals around the rituals' structure — separation, liminality, and reintegration. Originally proposed by Van Gennep in *Rites of Passage*, this three-tiered structure has remained at the forefront of ritual studies since Turner introduced it to America in the 1960s. This template illuminates the functional aspects of First Communion: the children move from their original position of separation from God's table and a lack of knowledge about one of the mysteries of the Catholic faith to a liminal period as they learn about the Church and demonstrate their knowledge of the Church and its symbols and gestures; they are then reintegrated after the ceremony as participants in the major ritual of their faith that unites them with God and all other Catholics past and present. In this sense, First Communion is a rite of passage in which initiates move from one status to another in their religious community. Joined to the Church through Baptism, the children can now unite with God and the Church through the partaking of Jesus' body and blood in the consecrated bread and wine of the Eucharist. But, however helpful this template is as a structural analysis of collective transformation, it fails to attend to individual participants, who remain anonymous, even invisible. Even those who emphasize individual experience do not turn ritual studies from structural analysis to participant experience. In his *Ritual Process*, for instance, Victor Turner spends seventeen pages discussing boys' and girls' puberty rites without including one quotation from a child.[7] In this and other studies on ritual structure, children's bodies, but not their voices, appear in the analyses of religious ceremonies in which children are the primary participants. There is no variation from the official ritual purpose here — variations that become ubiquitous when you watch or talk to the children. Turner's work would disclose no children spitting out the Host, participants saying that their standing within the universal Catholic Church had not changed, or communicants surreptitiously practicing different movements when they are supposed to be praying. Working directly with the First Communicants, however, allowed me to realize that, for the participants, things which seemingly had so little to do with their initiation into the Body of Christ, in many ways, defined it.

Attending to the communicants as individuals with varying opinions and experiences, rather than as a monolithic cohort of initiates, made the importance of the physical and sensory aspects of ritual immediately clear. As ritual studies scholar Catherine Bell demonstrates, focusing on performance suggests "active rather than passive roles for participants who reinterpret the value-laden symbols as they communicate them."[8] The children were constantly practicing, and being reminded to practice, the gestures required to receive the Eucharist—making the sign of the cross, genuflecting before entering the pew, and bowing to the tabernacle before stepping onto the altar. Many of the communicants felt that they had to do these gestures right for Jesus, and others, for their family, who would be watching from the pews. Learning these movements along with the children offered me insight into how the participants related to the adults' attempts to teach them about the rite. And, as we talked about the process, the communicants told me in various ways how they brought together their sensual experiences, intellectual understandings, and personal lives to create their individual interpretations of this ritual.

Conceptions of Childhood

In this book I draw on several kinds of data to demonstrate that the children do, as Bell suggests, actively participate in First Communion: interviews with the children, their drawings, their classroom activities, their gestures, and their behavior during First Communion Mass. While this statement may seem obvious at first, replacing Bell's "participants" with Holy Cross's and Blessed Sacrament's seven- and eight-year-old "communicants" is to many adults —scholars, religious educators, parents, and others—counterintuitive. For it challenges our common social understanding of children as little sponges who passively soak up knowledge and instead states that children are capable of complicated forms of thinking. It forces the reader to see that children do more than repeat adult definitions; they "reinterpret value-laden symbols."

The view that children simply "soak up knowledge" reflects a continuation of John Locke's belief that infants' minds are a blank slate, or tabula rasa, that naturally acquire the sense of morality to which the children are exposed.[9] In this model children become receptacles of the knowledge imparted to them by adults. This perception of children as passive and empty receptacles served to counter the Calvinist belief that children were naturally sinful. Locke's empty child soon took on a distinctly positive spin in the late eighteenth century through the writings of Rousseau and the Romantics. Among other things the Romantic child was naturally innocent and closer to God. For instance, in "Intimations of Immortality" Wordsworth wrote:

Heaven lies about us in our infancy!

. . . .

The Youth, who daily farther from the east
Must travel, still is Nature's Priest,
And by the vision splendid
Is on his way attended;
At length the Man perceives it die away,
And fade into the light of common day.[10]

For the Romantics, children were, as James R. Kincaid argues, "uncorrupted, unsophisticated, unenlightened."[11] Children were reminders of the purity and innocence that adults had left behind as they grew further and further away from God, having become embroiled in the corruption of the world. In the popular imagination, this understanding seemed, in large part, to have replaced theological understandings, like the Catholic Church's perception of children as naturally inclined to sin. By the twenty-first century, however, even within the Church children were more likely, although not always, seen as closer to God, open, and eager to learn than as inclined toward evil. As a result, adults acted as protectors of children's innocence and shapers of their future rather than as bulwarks against the temptations to which children would naturally succumb. Therefore, to analyze children's interpretations of First Communion, I had to understand how the adults thought they were using the ritual to form children's faith as well as the information that adults provided the children in the service of this goal. But at Holy Cross and Blessed Sacrament, I did not find beings you could call "empty" and "passive." On the contrary, they had their own ideas about what they learned in Faith Formation classes and their own ways to make those ideas heard.

As the children with whom I worked asserted their own agency, they, like many other children, continually came up against boundaries imposed by adults, boundaries that shifted only when the child reached a certain age: when the child was developmentally ready. In the twentieth century the passive and innocent child became wrapped in the protective blanket of developmental psychology, which represented children as "people in the making." Developmental psychology naturalizes the common understanding that children are passive travelers propelled on a journey toward maturation, a journey that dictates their intellectual and social as well as biological growth.[12] In this developmental model of the child, as anthropologists Alan Prout and Allison James assert, scholars treat "children's activities . . . as symbolic markers of developmental progress. . . . They are seen to prefigure the child's future participation in the adult world."[13] Similarly, understanding children as innocent adults-in-the-making precludes interpreters, including myself at times, from recognizing moments when children are corrupt or moral or sophisticated, just as it keeps the adults' energies trained on future threats to that innocence. Keeping an eye toward innocence and growth means that scholars' notions about children are always focused on some later developmental stage, making it difficult to assess how children are engaging in the world around them now—or even who they are now.

Within this developmental model, focused as it is on age groups, "the child continues to be realized as an instance of a category," which ignores the significance of children as distinct individuals with experiences all their own.[14] Thus, many researchers' understandings of children revolve around changes in the processes of *how* they think at different ages rather than considering *what* they think. And views of *how* children think commonly presuppose Piaget's universal stage theory of development, which outlines children's capabilities at particular ages.[15] Most religious educational material, for example, relies on Piaget's stages for its structure. Thus, First Communion books are built around the belief that seven- and eight-year-olds think "concretely" rather than "abstractly." While the broad patterns of development might be here, patterns never hold a one-to-one correspondence with individuals. Having children's limitations as the starting point for adults' work necessarily restricts understanding of children's perceptions to a rather narrow set of possibilities. Further, it encourages researchers to label behavior outside a set of possibilities as exceptional and thus beyond the scope of a "normal" child's capabilities.

There is nothing natural, however, about Piaget's categories. Perceptions of children and their limitations change from one culture to another and from one age to the next. Beginning with the art historian Philippe Ariès, many scholars, particularly those in cultural studies, have argued that childhood is not a natural category; rather, like time and gender, it is socially constructed.[16] The twenty-first-century understanding that children are innocents seems like a natural fact, a given, in the West; and Western culture, therefore, treats children as incapable of having their own thoughts or conclusions. The Western characterization of children as innocent implies (almost requires) that adults must protect them. And protection means, in part, that adults must speak for children because they are not informed enough to interpret the world around them.[17] If this is the case, then it is understandable that adults, not children, dictate the meanings of events.[18]

This view of children affects both how adults perceive children and how children understand themselves. First, this view of adults as protectors may be one reason that authors, both scholars and nonscholars, tend to focus on "children of crisis," as psychologist Robert Coles termed them. Adult fascination with youth-at-risk, however, obscures the lived reality of most American children, perhaps fulfilling adults' needs rather than children's.[19] Spotlighting these children, so obviously in need of protection, reaffirms the adult's place within their understanding of the adult/child relationship. Similarly, viewing children as innocent and in need of protection furthers the adult perception that children are vulnerable and unthinking. One Hopi girl whom Coles interviewed, for example, inferred this message of the unthinking child from her teacher's smile: "You kids are cute, but you're dumb. . . . And you're all wrong."[20] This child's understanding of how adults see children like her, young Native Americans, seems to echo the perceptions of many other children regardless of their race. This girl understood that the teacher believed she was dumb and wrong, so she did not answer the teacher's questions, which only reinforced the adult's interpretation of the Hopi girl. In adapting themselves to adults' perceptions and practices, children demonstrate that they internalize the social characterization of "children" into their self-definitions.

As historian Karin Calvert argues, "Every culture defines what it means to be a child, how children should look and act, what is expected of them, and what is considered beyond their capabilities." She goes further to highlight that "older children learn to adapt themselves to the personas encouraged by their society."[21] In her research on children's integrity, childhood studies scholar Priscilla Alderson also found that children were highly affected by adults' perception of them: "Our interviewees illustrated how parents' perceptions of a child's competence affected the children's confidence. It could be argued that children become confident by first being treated as if they are confident."[22] Instead of seeing themselves as people who interpret the world differently from adults, young people are constantly told, "You'll understand when you get older." This statement implies that children do not have the knowledge to form an understanding of events at the moment and simultaneously that any interpretation which they might have developed is unimportant. Therefore, young people often believe that those classified as "children" lack essential knowledge of the world.[23] As I began working with the children in my study, I sought ways to let them know that I believed they were knowledgeable and capable, such as asking them their opinions about the project and how I could make it better as well as having them sign an assent form when they agreed to participate in interviews. In so doing, I hoped to create a situation in which they felt less pressure to act in some prescribed "childish" way. I also hoped this approach would force me to attend to the communicants as I had attended to adult consultants in other ethnographic projects, not as I thought seven-year-olds needed to be approached. Considering these drawbacks of adult-set definitions of children and children's development, I tried to design my research differently. Rather than rely on Piaget, the Catholic Church, or other adults, I tried as much as I could to let the communicants define themselves as artists, athletes, children, nonchildren, happy, angry, or whatever they believed themselves to be during the time we spent together. In so doing, I found that while four-, five-, even ten-year-old children can rarely express themselves with sophistication, they often do have sophisticated interpretations to share. Through this study I hope to demonstrate that all children, the healthy and well-loved as well as the sick and neglected, have important observations to share about their religious lives.

Child-Centered Research

By placing children's reinterpretations of the symbols, gestures, and functions of First Communion at the center of this book, I have tried to shift from the "adultist" perspective (as sociologist Ann Oakley has termed this approach) to a child-centered one.[24] This shift does not mean that I researched only the "children's world," for the children and the adults live together and learn from one another. Thus I could not study children without studying the adults who taught them both at home and at church. What the communicants learned came in large part from the different experiences to which adults exposed them. Therefore, I spend time discussing the Faith Formation lessons and adult attitudes that helped shape the children's understandings of the Sacrament. In so doing I hope both to contextualize the communicants' statements and to demonstrate that they do indeed develop understandings that are distinct from those of their parents and teachers.

From our conversations, I am convinced that Katie and the many other Mexican, white, and African American children with whom I spoke during the past four years had their own important questions about First Communion and their own revealing interpretations that could add to scholars' collective understanding of ritual. In 1990 Coles published *The Spiritual Life of Children* in which he analyzed conversations he had had with children of many faiths during his research for his *Children of Crisis* series, published between 1967 and 1978, and his two other works on children from 1986, *The Moral Life of Children* and *The Political Life of Children*. Here, Coles placed his emphasis "not so much on children as students or practitioners of this or that religion, but on children as soulful in the ways that they themselves reveal."[25] His effort to understand children's religious lives in the children's own words seems to have interested some religious studies scholars to consider how different communities perceive a child's role within them.

Since 1990, a few theologians and religious historians have begun to examine the child's role in different religious traditions. *The Child in Jewish History*, by John Cooper, and *The Child in Christian Thought*, edited by Marcia Bunge, represent two of the most recent works.[26] Only a few works before this time, such as historian Philip Greven's *The Protestant Temperament*, seriously considered the young in a sustained way. Studies of prescriptive literature like Greven's offer scholars interesting insights into how *adults* hope to form children into people who will conform to their community's religious beliefs and social norms. These works rely, however, on adult-authored texts (for example, adults' diaries and memoirs) to reconstruct adults' interpretations of childhood religious experiences. Such studies offer great insight into how adults have thought about children and childhood. But they do not attempt to analyze children's perceptions of what adults have taught them at Sunday schools, temples, and dinner tables. Children, however, are still the "purloined letters" of religious studies: like the key piece of evidence prominently displayed, but completely overlooked, in the Edgar Allan Poe story, children are some of the most obvious participants in religious life as they stand before the congregation during their bar mitzvahs, First Communions, pageants, and choir performances, yet all but a few scholars continue to overlook them.

This hole in the research leaves the impression that scholars assume that children are incapable of thinking seriously about their participation in religious life. Robert Coles, though a psychiatrist, not a religious historian, stands as the one notable exception to this trend. Perhaps scholars of religion assume that adults' perspectives on children accurately reflect children's experiences, or perhaps they have neglected children's feelings about their religious practices in part because they presume that children are too young to understand religious experiences so as to formulate their own interpretations of them. Scholars almost never challenge adult first-person accounts found in dairies and autobiographies before using them to construct arguments about children. By taking the adult narratives at face value, researchers ignore the problems inherent in using memory to reconstruct history. As Kincaid reminded his readers, recollections "are not stored in some computer memory, but mixed together in various parts of the brain, recalled in narrative form and constructed anew each time we summon them. This invented story is 'memory,' always 'fabricated' and not just recalled."[27] Because of the problems of unraveling the different meanings of memory, scholars cannot understand how children interpret religious ritual by examining retrospectively only adults' prescriptions and perceptions. Speaking generally of remembered ritual, Grimes stresses, "Ritual recalled is not identical with ritual performed, ritual experienced, or ritual as prescribed in religious texts."[28] While it is true that scholars cannot get at ritual as it is experienced, it is also true that we must attend to the significance of the distance between rituals as they are written, performed, interpreted, and remembered. One cannot replace the other: a written text cannot equal a ritual performed, and an interpretation of a ritual that occurs while a participant is performing that ritual will differ from that same participant's memory of the event at a different moment in his or her life.

Since adults necessarily reconstruct their childhood faith in light of the intervening years of experience, the passage of time shapes how adults remember their childhoods. These memories, as Oakley argues, are also "filtered through the lens of how we have learnt as adults to think of childhood."[29] Therefore, many of these works that center children's religious lives through adult recollections are really *about* children rather than informed *by* children. The two most commonly used sources to examine children's religious lives — the prescriptive and the autobiographical — seem to support Kincaid's conclusion about the position of children in American society: "What the child *is* matters less than what we *think* it is." [30]

To access children's perceptions, scholars must first gain access to the children — a task that is understandably becoming increasingly difficult within the Catholic Church and in the wider society. From the time when I began my research in 1997 until I concluded it in early 2002, parishes welcomed my interest rather than questioning my intentions. My reception might have been quite different had I attempted to begin this research after the Catholic Church "sexual abuse crisis" of 2002. I continue to wonder whether I would have even been able to do this project given the current climate. If I had been invited into the church, would the children and I have had to talk in the back of their classroom as it bustled with activity, rather than in the privacy of an empty classroom or vestibule? How would this have changed their answers or my perceptions? Although issues of sexual abuse seemed to be far from my consultants' minds when I conducted this research, they may not be far from the reader's mind today. Read in light of the sexual abuse scandals, the parishes' openness and the fact that I spent a great deal of time alone with the children might seem startling. Yet, just as time changes people's interpretations of the past, it also transforms the way readers understand texts. In 1997, when priests, catechists, and parents spoke of the Church as a safe haven for children, they did so without reservation, and I recorded their comments without suspicion. Parish boards, priests, parents, and children welcomed me freely into their First Communion preparation classes. As I participated without restrictions in their preparation for the Sacrament, I came to understand the complexities of the First Communion ritual and the religious life of children in new ways.

Watching the children practice the sign of the cross before First Communion and listening to their exclamations of delight or disappointment over the taste of the Host after Mass emphasized many aspects of ritual that are hidden from those scholars who analyze only prescriptive texts or who focus on rites as they are enacted by ritual experts—be they those who organize the ritual or those who have performed it many times. Letting the children speak for themselves—through their words, drawings, and actions—focused my attention on the importance of rehearsal, the impact of expectations in the interpretation of rituals, and, as Grimes has stressed, the significance of local variations in what are commonly thought of as universal rituals.[31] Working with two very different Catholic parishes highlighted these local differences in terms of region, race, and mission. Most important perhaps, going through First Communion with children at both Holy Cross and Blessed Sacrament allowed me to understand that often some of the greatest variations in how groups perceive and enact a particular prescribed ritual come not from contrasting the practices of different parishes but from comparing various generations' understandings of those practices. For the interpretations of these communicants had more in common with those of the children in the other parish than they did with the interpretations of their parents, priests, or catechists. Analyzing the perceptions of First Communion expressed by the communicants in these two distinct parishes demonstrates that age is a significant factor in how participants interpret their religious experiences, a factor that scholars must consider if they wish to understand a ritual fully, how it is taught to its participants, how the participants learn it, and how the communicants comprehend their role in it.

In four thematic chapters in this book, I explore the children's understandings of First Communion and how those interpretations both reflect and reimagine what adults teach them about the ritual. Chapter 1, "Children Seen and Heard: First Communion Celebrations," introduces the event that both the children and I began Faith Development hoping to find out more about. Here I provide a detailed description of the three different First Communion liturgies in which the children participated. This discussion highlights the unique position of southern Catholic parishes and ways in which each celebration reinforced the distinctive identities of these three congregations: Holy Cross's African American parish,

Blessed Sacrament's Euro-American parishioners, and Blessed Sacrament's Hispanic congregation. I conclude with a brief overview of Catholicism in North Carolina that explains why I chose to study these parishes.

Chapter 2, "Drawing, Playing, Listening: A Method for Studying Children's Interpretations," takes a closer look at how I came to understand these celebrations. Here, I offer an account of the methodology that I brought together from different approaches used in anthropology, psychology, and sociology, as well as from situations that emerged from my own interactions with children. In particular, I recount how I came to work with each of the parishes, built relationships with the children and adults, and employed multiple techniques to help the children express their beliefs, values, and feelings about First Communion. In Chapter 3, "Learning the Mysteries of the Church," I apply the previously described methodology to the children's First Communion preparation. This chapter attends most specifically to how both the children and the adults view the Sacrament as having the potential, which it sometimes fails to meet, to unite the communicants with the Catholic Church and to cement their own parish identity. Finally, in Chapter 4, "Connecting to Parish and Family," I investigate the communicants' understandings of the Eucharist's effects on some of their most important relationships. Rather than examine how the Eucharist invites all communicants to belong to the Church in a new way, I focus here on how the rite celebrates the change in each child's status in the Church as it simultaneously brings about that change in the communicants' attitudes toward their place in their parish.

Throughout this book, I explore the adults' efforts to teach the children that First Communion is a rite of initiation which allows each person who participates in it to sit at the altar table with fellow Catholics, especially with family and parishioners; I will also demonstrate that the children perceived it as an opportunity to be seen as individually important and capable by the adults around them and by Jesus, who watched over them. Through First Communion, children came to see their roles in the parish, in their families, and in the eyes of God differently, just as they hoped that the adults around them would perceive them as worthy of their new status.

Examining the degree to which the children and the adults valued these two levels of transformation—the group and the individual—reveals that the communicants saw themselves as outsiders in their parish before the Eucharist, whereas the adults simply saw them as children. Further, while the adults centered the children's reception of Communion as the moment of initiation, the children understood initiation as a much more complicated process. Bringing these many voices together clearly demonstrates that although the two generations seemed to agree on certain more universal aspects of the ritual, each interpreted the specific knowledge the children received differently. But before I can explore the complexities of the children's and the adults' interpretations, I turn to the Eucharistic celebrations that were the focus of everyone's efforts and excitement.

children seen and heard

> *All during the Mass, we prepare our hearts to welcome Jesus,*
> *who comes to us in Holy Communion. When Communion time*
> *comes, the priest or Eucharistic minister holds the Host up to each*
> *of us and says, "The body of Christ." . . . After we receive Jesus in*
> *Holy Communion, we return to our places to pray and sing. The*
> *word Communion means that we are united with Jesus Christ*
> *and one another.* —Coming to Jesus (1999)

Blessed Sacrament's textbook, *Coming to Jesus*, from Sadlier's Coming to Faith Series, tells children what to expect during their First Communion. In just a few sentences, the children learn what they should do during Mass—prepare their hearts, pray, sing —and the result of receiving the Sacrament—it connects the children with Jesus and fellow Catholics. As the children would soon learn, however, First Communion encompasses much more than this generalization reveals. It is a rich, complicated, and dynamic ritual that has the potential to do more than unite the children with Jesus and the Church. In the children's First Communion Mass, they would dance, present the offering, and speak before the congregation. And in so doing they would enact and help shape their parish's ethnic heritage as well as its Catholic traditions. The usual descriptions erase these aspects of heritage and action. They focus instead on the uniform structure of the ritual and its intended universal result. This focus both flattens the ritual and assumes that it will succeed in bringing the child and the Church together. Though this union may occur on a theological level, it is not necessarily true that every child leaves the altar table feeling connected to the Church. I would have to wait until I talked with the children after their participation in the Eucharist to see if the ritual succeeded in the ways that they were told it would.

Although I could not learn how the Sacrament affected individual children from the liturgies, the ceremonies did offer great insight into the parish's self-understanding. For, in this moment of celebration, both Blessed Sacrament Catholic Church and Holy Cross Catholic Church brought together the characteristics that catechists felt best represented the parish's unique identity. Within these liturgies the parishes signaled their ethnic as well as regional identities. In the South (unlike in most other parts of the country), to be Catholic, let alone an African American or a Hispanic Catholic, is to be suspect. Each of the First Communion Masses, however, demonstrated that regional and ethnic identity were of a piece with their Catholic practices.

I begin this chapter with a description of Holy Cross's First Communion day, a description that raises many themes that I will discuss more fully in the following chapters, such as the children's understanding of gestures, dress, and transubstantiation, the process by which the bread and wine become Jesus' body and blood during the Mass. I follow this description with an analysis of what this liturgy revealed about the parishes' identities and what they hoped to pass on to the communicants.[1] I then follow the same format to examine Blessed Sacrament's bilingual First Communion Mass as well as its supplemental Spanish Mass. From there, I move to a discussion of how these liturgies reinforced the participants' Catholic and parish-specific identities that the adults sought to pass on to the children, paying particular attention to how the history of Catholicism in the South and patterns of migration have shaped these identities.

Holy Cross's First Communion

As I opened the door to the Activity Center just before 9:30 A.M. on a rainy First Communion Saturday, I could see Ryan, who was standing just inside the door, greeting his friend Michael with a big hug, exclaiming, "Today is the big day." When I walked in the building, near to where Cara's mother was fixing Cara's makeup, I quickly became aware that First Communion preparations were well under way. The boys had gathered in one classroom where some of them were dancing, others were drawing on the blackboard, and still others were checking to make sure everyone's tie was hanging correctly. Meanwhile, the girls wandered up and down the hallway showing off their dresses, adjusting their veils, and offering each other good luck.

Soon, however, the rain had stopped, so Mr. Thomas, a catechist and the parent of a communicant, took the class outside and lined the communicants up for their procession into the church. As the class made its final preparations, I hurried over to the church. Family and friends already crowded the sanctuary. I found my place next to Ms. Williams, the assistant catechist, on a folding chair in front of the first pew on the right side of the room. From here I watched two African American communicants, Cara and John, who had entered the church through a side door, talking with each other as they waited to begin the welcome dance. The drumbeat started, and the chorus began singing in a mix of Swahili and English, "Funga la fia. Ashé, ashé," to which the children answered, "Funga la fia. We welcome you, Funga la fia. Ashé ashé," in a traditional African call-and-response pattern. Then John, Cara, and Ezekiel, who was too far back in the wings for me to see him before Mass, moved out from the wings on the right, sashaying toward the center of the church as they brought their arms out to their sides and in close to their bodies, matching the movement of their feet. At the center aisle, they met the three children who had begun the dance from the left-hand side of the altar, and together they danced up and down the aisle. The congregation began to clap in time to the drum, a beat that Ms. Michael, an African American dancer and lifetime member of Holy Cross, played at the front of the sanctuary. This dance simultaneously announced the start of the First Communion celebration and the parish's African American heritage. Once these dancers reached their pews, the rest of their class, which had been waiting in the vestibule at the back of the church, proceeded two by two down the aisle to the drumbeat. They marched behind the 1997 First Communion banner, which was emblazoned with Jesus

FIGURE 1. *Holy Cross's 1997 First Communion banner*

standing in the middle of his sheep—pink, orange, and blue—with one sheep for each child (Figure 1).[2] The banner reflected the theme for this year's Communion class: "The sheep hear his voice, and he calls them by name" (Jn 10:3).[3] The children found their families' pews and sat at the end closest to the center aisle. As Father David E. Barry, S.J., began the Mass, I turned to look at the children sitting in the first few pews behind me. Many of them had begun sucking or biting on their fingers by the end of the first reading. Halfway through the second reading, the communicants began shifting in their seats. As the murmur from the children quieted, Father Barry, who now stood at the lectern, began reading from the Gospel according to John, which he followed with a homily that recounted his visit to a sheep ranch. He said, "It was during that time that I finally understood what John was writing about in this Gospel. There were more sheep than there are people in New York City. . . . When it came the time for the shearing, that's when I noticed that when each shepherd called out the word, those sheep who were all mixed together recognized his voice. . . . And all those particular sheep separated themselves from the other sheep and found their shepherd, . . . which brings us to the point. We hear Jesus say to us, 'Listen to my voice. . . . If you belong to me you will only listen to my voice. You will only follow me.' And this is what the good shepherd says, 'I love you. I need you. I want you.' And he says that to you constantly day in and day out."[4] The congregation then said, "Amen." However, I did not hear any of the communicants' voices, perhaps because they did not know when to speak, or perhaps because their minds were focused on the impending Sacrament.

After the prayers of petition, which the children had written themselves to thank their teachers, godparents, and God, the congregation sat while Ms. Smith, the African American woman who heads the gospel choir, played the opening bars of the gospel hymn "I'm in Love with Jesus Christ" on the electric piano.[5] One by one, parishioners began to clap until almost the entire congregation marked the beat together. When the music began, the stilted quality of the Mass disappeared, replaced by the usual comfort, rhythm, and fullness of Holy Cross's 9:00 A.M. Mass. "My First Communion was nothing like this," remarked one communicant's godmother, a white woman who flew in from Maryland for the event and sat in the pew directly behind me. Perhaps she was commenting on the more stereotypically Protestant style of the gospel music, the children's African dance, or the congregation's clapping. The soloist's voice grew in intensity, signaling the hymn's end. At this cue, Father Barry went to the front of the church. Simultaneously, four communicants and the altar servers headed down the aisle, bringing the gifts to the priest. The ruffling of dresses as the girls shifted in their seats and the general sense of movement in the church indicated the increasing excitement, as Father washed his hands with the holy water. From the children's surreptitious attempts to practice performing the sign of the cross and making "thrones for Jesus," it appeared that while they were trying to seem as if they were paying attention, they were anxiously anticipating receiving the bread and wine. (The sense of anticipation, I would learn, had a great influence on their interpretation of the Sacrament.) First, however, Father Barry had to consecrate the Eucharist, or as the children had learned in their classes, he had to bless the bread and wine, transforming them into the body and blood of Christ.

The recitation of the Our Father was the only part of the liturgy of the Eucharist that broke through these last-minute preparations and successfully encouraged the communicants to participate in the Mass. Now everyone in the pews held each other's hands saying the Lord's Prayer, "Our Father, who art in heaven," in an unbroken chain throughout the church.[6] When each person let go of his or her neighbors' hands, the congregation shared the Kiss of Peace. At this point most people left the pews to give hugs and kisses to their friends and neighbors (as they did each Sunday) and to wish the children congratulations. They offered signs of peace to those whom they could not reach, especially those in the balcony with the choir. Soon the piano music let the congregation know that it was time to return to their seats.

The boys in their white shirts and red ties and the girls in their white Communion dresses watched intently as Father Barry lifted the Host before the congregation. Again, the rustle of lace attracted my attention, and I turned to see Maureen, one of two white communicants, with short brown hair pulled back by a white headband, scooting to the edge of her pew as she sucked on her thumb. Since she sat in the first pew, Maureen would be the first one to receive the Sacrament. She looked over to her mother and her godparents for reassurance as the priest offered Communion to the two altar girls who stood on either side of him. The choir began to hum a gospel hymn, and a ripple of energy moved through the church. The 1997 First Communion class at Holy Cross was about to receive the Eucharist. Maureen's godfather signaled that the time had finally arrived. After Maureen had watched the congregation receive Communion countless times in the last seven years, her turn had come at last. She slowly rose to her feet, holding her palms together in front of the white sash that defined her waist. With her godfather's hand on her shoulder, Maureen walked anxiously toward the priest, whose white vestments of celebration had replaced the green worn on ordinary Sundays. "The body of Christ," he said, as he placed the consecrated Host in her hand. She put the Host into her mouth and then slowly walked to Ms. Hudson, the director of religious education, who held the chalice full of wine. Maureen sipped the wine. She performed the sign of the cross and returned to her pew, where she knelt and said her prayer of thanksgiving as Father Barry held aloft the consecrated bread that Maureen's classmate Matt, a Filipino with short black hair, had also waited so long to taste. With each step down the aisle, Matt's excitement (and self-consciousness) seemed to increase, for he knew that everyone was watching only him. With wide eyes and an anxious smile, he walked stiffly to the priest. His shoulders relaxed and his smile broadened as Father Barry placed the Host in his hands. As Matt put the Host in his mouth, the clicks of picture taking were emphasized by the burst of a flash, just as they were for each communicant.

I looked at Matt's face as I would look at those of his nineteen classmates as they received their first taste of the Sacrament. When the communicants reached the altar their usual smiles left their faces, replaced by serious expressions that remained as they placed the Host in their mouths. Those communicants who remembered crossed themselves as they shifted over to Ms. Hudson, who offered them the wine (Figure 2). Others bowed, and still a third group forgot to make any motion and just stepped quietly to the right. Standing in front of Ms. Hudson, they carefully took the cup. They became a bit shakier as the tart wine touched their lips. Many of them scrunched up their faces as if they had just bitten into a lemon. Some of the children recovered from the taste and burst into big grins as they returned to their seats. Others returned to their pews with puckered faces, eliciting laughter from the congregation.

Once the communicants and the other eligible Catholics in the congregation had received the Eucharist, Father Barry returned to the front of the church. He stood by the paschal, or Easter, candle and said: "The second sacrament of initiation is First Communion. So we return to that great symbol of lighting the candle for the light of the world, using the Easter candle, which is the light of Christ and the light of the world." Father Barry then moved behind the

FIGURE 2. *A First Communicant receives the Eucharist*

lectern and the Easter candle as the children walked one by one with their godparents to light their candles. The soloist began an impassioned rendition of "Jesus, You're the Center of My Joy," as Maureen's godmother lit Maureen's First Communion candle from the Easter candle and then handed it to her goddaughter. Her classmates followed, having their candles lit by their godparents and taking their places on the dais. With candles in hand, the children then lined up for a final picture with their godparents and Father Barry behind them. After the congregation took what the communicants believed were "too many pictures," the children blew out their candles, and to the hymn "I Just Want to Thank You, Lord," they moved back down the aisle in haphazardly assembled pairs that quickly formed a mass in the middle of the aisle, unlike the two straight lines by which they had entered the sanctuary.

After the children proceeded out of the church, everyone headed to the Activity Center. Walking into the downstairs meeting room, I heard Julie, a shy blonde white girl, describing her dress to Father Barry. "It's a bridesmaid's dress really," she explained. Father Barry replied, "You're like the bride of Christ now." Julie had no reaction to this comment, if she even heard it, which did not surprise me, since none of the teachers or parents ever mentioned that the communicants might become brides of Christ. However, this comment turned my attention to the power of dress. Although Julie did not explicitly make the connection between her dress and being a bride, Father Barry's comment emphasized that there was a relationship that many adults recognized between this dress and the bridal gown Julie might wear someday. While I pondered the dress's symbolism, Julie spun around in circles watching the dress's skirt puff out around her (an activity I remembered well from my own girlhood).

Listening to the conversations as I walked through the room, I headed to the kitchen to help the older women of the parish fix the plates for lunch. Each plate displayed the feast of a true southern celebration, marked most clearly by the presence of congealed salad. Each plate held a square of red Jell-O salad centered on a lettuce leaf, candied yams, wild rice, turkey, and gravy. Each person also received a piece of sheet cake, which had been decorated with a Bible and a scroll.

Once everyone had been served, I carried my plate out of the kitchen and found a seat with Ms. Wright-Jukes, the lead catechist, her parents, and her son, a First Communicant. Before long, Father Barry joined us too. He quickly confessed that he had never seen a sheep or a sheep farm, despite the claims he made in his homily. I was shocked and a little saddened by the confession. No one else seemed bothered, although they were all somewhat surprised. We lingered together a long time. By the time we got over our surprise and finished laughing, we were the only people left in the room. Everyone else had probably gone to their own family celebrations. I walked out to the parking lot thinking about how the communicants would later interpret this experience. I would soon learn some of the children's perspectives in Faith Formation class the next week and later in follow-up interviews.

An Analysis of "the Big Day"

As the primary participants in this ceremony, the children learned aspects of Holy Cross's identity that they could not learn solely from textbooks and teachers. Artifacts, food, music, dance, dress, gestures—all conspired to enrich the children's experience and convey crucial messages about their Catholic identity.[7] At Holy Cross, food marks every occasion; many of the parishioners referred to the church as the "eatingest church around." The parish holds monthly parish brunches, for instance, where Holy Crossers pile their plates with French toast, sausage, fried chicken, and fruit. This practice reflects both Holy Cross's location in the Protestant Bible Belt and its African American heritage. Jualynne E. Dodson and Cheryl Townsend Gilkes have argued, for instance, that "African American church members in the United States feed one another's bodies as they feed their spirits. . . . In the process, an ethic of love and an emphasis on hospitality emerge, especially in sharing food, which spills over into the larger culture."[8] With this meal, then, the Holy Cross community fed the children's bodies and their spirits just as the Eucharistic meal had fed their souls. This meal, like the one before it, helped to bind together the children, their families, friends, and fellow parishioners, for this traditional southern Sunday dinner was served after First Communion to everyone who chose to stay after the Mass. With this show of southern and African American hospitality, Holy Cross reinforced and helped to create the welcoming and nurturing spirit that they held as a hallmark of the parish.

Teaching the children Swahili and the movements of African dance told them that the parish took its African roots seriously. The children seemed to connect with the dancing, although they did not put their feelings in ethnic terms. Instead, some children, like Sarah, said that they "liked the dancers" because they were "cool," while others appreciated it for being something other than just praying.[9] Similarly, inviting the gospel choir to sing at this most important Catholic celebration demonstrated that African American culture and Catholic ritual could blend harmoniously in worship, although this blending did not suit everyone, as I will discuss below. Finally, and perhaps most important, by following the unspoken weekly Our Father protocol with the handholding, kissing, and hugging of the Kiss of Peace, the liturgy provided a space to express to the children that they belonged to Holy Cross and the larger Catholic family. Going through First Communion with their godparents and receiving the First Communion candle from the older generation also helped to reinforce the congregation's focus on community and continuity. Yet, simultaneously, creating a banner on which each child had his or her own sheep emphasized the individual importance of each parishioner in the flock. This theme was so important that Father Barry in his homily felt the need to invent his personal experience with the shearing of sheep to emphasize it. Woven seamlessly into the liturgy, these African American and community-focused practices and artifacts seemed to reflect and shape Holy Cross's First Communicants' interpretations of First Communion. These characteristics were very different from those expressed in Blessed Sacrament's bilingual First Communion liturgy, in which the catechists hoped to honor the talents of its Spanish- and English-speaking parishioners.

Blessed Sacrament's Bilingual Liturgy

Kim still seemed hesitant about where she was supposed to stand—was she in the right-hand line or the left-hand line? Unsure, she was standing in the middle of two rows of children ranging in age from seven to fifteen, some talking to each other, some practicing the sign of the cross, and some focused, staring straight ahead. I watched Kim and a few other children try to find their place in line as I hurried past them on my way to the sanctuary. "Remember to walk slowly," I heard Ms. Fabuel, the head catechist, remind the children as I opened the sanctuary door. As I stepped in, the sounds of the organ and whispers replaced the children's voices and giggles that I was certain were continuing outside. I walked down the red-carpeted aisle and sat down with the Staples family as the piano player began the processional. Two lines of approximately twenty-five children each from the Faith Formation classes, the parish school, and the Hispanic ministry walked slowly into the sanctuary. As I was saying "thank you" to Mr. Staples for allowing me to join his family, Ms. Tackitt, Blessed Sacrament's religion teacher and vice-principal, and Ms. Jeffries, the bilingual catechist, welcomed the congregation (in English and Spanish, respectively) to the bilingual First Communion. After the introduction, the children walked two by two down the center aisle to their seats. Ms. Fabuel and Ms. Tackitt stood at the end of the pews, making sure that the communicants either bowed or genuflected as they entered the rows.[10]

Once everyone had entered the pews, the children sat, and Ms. Fabuel brought those who were to "dress" the altar back to the other end of the aisle, while Ms. Tackitt took the readers over near the lectern. As the ceremony began, one child at a time brought down objects—a textbook, a ring from First Reconciliation, a stole, and more—to symbolize what the class had learned throughout the year, as one of their classmates read a short description of each object to the congregation. Once the altar was "dressed," the priests and altar servers processed to the front of the church. Father Briant, in a cream and gold robe, welcomed the congregation. The children sat together as a class in the first four rows of the sanctuary. They faced forward and remained relatively still as they listened to their classmates recite the first and second Gospel readings, alternating English and Spanish, from the lectern. Although some communicants in the pews paged through the program, they did so quietly, while their classmates listened, daydreamed, or worried. Having the children read from the lectern seemed to reinforce one of the teachers' primary principles: to get something out of the Mass, the children had to participate in it.

The participation they had been anticipating for so long, however, would have to wait until after the Gospel reading and the homily. For the Gospel reading, Father Bob, the associate pastor, recounted the Emmaus story in Spanish, telling the congregation that the apostles recognized the risen Christ only after he gave them blessed bread. Father Briant then recounted this same long Gospel in English. As the priests read, some communicants looked around for their parents, while others started putting their feet up on the pews in front of them. When he finished the Gospel, Father Briant regained the children's attention by beginning his homily, asking what the rule was for the day. Most of the communicants answered loudly, "Relax." Father Briant then reminded them of what he had told them before Mass: "I am going to ask you some questions, but you only have to answer them if you feel like it." He continued: "What is the oldest story?" No one raised his or her hand, so he told the group that it was Genesis, the story of when God created the world. "First, God made light, then the sky." Father Briant asked, "What did God put in the sky?" "Stars," one child said. "Birds," added another. "Meteors," answered a third. Looking out over the three pews of children, all in white dresses or khaki pants, Father Briant continued with the story, going through each day of creation with the children until he took a long pause on the day when God made men and women: "So God made people," Father continued, "and then we screwed it all up with sin. Where there was life, we made death, and where there was joy, we made sorrow. So what did God do? He sent us Jesus, who gave us back life. And what did Jesus do for us?" One communicant answered, "He gave us his body and blood." "Right," Father Briant responded. Then he went on to talk of his own First Communion: "My parents once said to me that this was the happiest day of my life. I thought that the happiest day was the day I got another train, but they said it was my First Communion. As I got older I began to see that they were right because that . . . was the day I got to become one with Jesus in a real way. Today Jesus makes a home in you, so that one day you will be able to make your home in him. God bless you." Here Father Briant emphasized the importance of the children's union with Christ and the adult desire that this rite be but one step in their faith development.[11]

As he talked, however, the children in the pews became increasingly antsy, while other First Communicants waited at the top of the aisle to bring down the gifts for the offering. Soon, these communicants did the presentation of the gifts. One group read as the other group brought down the books, wine, grapes, and wheat. We sang "Pescador" followed by "Here I Am, Lord" from the church missalette, while the three parish priests—Father Briant, Father Bob, and Father Terry—prepared the gifts. The excitement mounted as First Communion time drew nearer. Although the communicants were still quiet, there was more shifting and a few additional efforts to make eye contact with family.

After the Our Father, Father Briant offered Communion to the Eucharistic ministers. Once they had received the Sacrament, the Eucharistic ministers stood on either side of him with the wine, and the photographer focused the camera on the place where the children would receive Communion for the first time. In a few moments, Ms. Matterson, the director of the Hispanic ministry, began calling the communicants' names. The children proceeded to the altar alone. Some of the children seemed nervous, walking with halting steps and eyes focused on the carpet, but others approached the priest with confident gaits and heads held high. Many of them forgot to cross themselves after receiving the Host, but only a few contorted their faces at the taste of the wine, perhaps because they had practiced with the wine in class. Ms. Matterson sometimes had to speak unnaturally slowly so that the photographer could get all the pictures, and once there was a break for him to change film. I watched as Kim and Christy forgot to cross themselves after they received the Host. Their mother, who sat in front of me, noticed this too, commenting to the woman next to her that they would work on that at Mass. A boy from the school seemed to have kept the Host in his cheek upon his return to his pew. It was still clearly visible when he knelt to pray. I wondered if he went home with the Host or, depending on his understanding of transubstantiation, with Jesus in his pocket.

After all the communicants had received the Sacrament, other Catholics came to the altar. They did not go in an orderly fashion, as is customary at the English-language liturgy; they went down randomly, like parishioners often did at the Spanish Mass. After everyone received the Host, the children applauded their parents and teachers for their help. Then the children went to the altar for the closing song. As Ms. Jeffries arranged them for the song, Father Briant told the parents that "just for this once, he would bend the rules and parents could take pictures." Then the children, in four lines on the steps up to altar, began to sing "Shout to the Lord / All the earth let us sing. / Power and majesty / Praise to the king," complete with hand signs taught to them by Ms. Tackitt, who translated

FIGURE 3. *Blessed Sacrament's 2001 First Communion class*

for deaf students in addition to working at the school (Figure 3).[12] The song ended with the children singing the hopeful verse: "Forever I'll love you. / Forever I'll stand / Nothing compares to the promise I have in you." The communicants remained in the front of the church for some last-minute pictures, while many parents wiped tears away from their eyes and made their way back to their seats.

Just before the hasty recessional, Father Briant invited everyone over to the Koury Center, the parish hall located in the old Blessed Sacrament school building across the parking lot from the church, for a celebration. By the time I got into the Koury Center's gymnasium, many of the communicants were leaving with their certificates and First Communion candles in hand. Some communicants remained, however, talking to their families and their teachers. These families sat eating cake at the long white tables with hydrangea centerpieces or took pictures under the flowered arch (which Ms. Key, the director of religious education, had designed) next to the statue of the Virgin Mary. Most parishioners seemed to stay only long enough for a few pictures and a piece of cake. Some parents talked to each other or offered to take another family's picture at the grotto. As I watched the families at the reception, I realized that the unified parish that Blessed Sacrament hoped to create, primarily through its bilingual youth activities, would take many years to come together.

What First Communion Taught

This First Communion at Blessed Sacrament (the Saturday bilingual Mass) displayed the symbols of the parish and, like the one at Holy Cross, worked to promote the children's participation in the Mass. Again, all the elements in the actual performance of the ritual conveyed messages to the children that words alone could not. Yet important differences emerged at Blessed Sacrament. Here, the children read from the lectern, in addition to singing songs and saying prayers as did the children at Holy Cross. Allowing the communicants to read from the altar as they saw the adults do each Sunday marked one of the greatest differences between the children's participation in the First Communion Mass at each parish. By allowing the children to proclaim the Old and New Testament readings, the catechists created a ritual that reflected the children's new ability and a new responsibility to perform adult activities. This tacit acknowledgment of the children's capabilities did not go unnoticed by the participants. After she received her assignment for the First Communion liturgy, Melissa proudly reported that "I get to read first . . . I get to read from the book."[13] Her fellow readers were equally as excited by this opportunity. Whereas those children who brought the gifts to the altar did not mention their jobs, all the readers told their parents, and often me as well, that they had been chosen to perform such an important duty. By offering them opportunities to read before the congregation, a task that only the catechists performed at Holy Cross, the Blessed Sacrament catechists provided the children with a reminder that they were able and important members of the parish community. This reminder of the communicants' valued participation, perhaps, supplemented the handshaking during Blessed Sacrament's exchanging of the peace, which replaced the more demonstrative hugging of Holy Cross' Kiss of Peace.

Blessed Sacrament worked to realize the gifts of all its parishioners (both children and adults) in all aspects of the Mass. First Communion provided an opportunity for each child to participate individually and actively in each part of Mass for the first time, whereas at Holy Cross the adults did the readings, while the children offered prayers and presented the gifts during the Offertory. Consequently, at Holy Cross the children—because they were children—had a reduced role in the ritual. Having both the Latino (primarily Mexican and Mexican American) and the white communicants celebrate the Sacrament together, learning songs and prayers in both languages, seemed to emphasize the importance of the sense of unity that was one of the most important objectives of Blessed Sacrament's emerging identity.

Yet even as Blessed Sacrament hoped to be a multicultural church, the Mexican children participated in a distinctly Euro-American ceremony. For example, although candles are an important part of Hispanic Catholicism, the bilingual mass did not allow lit candles, highlighting the distance between this Mass and one that included Hispanic *culture*, not just its language.[14] This lack of Hispanic culture may have come from the parish's understanding that the Church centered on faith rather than action, as I discuss later in this chapter. Thus, while this approach resulted in a liturgy that privileged Euro-American over Mexican traditions, the sacramental preparation process did, in a limited way, begin to bring the two lines of the congregation, Spanish-speaking and English-speaking, together through the children's activities. The children had been in this bilingual system for their entire tenure at Faith Formation class, so they never commented on the class's structure. The communicants did, however, include both their Mexican and white classmates in our conversations and occasionally in their drawings.

The Latino Communion Celebration

Unlike the Saturday bilingual Mass at Blessed Sacrament, at which the children had bare hands and approached the altar alone, during the Sunday Spanish Mass at Blessed Sacrament the seven (of sixteen) Hispanic children who attended this Mass as well as the bilingual one, along with older Spanish-speaking children who took age-appropriate classes in Spanish to prepare for First Communion, could and did wear their white gloves and approach the altar with their *padrinos* (godparents). Although none of the parishioners mentioned to me that they were troubled about the bilingual Mass, the inclusion of a second "First Communion" Mass began in response to this parish's desire to unite the two parish communities in the liturgy. At this Mass, the Mexican communicants could celebrate the Sacrament with all the Hispanic cultural elements—the inclusion of their padrinos, lit candles, and white gloves for the girls and ribbons for the boys.

When I walked into the vestibule, I saw Carolina and her sister dressed in their First Communion dresses, carrying big white boxes that contained a rosary and a missalette (a small book of Catholic devotional prayers). As I made my way through the crowded vestibule, I noticed that only one boy had a white First Communion ribbon on his sleeve. He had not worn the customary First Communion ribbon at the bilingual Mass the day before, nor did any of the other boys have it on today. Clearly, however, for this little boy and his family, this Spanish Mass offered an opportunity to proudly display his Mexican heritage.

The altar was still set up from the preceding day, so after checking if I could do anything to help Ms. Matterson prepare for Mass, I found a spot in the pew behind Juan's sister, who sat two rows behind the altar servers on the right-hand side of the sanctuary. The church was much more crowded than I had seen it during other Spanish Masses, except for the feast of Our Lady of Guadalupe, the patroness of Mexico. I was surprised that none of the white catechists were there to support the children. Only the Latina catechists came to the celebration.

The Mass began with a gathering hymn, sung with enthusiasm by the whole congregation and accompanied by the piano and bells. As everyone sang, the children dressed in their traditional attire, including appliqués of Our Lady of Guadalupe on the girls' skirts, processed into the sanctuary, with their padrinos walking behind them, and sat in the first two pews. A guest priest, Father Michael, and the altar servers followed this procession. Once everyone was seated, the Mass began. For the most part, it followed the pace of a Spanish-language weekend Mass. Unlike the bilingual Mass, which the catechists had designed especially for the children, the Sunday Spanish Mass was not geared toward First Communion. Father Michael's homily, for instance, discussed religious vocations (it was vocation Sunday). Furthermore, the communicants did not perform the readings or bring the offering to the altar as they had the day before. Overall, the communicants seemed bored: Sergio slept through most of the Mass, or at least his eyes remained closed throughout; Maria and her sister played with their rosaries; the remaining First Communicants amused themselves in other quiet ways. There were so many babies crying and little children talking that Father Michael was continually raising his voice, not only for emphasis but also to be heard over the clamor.

As the time for their second Communion drew nearer, it seemed that the children moved to the edge of their pews, either in anticipation or as preparation for kneeling. When Father Michael was passing Communion to the Eucharistic ministers, the two padrinos who sat in the aisle seat of the first pew behind the children went up and lit their godchildren's First Communion candle from the paschal candle, which symbolizes Christ's resurrection. They then returned to their seats and lit the candles of the godparents who sat next to them. The flame traveled down the line until all the candles had been lit. The lighting of the candle signaled to José, the first child to receive the Eucharist, that he should stand up and walk to the aisle, where he met his padrino. Together, they proceeded to the altar to receive First Communion. Unlike the day before, most of the communicants remembered to cross themselves, one of a few small signs that their anxiety had decreased. I was not sure whether this more relaxed feeling came from their having received the Sacrament the day before or from the reassuring presence of their padrinos at the altar. As the ten communicants, including seven from the Faith Formation class, made their way to the chalice after receiving the Host and back to their pews, I wondered which Mass these seven really considered their First Communion.

If they centered on the bilingual Mass, what would this mean for the continuation of their ethnic traditions? If they focused on this Spanish Mass, what would that say for their relationship with their parish? And, finally, if they blended certain aspects of each celebration into one First Communion memory, what might that blending say about their relationships with their families, their Church, and the effects of Blessed Sacrament's experiment of bringing the two communities together?

As I continued to consider these possibilities, the remaining children received the Eucharist, the padrinos blew out their candles, the priest congratulated the communicants, and the congregation exploded in applause. Then all the worshippers were invited to approach the altar for Communion or a blessing. At the conclusion of the Eucharist and the announcements, the children recessed with their padrinos. The priest and the altar servers followed them. As I exited the sanctuary shortly after the priest, I passed communicants in the vestibule who were holding their rosaries and waiting for their families. Once I made my way outside, I greeted some families who were taking pictures of their children in front of the statue of the Virgin Mary (Figure 4). I also received some *recuerdos* from the children, simple silk ribbons that recorded the place and date of their First Communion. These recuerdos marked an important Hispanic tradition that the adults hoped the children would now associate with First Communion and, perhaps, Catholicism.

Learning from the Spanish Mass

While the Hispanics at Blessed Sacrament spoke of family in Mexico and many girls had the Virgin of Guadalupe embroidered on the front of their First Communion dresses, only some of these children had attended the Spanish Mass to supplement the bilingual celebration of the day before with Mexican traditions and the Latino congregation looking on. This Spanish Mass—from the time when the girls were putting on their gloves to when the girls and boys handed out their recuerdos—taught, reinforced, and announced the children's Hispanic heritage. In contrast, the bilingual Mass emphasized individualism, which may have seemed

FIGURE 4. A boy poses with a statue of the Virgin Mary after the Spanish First Communion

Euro-American to many Spanish-speaking participants and their parents, who traditionally approach the altar with their godparents for First Communion. During the bilingual First Communion, the children at Blessed Sacrament approached the altar alone. The individuality of the Saturday Mass, however, turned on Sunday into a family celebration as the children walked toward the priest with their godparents behind them. Further, the family was extended to the entire parish as the children handed out their recuerdos, inviting everyone into their personal celebrations and bringing that celebration home with them. Although this Mass did not have the formality of the Saturday Mass and although it did not have the pastor presiding, it did aim to connect the children to the Hispanic congregation, their heritage, and their Church. In these important respects, this Sunday Mass and the celebration that followed shared more of the characteristics of Holy Cross's First Communion liturgy.

Like Holy Cross, this Mass also included candles, which the bilingual one did not. In the fall of 2000, Blessed Sacrament had ruled that no one could light candles in the church, citing fire concerns. This ruling upset many in the Latino congregation who had been carrying on their premigration tradition of lighting candles around the picture of the Virgin of Guadelupe, which is placed on the altar during the Spanish Mass, as well as during their prayers in the sanctuary before and after Mass. Despite the protests, Blessed Sacrament enforced the ruling during ordinary Sundays as well as special celebrations such as First Communion. But at the request of Ms. Matterson, who knew the religious and cultural significance that candles held for this congregation, Father Briant made an exception for the Spanish First Communion Mass.

The candles, as well as the inclusion of padrinos, did set the Spanish Mass apart for at least one of the seven children who attended both Masses. The only child who spoke with me about the Spanish Mass did not interpret this liturgy as a significant event. For José, First Communion was with the entire Faith Formation class on Saturday. When I asked him if he had had another First Communion during the Spanish Mass on Sunday, he replied, "No, we just got to take our Godmother and our Goddad to church. . . .

Our godparents had to take our candle up to light it."[15] Although he did not mark this event as his First Communion, José did seem to note the differences between the two, and throughout our conversation he highlighted the importance of these inclusions in the ceremony. He was "never going to give it [the candle] away," for instance, "because it was light [*sic*] up by the candles that the church has and those candles are blessed by God."[16] The significance of the candle to José may have reflected the importance that his family placed on candles in their own religious devotions. Wherever his understanding came from, for José it seemed that the Spanish Mass allowed him to take God's blessing home with him, not only through the Eucharist, as the previous day's celebration had, but also through an object that served as a significant cultural marker for many of the adult Latinos in the parish.[17] This Mass, however José defined it, reinforced the importance of ritual objects and their significance to the culture of his congregation; it also connected him to his congregation and the Church in a tangible way. That kind of connection, both cultural and congregational, seemed to be the goal of each of the three liturgies.

Performing Heritage and Joining Parishes

These liturgies clearly expressed the adults' desire to continue their Mexican, African American, and southern Euro-American traditions and to educate the children about their own family's heritage. As sociologists Helen Rose Ebagh and Janet Saltzman Chaftez explained about immigrant parishes in particular, the parish "provid[ed] the physical and social space in which those who shared the same traditions, customs, and languages [could] reproduce many aspects of their native culture for themselves and attempt to pass it on to their children."[18] As we have seen, the Hispanic congregation of Blessed Sacrament was not the only congregation in this study that needed this space to construct its ethnic heritage. Holy Cross, as an African American Catholic Church, also sought a place to bring together both its African American and its Roman Catholic identities in its parish life. Within these protected parish spaces, traditions, like the festival of Our Lady of Guadalupe or Holy Cross's gospel choir, can become "like the air that is breathed," as historian Dorothy C. Bass described it, "so taken for granted as not to be noticed."[19] The children's lack of discussion about their parish culture seemed to evidence that these parishes achieved this kind of cultural transmission. Elizabeth, for instance, seemed bewildered when I asked her to describe Blessed Sacrament; she replied, "It has Communion and a children's liturgy. . . . And it's really nice." One of Elizabeth's classmates, in response to my question about what made Blessed Sacrament special, said, "It's my church."[20] Similarly, the children at Holy Cross never commented specifically on the character of their parish, and the absence of comments may reveal that the communicants took their parish identity for granted.

Although the children may believe that their parishes have an inherent, unchanging identity, the First Communion liturgies show that parishioners work hard to create and maintain this identity. When those "taken-for-granted" elements are threatened, however, efforts to create or sustain traditions become much more overt. Although the number of Catholics is continually growing in North Carolina, none of these congregations—including Blessed Sacrament's white congregation—can be assured that its children will gain an understanding of themselves as members of their ethnic group, their parish, or their Church. Because they are in the Protestant South, these congregations cannot depend on religious dominance, nor can any but the white members of Blessed Sacrament rely on ethnic advantage to maintain the ethos of their local congregation. And, as I discuss below, given the growth rate of the Hispanic population in North Carolina (more than 500 percent over the last decade), that ethnic advantage for white Catholics may soon diminish drastically or disappear entirely.[21]

Congregations such as those at Holy Cross and Blessed Sacrament must therefore continue to assert their congregational identity, especially in public displays like First Communion celebrations, reminding the participants and their viewers about their ethnic and religious heritage. While the Faith Formation classes taught the communicants about their Catholic faith, the Masses revealed their parish community's unique blend of religious and ethnic heritage. The children learned the character of the parish they were joining, and the parish reaffirmed its identity before all those in attendance. As these seven- and eight-year-olds performed the ceremony of the Sacrament, they gave comfort to their audience that the community would survive another generation.

Catholicism in the Bible Belt

Survival has never been certain for southern Catholics. In the minds of many, to be southern is to be Protestant, thus there is no room for a southern Catholic. In the Northeast and the Midwest, the vast number of Catholics has meant that Catholics had their own social clubs, youth organizations, and neighborhood groups through which to teach young Catholics the value of their Catholic identity. This has not been the case in the South. The children's Catholic identity, many adult parishioners believed, was more at risk in the predominately Protestant Bible Belt than at other places in the United States. Although the children's understanding of their minority religious status revealed itself only in a few comments about not talking to their friends at school about First Communion, this choice, to whatever degree it was conscious, does demonstrate that the communicants realized that their experience was not in the mainstream. When their Protestant friends discuss their baptisms, which usually occur around age twelve or thirteen, the children may become more overtly aware of the difference between themselves and their public school classmates, particularly when those classmates ask whether these young Catholics have been "saved." Then the children would need to know what differentiated them from the southern evangelical mainstream. One pastor at Immaculate Conception, another Catholic church in Durham, who had recently been transferred from New York to North Carolina, explained: "In the North, . . . being a Catholic is somewhat commonplace, you . . . lose your identity because you don't have to think about it—being Catholic. Lots of people are Catholic. You don't have to explain it. But down here lots of people are puzzled about that [and] you are forced to think, well, who are you?"[22] Through the Faith Formation classes and First Communion liturgies, the adults hoped to teach the children that the answer to this question was "Catholic," and they also hoped to teach them what that answer meant, a meaning that varied from person to person and from parish to parish.

In the South (where as recently as 1995 fewer than four in one hundred people were Catholic), passing on Catholic traditions through Faith Formation classes became more important because the children were not going to experience their traditions very often outside their parishes and their homes.[23] Neighborhood activity centered around Protestant organizations. Therefore, rather than being celebrated and supported, Catholics were excluded from much of the customary neighborhood networking and community events. One fifty-year-old Anglo man from a small town in South Carolina described such exclusion this way: "A lot of the social events were routed through the town's churches, and since 99 percent of the churches were Protestant, well, Catholics weren't included."[24] Southern Catholics have always been considered suspect: Catholic children are continually asked if they have been saved and, more pointed, if they are Christian. Further, neighbors look upon Catholic practices, such as saying the rosary and venerating the Virgin Mary, with much suspicion. The diocese with which I worked clearly recognized that this mistrust existed in the wider community and the social pressure it put on their children to behave like the majority. Thus as they taught the children their religious and ethnic heritage, the catechists and parents hoped that they would make the children understand that this heritage was a part of their identity (a part about which they could be proud) and not simply an alternative they could choose. While this attitude toward their Catholic heritage may seem less important today as more and more Catholic migrants have come to North Carolina, it has developed from Catholicism's long history as a minority religion in the South.

In the early nineteenth century, when Irish immigrants to the United States began flooding parishes in the North, the number of Catholics in Georgia and the Carolinas warranted the creation of only a single diocese, the Diocese of Charleston. The Diocese of Raleigh did not become a separate entity until 1926.[25] Between 1820 and 1860, nearly three hundred thousand Irish had joined parishes in the Northeast, while North Carolina claimed only five Catholic churches and had almost no ecclesiastical infrastructure.[26] Without the influx of European immigrants that so transformed the North, the southern Catholic Church grew slowly, even after the Vatican sent the Church's first vicar to the region at the close of the Civil War. That priest, who would become Cardinal James Gibbons, estimated that there were three hundred Catholics in North Carolina when he arrived in 1868.[27] In the nearly one hundred years that followed the Civil War, the Church barely made a mark on the state's religious landscape. It was not until the late 1960s, when northerners came south to enjoy the economic and climatic benefits of the Sunbelt, that the Catholic Church began to garner a visible membership in the South.[28]

Most parishes in North Carolina served fewer than one hundred families before the development of the Research Triangle Park near Raleigh, North Carolina, in the late 1960s.[29] This area attracted technical and research firms from across the United States such as Bell Telephone, IBM, and, later, GlaxoSmithKline. Job opportunities brought northern Catholics to the Triangle in great numbers. Almost all the white children at Blessed Sacrament and Holy Cross travel to the Northeast to visit their relatives, whereas the African American children at Holy Cross had their families in the parish.[30] Brian, an energetic white nine-year-old boy, from Blessed Sacrament, who had moved to Burlington, North Carolina, when he was younger, lamented, for instance, that many of his relatives could not come to First Communion: "All my family lives in Pennsylvania, and they don't have time. . . . It takes five or eight hours and then [to] go back [another] eight hours."[31] Ms. Key commented on the increase in non-Hispanics she had witnessed in her parish in the past five years, stating that there has "been a tremendous amount of growth in this area, which has tended to bring people from other places like Ohio, where they might have more Catholics."[32] Similarly, Britney listed the family that would come to see her: "I know . . . probably my godparents, my grandma from New Jersey. I don't know if my other cousins from Pennsylvania are coming."[33] These Anglo children and their families emigrating from the North represent one reason why in 2001 North Carolina was reported to be the ninth fastest growing state in the nation.[34] This growth, as journalist Richard Stradling has noted, gave the Triangle (Raleigh, Durham, and Chapel Hill) a "different vibe than [in] 1995." He went on to note that according to the census, "one in three Triangle residents in 2000—about 360,000 people—lived in a different county, state, or country just five years before."[35] Given the transient nature of much of North Carolina's population, churches have often found themselves struggling to deal with the competing expectations that the various migrants bring with them to Mass as well as those expectations of the native population.

Catholics from the North have not been the only recent additions to such parishes as Holy Cross and Blessed Sacrament. These parishes have also had to contend with an ever-increasing number of Latino Catholic migrants. The Latino population in Durham, North Carolina, has grown from a barely visible minority in the early 1990s to a group whose strong presence in the area is evidenced by the number of Mexican restaurants, bilingual signs, and Latino markets. The 2000 census showed that Durham County, which extends just beyond the city, had a 730 percent increase in its Latino population since 1990. With this increase in Latinos and the coming of immigrants from Asia as well, Durham (the home of Holy Cross) became the first "all-minority" city in North Carolina.[36] Large numbers of Hispanics, chiefly from Mexico, began settling in North Carolina in the early 1990s to work in construction, poultry plants, food services, and businesses that grew in response to the population boom in the Triangle. Although the number of Latinos currently living in the Triangle is difficult to measure because of their immigration status and high mobility, the 2000 census counted 378,963 Latinos in North Carolina, an increase of more than 550 percent in the last decade.[37] Some of the Latino children in this study and nearly all their parents were among these newcomers. Given their age, however, the children remembered little about Mexico, particularly their religious participation. Virginia seemed frustrated when I asked her what she remembered from Mexico. She replied, "I don't remember that but my mom told me, but I forget everything."[38] The adults feared that young children like Virginia would forget, particularly in North Carolina where the small immigrant community has been struggling to translate its traditions within the confines of its new home.

While other parishes in the United States have also witnessed a great increase in Latino parishioners, migrants to North Carolina and other southeastern states (unlike those who settle in the borderlands of the Southwest, with its long-established Latino populations) have found churches that know little about Latino religious practices and cultures. Like the earlier European immigrants to the North, however, many of these Latinos have turned to the Catholic Church to help them maintain their traditions and to learn the customs of their new home.[39] In most towns in North Carolina, these parishioners entered small parishes that were largely unprepared for the new arrivals. In recent years, therefore, parish councils throughout the Raleigh diocese have spent much time trying to develop a plan that incorporates new Latino members into their parishes in a way that honors both Anglo and Hispanic religious traditions.

The speed and size of this migration, combined with the continuing influx of northern Catholics and the diocese's relative lack of existing resources, have created serious challenges for these parishes. Churches have been stretched to find space within their sanctuaries and classrooms for their new parishioners as well as the financial and human resources needed to meet all of their parishioners' spiritual and physical needs. Most churches have been devising ways to accommodate the swelling number of worshippers (even if it means holding Masses in unusual places, such as school cafeterias, while they build new sanctuaries). Finding room for new cultures and, an even more immediate need, new languages can be more difficult.

In deciding how to respond to growth, each parish has had to decide how it can meet the needs of these new parishioners while continuing to be able to effectively pass its religious beliefs and parishwide traditions on to the next generation. There seem to be three responses to this growth. First, many parishes have formed parallel Hispanic congregations with separate Spanish Masses, Faith Formation programs, and social events. Blessed Sacrament has been trying to clear a second path that seeks to unite all its parishioners —Anglo and Latino, northern and southern—into one multicultural community. In a third approach, Holy Cross has chosen to have Masses only in English, thereby excluding the vast majority of Latinos and creating a unicultural African American–based congregation. For each of the parishes I studied, the decisions about how to respond to growth reflected the goals of the congregations: Holy Cross's desire to remain an African American Catholic Church and Blessed Sacrament's hope to create a community that respects everyone's ethnic heritage were particularly evident in their parish life. These goals have affected more than the history written on their Web pages. They also influenced how the catechists taught the children. For Holy Cross, a unicultural parish, these objectives meant that the catechists would teach the children that regardless of their individual ethnicity, as members of Holy Cross they were part of a black Catholic Church family that had been a vibrant part of Durham's religious landscape for nearly sixty years.

Maintaining African American Identity

Holy Cross Parish began in 1939 as a Jesuit mission to African Americans under the leadership of an Anglo priest, Father John Risacher.[40] Father Risacher held the mission's first Mass in an 8″ × 8″ anteroom of a dental office on 5 December 1939.[41] Although it began with only one African American family and a few students from North Carolina's College for Negroes (now North Carolina Central University), by 1999 membership at Holy Cross had grown to approximately seven hundred. Father Barry, who had come to the parish in 1996, described this congregation as primarily middle to upper middle class, comprised mostly of professionals and community leaders.

The middle-class status of many of the members was due to their involvement with North Carolina Central University, Duke University Medical Center, and other Triangle industries such as North Carolina Mutual Life, which in 1919 began to attract many African American businesses to Durham.[42] In the area nicknamed the

"Hayti" district and once called "a Mecca for Negroes" by W. E. B. Du Bois, black business grew largely without interference from whites.[43] At the end of World War II, however, the Hayti district, like Durham's downtown itself, began to decline.[44] This decline in the downtown was countered by the creation of the Triangle. The Triangle, as I noted above, brought with it increasing numbers of Mexicans and nonnative Euro-Americans to the city. Over time, Holy Cross's membership began to look much more like the Durham of the 1990s than the Durham of the Hayti era. By the end of 1989, the increase in white attendance (which began in large part from efforts to build a relationship with nearby Duke University), combined with the membership of newly arrived Mexican workers, meant that the church could "boast more than 225 households." And that number should probably be increased to include nonregistered Latino families.[45]

As a middle-class, African American parish, once known as the "home of the immigrants," Holy Cross has often found itself in a battle to maintain its identity against the forces of white, immigrant, and marginalized Catholicism. Holy Cross's efforts to maintain its African American identity conflicted with its other desire to be a diverse and open parish. Therefore, although many white parishioners thrive at Holy Cross, acting as godparents to the community's children and being elected to the parish council, those who do generally follow Ms. McLean's advice: they are "in a black church, and so when in Rome."[46] For those whites, however, like Ms. King, a former member of the parish, who wanted to express their own cultural understanding of Catholicism, the church's welcome seemed to extend only so far. She commented: "I felt very welcome by people [at Holy Cross] in a sort of formal sense but . . . I never felt like I could dive in and really become a part of the activities because it was presumed that the emotional center would be with the African Americans in the congregation."[47] Although the relative lack of whites on all the parish's committees seemed to confirm Ms. King's assessment, both black and white parishioners preferred not to talk about things in racial terms, which tended to obscure these inequities.

Instead, many parishioners at Holy Cross spoke enthusiastically about its diversity—noting the rainbow of brown, black, yellow, and white hands they saw raised in the air during the Our Father. Still, some members were much less comfortable with the changes in the church. When the proportion of Hispanics reached nearly 20 percent and the pastoral leadership changed, the parish board decided that it must remain true to its original mission as an African American church. The mission statement reads: "Holy Cross Church was founded by the Society of Jesus to serve the African American Catholics of Durham. . . . Our special character as an African American parish continues to shape our worship, our ministries, and our contribution to the wider church."[48]

In accordance with this goal, when a new priest came—Father Barry, a white priest from Maryland who did not speak Spanish—the parish board voted to end its Spanish Masses. Some parishioners told me that the church ended its Spanish Masses to integrate the Hispanics into the larger English-speaking, African American–centered parish. Most of the Latino parishioners at Holy Cross, however, interpreted this cessation as a call for their departure. The majority of the immigrants who attended Holy Cross walked out of the church in October 1996, taking their statue of Our Lady of Guadalupe with them. With the walkout, there were no Mexican parishioners with whom I could speak. However, African American members often commented on their disappointment over the split. "I think," said Mr. Green, "it's one of the most Christian gatherings I've been to in a while. I say this especially as related to Holy Cross when we first got here and there was a large Hispanic population. The situation with the Hispanic folks leaving bothers me because it takes away from what I like about the church."[49] Thus, while Mr. Green and others put their emphasis on the church's "multicultural" reality, an equally large—and in the end more powerful—portion of the parishioners feared the dilution that this kind of truly multicultural interaction would have on the church's African American atmosphere.

In the days and weeks following the walkout, Holy Cross's parish board met to consider the matter and resolved: "As Holy Cross has become an increasingly diverse parish, we see the need to retain that which is fundamental to our foundation, the African American culturally based Mass."[50] The African American elements of the weekly Mass, particularly of the 9:00 A.M. Mass, including the gospel choir and fabric with African patterns covering the altar table, were emphasized in the First Communion celebration: the children performed an African dance in time to the drum's beat and sang in Swahili; there was no room for Spanish here.[51] Only a few months after the walkout, all of these aspects—the catechists' musical selection, the congregation's involvement, and the children's scripted movements—evidenced to me and to everyone else in the congregation that this was an African American Catholic Church.

· · · · · · · · · ·

Building a Unified Parish

Blessed Sacrament, however, took a different course in creating a parish identity that included the Mexican migrants by inviting all the children to learn songs in English and Spanish as they prepared to receive the Sacrament. Like Holy Cross, however, it also looked to its history and its mission statement for guidance and justification. While Holy Cross was founded specifically to support and increase the African American Catholic community in Durham, the diocese created Blessed Sacrament in 1929 to minister to Catholics in the parish's geographic area. In the beginning, the goal was simply to establish a parish. In the early days of the twentieth century, a single priest served the only *two* Catholics of the Burlington area, a region whose population was estimated at four thousand. In 1929, the new Diocese of Raleigh, which had been created three years before, formed Blessed Sacrament Parish under the leadership of Father George A. Watkins. Within five years, the parish had celebrated its first marriage, had begun ministering to eight families, and had built a school for its children. The membership grew slowly until Western Electric moved to Burlington in 1946, bringing with it many Catholic workers from the Midwest and the Northeast. By 1982 the parish had six hundred families, some of them migrant workers from Mexico.[52]

Together, these worshippers, under Franciscan leadership, developed a mission for their parish. In part, the parishioners wanted to "devote ourselves to deepen our relationship with Jesus Christ and to continue his mission to bring all to a knowledge of and union with his Church, its sacramental, scriptural, educational, and social life—to recognize, to encourage, and to utilize the unique God-given gifts of all parishioners."[53] This mission reflects the white English-speaking community's more meditative character and its desire to appreciate the diversity of its parishioners' traditions, the gifts they bring to the community.

During my stay at Blessed Sacrament, Father Briant Cullinane, O.F.M. Conv., had the task of overseeing the efforts at community building. "The goal is to respect the culture," Father Briant explained, "because I think that's a richness that's brought. . . . [T]o bring the two communities together as much as possible 'cause the common ground doesn't have to do with culture. It's faith." "How does a church do that?" I asked, thinking that perhaps this distinction between faith and culture, which is often taken for granted in the United States, might make it more difficult to help the Mexican parishioners feel at home since their cultural practices are inseparable from their Catholicism. "I wish I knew," he lamented. Then, he explicated some of the difficulties the parish faced: "It is a topic that the Parish Council is trying to address, but we also find a high degree of mobility among the Spanish, so that exacerbates the challenge. Some relationships start to develop and then all of a sudden, one or the other is gone."[54] Perhaps more than the problem of mobility, the parish's efforts at unity were hampered by its lack of resources. The tremendous growth in both the Anglo and Latino congregations put a strain on Blessed Sacrament's budgetary and personnel resources. The sanctuary, which was originally built to hold four hundred worshippers, by 2002 had to accommodate two thousand families, for even as the number of Catholics in the area grew, the number of parishes did not.[55] In our interview, when talking about the parish's challenges, Ms. Key reminded me that Blessed Sacrament is "the only Catholic parish for two and a half counties."[56] To help alleviate the overcrowding, the parish's three priests said six weekend Masses as well as one weekday Mass when I conducted my study. On my first visit to the parish, I sat in the vestibule with ten other worshippers who could not find a seat in the pews or on the folding chairs that lined the aisles at the 8:30 A.M. Mass. As the parish tried to resolve these practical issues of space

and human resources, it also sought ways to bring the Spanish-
and English-speaking parishioners together through their bilingual
Faith Formation classes, which I discuss in Chapter 3.

Conclusion

Each of the three congregational identities I studied were
distinct, even if the head of the media center at the Raleigh Diocese
insisted, "They're all the same. They're all Catholic."[57] As Ronald L.
Grimes has suggested, for this Catholic diocese and many others
the label of "universality" had obscured the very important local
variations between these parishes.[58] As I compared these three communities, I quickly came to the conclusion that there was no "typical" Catholic Church, or even a typical *southern* Catholic Church.
In part, the children learned their congregation's identity by enacting it in the First Communion celebration. The First Communion
ritual offered the children an opportunity to take on their parish's
ethnic as well as religious identity, simultaneously transforming
it through their participation in the Sacrament.[59] The dynamics
of this transformation often get lost in scholarly interpretation of
liturgies like the ones in this chapter. So to highlight the multiple
meanings of the Sacrament, and how they are formed, I asked the
children, their parents, their teachers, and their priests to teach me
about the ritual. The next chapter explores the method I developed
to gain access to the participants' interpretations of First Communion, particularly the children's.

drawing, playing, listening

"Is that you?" I asked, pointing to the girl Cara has just drawn. "Umm-humm," she replied. "I couldn't really make a pony-tail; that's why I have my hair like that. But I still have my Communion dress—it was white." Cara, an eight-year-old African American girl, and I talked as we sat on the floor in the vestibule of Holy Cross's Activity Center. Although it seemed to me like a strange place for an interview, Cara decided that she wanted to talk there stretched out on the floor with the occasional latecomers stepping over us on their way to Faith Formation classes, which Holy Cross held in that building. So, on the white linoleum floor, we spread out the white construction paper, on which I asked her to "draw me a picture of First Communion." Preparing for our conversation, Cara found a comfortable position in which to sit, and I placed the box of sixty-four crayons in front of her. As she picked the appropriate colors for her drawing, I put the tape recorder that would record our conversation about a foot behind her right elbow in an effort to make sure that at least its physical presence would not distract her.

Before I began this research I had hoped that Cara might understand this situation as two friends coloring together and talking freely about First Communion, albeit with a microphone off to one side. As I began my work with the communicants, I still clung to the notion that children were completely trusting and accepting, even though my life experiences and my knowledge of childhood studies told me otherwise. As I spent time listening to the children and their fellow parishioners, I worked to create a methodology that would help my consultants express themselves as fully as possible. I soon realized that I would have to do more to get the children to share their thoughts with me than sit with them on the floor and color. In developing my procedure for doing fieldwork with the First Communion classes at Holy Cross and Blessed Sacrament, I tried to keep the many epistemological, practical, and legal concerns about working with children in mind. I worried constantly about my ability to enter the children's world. I was concerned about the power differential between children and adults. I debated ways by which I could gain informed consent from the children. And I asked myself continually if I was doing everything I could to help them understand what my study was about and why I was conducting it.[1]

In this chapter, I outline the methodology that I developed to learn the children's expectations for First Communion as well as how they interpreted the ritual after having received the Sacrament. I simultaneously address how adults' understandings of children, including my own, constrained the communicants' stories, as well as the means by which the children negotiated these adult-imposed boundaries, sometimes overtly challenging adult assumptions about the facileness of the children's interpretations, and the children's inability to express themselves clearly.

Children's Perceptions as Sources

In previous studies of children's culture, some anthropologists have proposed using fieldwork as a means of gaining access into children's interpretations and practices. Allison James and Alan Prout have argued, for instance, that "ethnographic approaches . . . could bring researchers close enough to this action [the action of everyday life] to elaborate on 'children's agency and action' through close attention to children's everyday lives in different settings."[2] However promising this approach might be, many practical issues are involved in doing ethnography with children. (This might explain why so few have tried it.) Religious studies scholar Robert Orsi highlighted some of these issues in his report on the Lily Foundation's Consultation on Religion and Children, "Mapping the Ground of Children's Religion: A Beginning." Orsi asked: "Is it possible to know their religious worlds from the inside? How can adults be present in such conversations without being overwhelming?"[3] And how is it that one can get children to understand what their participation in a certain project means both for the present and the future? Except for the last one, these concerns apply to *all* field studies, not just those involving children. No researcher can ever fully or permanently enter another person's or group's symbolic world. An ethnographic interpretation is always constrained by the narratives told to the researcher by the examined community and by the position from which the researcher observes that society.[4] But by spending a significant amount of time with the community and attending closely to the consultants' words, artifacts, and practices, a researcher can gain some insights into that social world, insights that could not be achieved through the use of a methodology other than ethnography. Thus, while I would never claim to know the religious worlds of the children I studied, I can analyze how they *represent* those worlds through their words and their actions.[5] I try to make this most important difference clear throughout the book.

Finding Myself In Between

As I entered the field, I had hoped that both the children and the adults would come to see me as one of them in some way, thereby enabling me to break down potential barriers between us. This process proved to be slow, difficult, and ultimately impossible in both cases because of differences in religion, age, race, education levels, and socioeconomic class that, although unacknowledged by many of my consultants, continued to divide us. I frequently heard sentiments similar to Father Briant's closing comments in our interview: "Pleasure having you, Susan. You really fit. I mean you are very much at home. You're like an old shoe—a *young* shoe. You didn't seem to have any problems—I mean the people that you were with. You were just one of them."[6] Of course, it was not as simple as Father Briant suggested. I never "fit" completely, and I always remained an outsider in one way or another. Not being Catholic, for instance, allowed me to ask many questions that a Catholic would not have asked; at the same time, my religious affiliation excluded me from the central Sacrament of the Church and the ritual I had spent years studying. Because I am a white woman, I am sure that the African American parishioners at Holy Cross and the Hispanics at Blessed Sacrament did not disclose all they might have about the racial and ethnic issues in their parishes.

Although my race did not appear to have an obvious effect on the children at Holy Cross (although it might have had effects I did not notice), it seemed to have a significant impact on the Mexican children at Blessed Sacrament, evidenced most clearly in their insistence on speaking to me in English, even though I let them know that I spoke Spanish. Although many of the children whom I interviewed spoke English fluently, for all but two of them, Spanish did seem to be their first language. Scholars working with adult migrants have found that their consultants usually speak in Spanish, particularly when they discuss important, emotional events. Perhaps this discrepancy reflects that the children use their two languages differently from adults because they are growing up in a bilingual world. My consultants' persistent use of English may also have evidenced their desire to show me that they knew English and thus to gain a status that they may not have felt that they had in their Faith Formation or second grade classrooms. Depending on their ability to speak English, their choice of language may have limited what some of the children could share with me about their interpretations. It also continually forced me to recognize that just because they never spoke directly about race, the children—Mexican, white, African American—did not live in a world apart from the (adult) world with its concerns about class and ethnicity. Rather, it seemed that race and socioeconomics shaped the format of their interpretations and in so doing influenced our discussion in almost imperceptible ways.

Race and ethnicity may well have had more influence on the children's interpretations than the interviews, observations, and drawings revealed. An African American or a Mexican American researcher may have found other results. The Spanish-speaking children at Blessed Sacrament, for instance, may have assumed that because I am white, when I talked about First Communion I was referring to the Saturday Mass. Communicants at both parishes also may have felt uncomfortable discussing race or ethnic issues with me. I used the information that they did provide me, verbally and nonverbally, as carefully as I could to interpret their comments about their parish and First Communion. Whether rooted in ethnicity or age, I never believed that I could understand these events the way that the children and their parents did. What I have tried to do instead is to analyze the perceptions and emotions that they felt were most important to share with me.

My conversations with the parents, teachers, priests, and children seemed to occur with greater ease as the many weeks of my study progressed. As Mr. Dwyer, a catechist and parent at Blessed Sacrament, said during our interview approximately six weeks after my study began, "I didn't understand in the beginning of the year exactly what you do. . . . It did make me a little bit nervous . . . thinking that I was going to be judged every week." Any initial anxieties that existed about being "judged" seemed to disappear quickly among the catechists as we developed relationships and they came to a clearer understanding of the project—or at least they kept their worries to themselves. By the time of our interview, Mr. Dwyer, for instance, had come to understand his role in the study and said, "I like what you're doing. I think its cool. . . . It's the first time I ever heard of something like this."[7] The other adults with whom I spoke also seemed to be intrigued by this research. Although my primary goal was to discover how the children viewed the Sacrament, I also interviewed some of their parents to see what they emphasized at home and how these emphases may have influenced the children's interpretations of First Communion. In my interviews with five parents at Holy Cross (two white mothers and three African American mothers), as well as seven parents from Blessed Sacrament (four white mothers, two Mexican mothers, and one Nicaraguan mother), they told me their own goals for their communicants' religious education and, in that context, described what they said and did in their homes.[8] Although my conversations with the adults were structured, they each flowed with their own rhythm.

As I compared my discussions with the adults to the children's interviews, I could see how the children's beliefs, values, and feelings both paralleled and diverged from those expressed by the adults. The differences were most intriguing, since they seemed to challenge the widely shared notion that children do not come to their own conclusions about the world around them but simply parrot parents and teachers. As Robert Coles wrote of one of his young consultants, "No doubt she should offer some trite remarks, some memorized clichés—who doesn't? She seems to have her own slant on things, making it hers rather than mere rote replication of church truisms."[9] What I found among the children I interviewed fits this description, but it took time for me to understand that these "slants" were, in fact, unique interpretations rather than a mere parroting of adults.

Playing with the children and working hard to build relationships with them also prompted some of them to share their feelings about Faith Formation class and First Communion with me. To aid in this relationship-building process, I entered their classes without a set plan or schedule for my research. Rather, I took my cues from the children and the adults around them. As we got to know each other and they came to a greater understanding of my project, I asked them to participate more directly, just as I began to participate more directly in their church activities.[10] The more time I spent with the communicants, the clearer it became that Cara and her classmates would never treat me like one of them, regardless of my efforts. And, even if they did, I would never understand the world as any one of them did. Given these limitations, however, my approach to this fieldwork seemed to allow the children to place me into their own uniquely defined category. I did not come into the room asking to be treated or addressed like they treated their teachers (although some children did address me that way), nor did I pretend to be the seven-year-old that I was not. The children knew that I was not just a "big kid," but they also did not interact with me as they did with many other adults. Rather, I seem to have established an ambiguous place in the children's world. While the children knew I was older, they also knew that—unlike the other adults in the church—I was in school, was not married, had no children, and knew little about what they were learning in class. (Like them, I could neither make the sign of the cross nor genuflect.) All of these characteristics seemed to keep them from placing me fully in the "adult" category. After my first few visits to Holy Cross I began to see that my methodology would be built in part on my "in-between" status—

a status that I did not realize the children would grant me before I entered their classrooms. Nonetheless, this in-between status—neither a child nor a mother, neither a communicant nor an initiated Catholic, neither a teacher nor a classmate—became the key element in my relationship with the communicants. Just as they seemed not to know where I fit, much of the time neither did I. I realized rather quickly the advantages of my ambiguous position, and I worked hard to keep it. I played with the children, helped the teachers pass out paper, as many children did, and tried not to discipline the communicants who put their feet on the desks or played too closely to the street while they waited for their parents to pick them up. But, of course, I am an adult, and I, like other adults in the children's lives, felt an obligation to keep them safe and to ease their anxieties as they practiced for First Communion. And I did so.

Although I sometimes helped the teachers by handing out scissors or cookies and occasionally admonished the communicants' dangerous or disruptive behavior, most of the children did not see me as a teacher either. At the last class before Christmas, for instance, one little girl at Blessed Sacrament asked, "Are you a teacher, 'cause you don't act like it."[11] My willingness to sit on the floor and play hopscotch in the gym, where the children at Blessed Sacrament waited before their Faith Formation classes, may have prompted her comment. Throughout our time together this "in-betweenness" seemed to create a space in which the communicants could teach me about their perceptions of the Sacrament.

As one might expect, the majority of the girls at both parishes seemed more comfortable talking with me than did the boys. Of course, there were exceptions. Some of the boys came over often to show me their pictures or waved enthusiastically when we saw each other at church or around town. A few of the girls would smile at me from across the room but were too shy to talk with me after Mass, before class, or when I was helping them with projects. Most often the girls first opened up to me because of random personal characteristics. On my first day at the Holy Cross classes, for instance, Jennifer, a seven-year-old African American girl, waved to me as she asked in a quiet voice, "Do you want to sit next to me?" When I sat down beside her at the U-shaped table that surrounded the blackboard, she leaned over and whispered, "I like your hair." Likewise, the first time I wore my hair down at Blessed Sacrament, Stephanie, a shy seven-year-old Anglo girl, leaned over and whispered something in her father's ear. He then turned to me, smiled, and said, "She wants me to tell you she likes your hair." While I had anticipated that my age, gender, race, religion, and even my quiet demeanor would have influenced what the community allowed me to know and what they kept to themselves, I never would have anticipated that my long, curly hair would have shaped our encounters. As it attracted the girls' attention and gave us a starting point for our communication, it also may have influenced some of their artwork. While none of the girls in either of the classes had curly hair, curls appeared in some of their drawings. Britney, a friendly and confident seven-year-old white girl with straight shoulder-length brown hair, in particular spoke to me often about how she made curls in her hair. She even gave herself curls in her self-portrait.[12]

Although it was relatively easy to make superficial connections with a few of the girls, it took some time for the children and me to get to know each other. When I first walked into the children's classroom, most of them, aside from Jennifer, made little effort to interact with me. Week after week, our comfort level with each other grew. After a few weeks, I found the opportunity to introduce the children to my project. Contrary to some of the adults' expectations, especially the expectations of those who see children as naturally subservient, the communicants had many questions about what I was doing, both when I first discussed the study with them and throughout the year. At Blessed Sacrament, for instance, I told the children that I was at their class each week trying to learn what it was like to have a First Communion, since I had never had one. I went on to say that I wanted to understand what they were learning about the Eucharist and how they felt about receiving it for the first time. Britney then asked why I had never had a First Communion and whether I was sad about it. This led me to talk briefly about how I was not Catholic and to explain that my church did not have First Communion. I told them I had always wanted to have a First Communion, as my Catholic friends did.[13] A similar interaction occurred at Holy Cross. After my conversation with Ferris, an outgoing eight-year-old African American boy, he said, "I gotta two questions to ask you ask: What religion are you, and—I know you told us about it . . . but why are you doing this?"[14] Similarly, when I told Melissa that we did not have a First Communion in the church in which I grew up, she asked if my parents were Jewish.[15] Instead of creating an obstacle between us, however, my Protestantism seemed to engender a great deal of sympathy in these children who were so anxious to receive the body and blood of Christ that I would never get to taste. Katie expressed this when she explained, "God wants you to taste the bread and the blood. If you don't you'll be like you."[16] These conversations seemed to let the children know that even though I was older and bigger than they were, I *truly* wanted and needed them to instruct me. I think many children could sense this, and it seemed to invite them into a relationship with me.

Still, not all the children were as inquisitive or responded as enthusiastically as Britney from Blessed Sacrament or Ferris from Holy Cross. Some of the children were too shy to interact with me or their teachers, while some of the boys seemed to be uninterested or uncomfortable talking to a female, even—or especially—one who appeared to be an older girl with curly hair and lots of questions. Nevertheless, the ever-growing number of volunteers who raised their hands when I asked each week who would like to speak with me was my best evidence for the children's increasing comfort level with me.

Informing the Participants

Just as this conceptual issue about the distance between researcher and consultant has great import in all ethnographic studies, so do other legal and moral issues that are particularly relevant to an ethnographic study of children. Chief among these issues are: Should a researcher attempt to obtain consent from a minor consultant, and if so, how can a researcher get *informed* assent from children? Scholars and lawyers have debated often about this issue in different arenas. As a strictly legal matter, an adult parent may provide consent for his or her child to participate in a study which will bind the child and protect the researcher. However, if a child has the capacity to give his or her informed consent to participation in a study, shouldn't efforts be made to obtain this consent at least as an ethical matter? I believe that the special category in which scholars place children has much more to do with their presuppositions—in particular, the assumption that adults are competent and children are incompetent—than with adults' or children's capacity for understanding the consequences of their participation in a study. In general it seems that scholars pay a great deal of attention to issues like informed consent from consultants when researchers work with children, but they often minimize the importance of these issues when working with adults. Even if they are working with adults having no impairments, I believe that no consultants, adults or children, can be fully informed about what their participation in a project might mean for them in the future.[17] If, however, one takes care to explain the foreseeable consequences of participation in a project in terms familiar to a child or to an adult, most consultants can understand to a large degree the potential impact the consultant's participation in a study might have on him or her. To that end, the study and its possible affect on the young consultant could be explained using language and examples with which children are familiar, not legal language used on an adult consent form. Then, after a discussion with the child in which the researcher answers the child's questions, the researcher should be able to assess whether the child understands the possible implications of being in the study, at least at that moment, and then determine whether the child is comfortable in proceeding with participation in the study. As Priscilla Alderson stated, "Children do not have to be perfect to qualify as competent, that is, reasonably informed and wise."[18] And in field studies like mine, the researcher can make multiple ongoing efforts to do everything possible to try to ensure that the children are "reasonably informed." As an ethical matter, I believe such an effort is appropriate.

At both parishes, once I met the First Communion team, they welcomed me into their classrooms, if only because of their curiosity about me and my project. Soon after I began attending classes at each parish, I introduced myself and my project to the parents at a First Communion meeting. Of the sixty families at the two parishes, all but two parents from Blessed Sacrament consented to their child's participation, an exceptionally high participation rate.[19] From both parishes' viewpoint and as a strict matter of law, it seemed that once I had parental consent, I had all the permission I needed to record the children's comments and activities during the classes.

According to the parishes' procedures and their legal obligations, the children did not need to agree to the study, and with so many other things to think about each Sunday, getting their permission did not seem to occur to anyone. As a result, the adults greeted my suggestion that I introduce the project to the children and ask them for verbal permission with some surprise and many enthusiastic nods.[20] In this reaction the parents seemed to affirm a belief in "the innocent child," perhaps seeing themselves as protectors of the children while envisioning the children as passive entities who need not have a say in the activities in which they participated. Although parents may have asked the children at home if the children wanted to participate in the research, from their conversations at church it seemed that when the parents and teachers imagined children's participation in this study, they assumed that the children would not question adult behavior or instruction effectively. Thus, as with many other institutions, the parishes' procedures seemed to discount, although not actively discourage, any questions the children might have had about my actions as a researcher in their classroom, as well as any objections they might have had to the study.

While I could not know for sure how the children would react to my request for their permission, I wanted consent from my primary consultants, the children. I tried to ensure that the children were "reasonably informed" so that they knew what consent was and what they were consenting to. Once we found a place to sit—on top of a staircase, on the vestibule floor, at a hallway table, or in an empty classroom—I would set up my tape recorder as I verbally explained my project to the child again.[21] Then I handed him or her an assent form to sign.[22] I instructed the children more formally about how I would use what they taught me about First Communion to write something that would help to show how children thought about receiving the Sacrament for the first time. I gave the children time to read the form, which some of them did aloud. If the children agreed to be a part of the project (as all of my volunteers did), I asked them to sign the assent form. Then I signed it after them. Through this interaction I hoped that the children would see that I saw them as partners and teachers in this project. Just as their parents had to sign permission forms, so did they.

When the children were deciding if they wanted to participate, I went over what would happen in the interview with them and told them that I would give them a different name in print (a name they could choose) so no readers except me would know their identity. I could not, however, restrict the parent's access to our conversations or to their drawings.[23] Some children enjoyed picking their own pseudonym, especially Britney, who was thrilled to discover that she was the first girl to choose to name herself after the teen pop singer. Elizabeth, however, was less thrilled to find that the name had already been taken and so chose the name "Elizabeth."[24] Inviting the children to participate in the pseudonym process helped them to realize that their comments would be anonymous. Still, some children double-checked this fact before they revealed that they did not like Sunday school or that they found a particular catechist boring.

Drawing Conclusions

After spending six weeks building relationships at Holy Cross and three months getting to know the children at Blessed Sacrament, I began to ask for volunteers in each classroom to tell me in an interview what they thought of First Communion.[25] I chose to start this process early so that even after waiting a few weeks to help establish a relationship, First Communion was still many weeks away, which allowed those communicants who still felt uneasy speaking with me that first Sunday to do so later if they so desired. In the end, twenty-six out of the fifty-eight children volunteered to talk with me one-on-one about their expectations (and later, memories) of First Communion. At Holy Cross, I spoke with nine communicants: three African American children before their First Communion; five African American children seven months after the ceremony; and one Anglo Communicant both before and after. At Blessed Sacrament, I spoke with seventeen children: four Anglos and five Latinos before First Communion; two Anglos seven months after First Communion, and four Anglos and two Latinos both before and after reception of the Sacrament.[26] (This small group allowed me to observe certain patterns among the 1997 and 2001 Communion classes' interpretations of First Eucharist; it did not, however, allow me to draw firm conclusions about Catholic children in other places and at other times, or even about all the children at these two parishes.)

In an effort to ease some of the children's anxieties during these recorded conversations, I followed the lead of psychiatrist Robert Coles by using drawings to create a common visual vocabulary and to offer the children another medium through which to express their understanding of the Sacrament.[27] For a few children, this approach seemed to create more anxieties than it dispelled. These children did not want to draw or could not think of anything to draw: in such cases, the paper remained blank, and we simply talked about their experiences or expectations.[28] Using the knowledge that they learned in school, at home, and in Faith Formation classes, many of the children created pictures in response to my request that they "draw me a picture of First Communion." I hoped that this open-ended request might give them an opportunity to depict the most important aspect of the Sacrament or the liturgy to them. For those who had not yet received the Eucharist, I hoped their images might reveal their expectations of the ritual. Although I could have included a number of different elements, such as play, in the interviews, I chose art because it offered the children another way to represent how they felt and what they valued with no significant input from me other than what our conversation may have lead them to imagine.[29] In this respect, I agree with a number of art therapists who contend that many children "draw what is important to them . . . whereas speaking comes with more difficulty."[30] Some children took this opportunity to express themselves more than did others. My request for a picture resulted in a wide variety of drawings—from imaginings of what it would be like to receive the chalice from the Eucharistic minister (Figure 5) to a detailed picture of the Host itself (Figure 6), to a drawing of one child receiving

FIGURE 5. *José depicts himself standing before the Eucharistic minister*

the Eucharist from the Eucharistic minister. It did seem in many ways that the children drew the component of the ceremony that was affecting them most at the time of our conversation.

The paper and crayons also helped to put many of my young consultants at ease while supplying them with another means of self-expression and providing us with a common referent for our conversation. Many of the children appeared to enjoy this project. Communicants said that their favorite part of Faith Formation class were the art projects, which gave me some reassurance that they felt at ease, at least to some extent, with drawing. This method worked well for children such as Christy, who, when I asked her if there was anything else she thought I should know about First Communion, told me: "I don't know, but maybe the picture will tell you."[31] Other children were quite comfortable talking even before

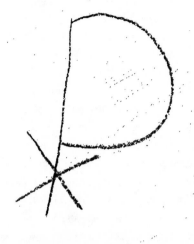

Eucharist

FIGURE 6. *Ryan draws a detailed sketch of the Host*

they began drawing. Maureen and Melissa, for instance, told me about their friends, family, and waking up early Sunday mornings, as well as First Communion.[32] With these children, my questions followed from their conversation. Occasionally, I did have to steer the child back to the topic if we became too deeply involved in a conversation about sleepovers, school projects, or cats. Generally, I did this by referring to the aspect of the picture that the child was drawing at the time. Although they all volunteered to talk, some children were much more reserved and anxious when we were sitting together than others. Christopher, for instance, could not remember his birthday when we first started talking. As we settled into our conversation, Christopher's sentences became longer, and his anxiety seemed to lessen. Still, he twisted his fingers under the table as he explained why First Communion was important.[33] In conversations with the more reserved children such as Christopher, I did direct the conversation to some degree. In these instances I asked very open-ended questions, such as, "Why is First Communion important?" (if we had already established that the child thought it was important) in order to stimulate conversation. Then I used their answers to formulate my next question. However nervous they may have been, as I sat with the children I got clues from their words, posture, gestures, and drawings about how they felt about participating in my ethnographic project and how they understood First Communion.

Through these many telling sources (art, conversation, and gestures), I learned that each communicant and parent had his or her unique views on the Eucharist's meaning. By the end of my research, I was able to compare the interpretations of twenty-six children to see the patterns, which comprise the substance of the remaining chapters, in how these two classes interpreted their First Communion experience—both the ritual itself and the months of preparation that preceded it. The children's drawings and their conversations, together with what I observed in their classes and learned from their parents, taught me much about how both the children and the adults perceived First Communion. Working closely with the children and their parents showed me that I could not prefer one means of expression over others in my effort to understand the children's interpretations of First Communion. Analyzing the interactions of children and adults—parents, teachers, priests, and myself with all of them—I found that everyone agreed that First Communion offered an opportunity for belonging. In the next chapter, I examine one important aspect of this belonging by focusing on each group's perceptions of the Eucharist, particularly the Eucharist's ability to connect the children to Jesus and the Church.

learning the mysteries of the church

After opening prayer, Ms. Williams introduced the lesson to the five communicants who had arrived on time at Holy Cross's Faith Formation class that spring morning, the first day of daylight savings time: "Today we will discuss basic Catholic beliefs and practices. Catholics share many special gifts. We believe, live, and pray as one family." Following this introduction she asked, "What does it mean to say that God exists in three parts?" The children sat around the rectangular grade school cafeteria-style table in the recreation room of Holy Cross's Activity Center looking at each other to see who would answer. Maureen reluctantly responded, "It means that God is one part the Spirit, one the Father, and then Jesus." "Yes," Ms. Williams said, "and what else can we say about God?" While she waited for a response, she handed that day's lesson plan to Maureen's mother and me. At the top of the first sheet of paper, in boldface type, was the heading: "What Catholics Believe." As I scanned the three-page lesson plan, I heard Maureen reply: "God is mysteries. You know, like the chicken and the egg." Michael, who had commented a few weeks earlier that he could give up everything for Lent but his Sega video games, added, "God gave us technology."

Trying to build on this burst of conversation, Ms. Williams responded, "What can we do with technology?" Michael, generating his own line of conversation, blurted out, "Electricity is man-made." "But God gave us the brains to make it," Hunter retorted. Ms. Williams broke the mounting tension by asking the children to "name one special thing that God gave us." The lesson plan suggested that Ms. Williams wanted someone to mention Jesus and the Eucharist. The children had their own plans. Switching from technology to religion, Michael, who had commandeered the conversation, responded, "He gave us everlasting life because he died for us."

Thirty minutes into the class, four more children arrived—their parents having forgotten to make the daylight savings time adjustment. The expanding group of communicants began discussing "who Jesus is." Offering one defining characteristic, Ferris commented rather seriously, "Jesus is patient." The moment Ferris finished his response, Maureen asked, "Why did God have to make Jesus a boy—is that because boys are better?" As Ms. Williams struggled to find an appropriate answer, Maureen's mother jumped in explaining the social context of the Roman world in which Jesus lived. She explained that at that time no one would have listened to a woman. After that digression the class went on to discuss the Holy Spirit. By the time the children left for Mass or home, they had completed only one of the three pages Ms. Williams had hoped to discuss. Next week, perhaps, the communicants would revisit this lesson to cover "We Believe in Mary and the Saints," "How Catholics Live," and "How Catholics Worship."[1]

As in each class, the children and the teachers had conversations based on the adults' goals for that day during which the adults shared their own understanding of key Catholic figures and beliefs. At times in these discussions, the official doctrines of the Catholic Church got lost in the interpretations and personal descriptions of both the children and the adults; at other times the official definitions were supported by personal testimonies. After all, neither the children nor the adults were working from a Vatican-issued script. Like the children, the adults also worked from their own ever-changing interpretations of "what Catholics believe." Although the catechists' lessons may have sounded more similar to the catechism than the children's comments did, they were still unique expressions based on the teachers' own experiences and beliefs. What the adults considered the most important goal of First Communion preparation, however, remained constant at both parishes: the passing on of Catholic beliefs and both universal and parishwide traditions to the next generation of Catholics. Therefore, the adults continuously pushed the children's interpretations to come into line with the adults' understanding of the faith they wanted the children to adopt. Through their conversations, rather than the memorization of Church truisms, then, the adults focused on nurturing their young parishioners' faith.

Both in response to and in spite of the adults more theological and intellectual concerns, the children emphasized the ritual and its immediate effects both physically (through new sensory experiences and participation in new activities) and spiritually (in the nearly instantaneous change in the children's relationship with Jesus). Similarly, those who engaged in the lessons each week also sought to make the abstract "fundamentals" relevant to their own lives. The children demonstrated one means of controlling the class content in the example of classroom discussion that began this chapter when they shifted the focus on Jesus' miracles from the Resurrection (the teacher's intended focus) to video games (some of the children's focus) and by asking questions about where women fit in this male-dominated story. As the communicants sought to make Faith Formation class pertinent to their own experiences, they took varying levels of interest in the adult efforts to teach them about Jesus' love, their place within the Catholic Church, and the meaning of the Eucharist. So, just as the parents and teachers were crafting a First Communion experience for the classes that met their objectives, the children were crafting an interpretation of their own understanding of Jesus, the Church, and celebration that resonated with their individual experiences.

In this and the next chapter, I explore how the children's understandings of the Sacrament both intersected with and diverged from the adults' prescriptions that informed them. The children understood certain elements as the adults intended, whereas in other areas, their interpretations differed from those of their parents and teachers. And still another portion of the required teachings remained almost entirely absent from the thoughts and memories that the communicants shared with their classmates and me. Throughout this chapter, I try to follow many strands of conversation, both those coming from the adults at the front of the classroom and those between the students in the back, to analyze how the adults expressed their primary goals for First Communion formation, how (and, in some cases, if) the children interpreted them, and how the adults then hoped to shape these newly formed interpretations.

I begin this chapter by discussing the official meaning of First Communion and the diocesan guidelines that dictated much of what the catechists taught each week. Then, by examining the classes themselves, I analyze how the teachers conveyed this information and how the children responded to the instruction. To understand the context within which these conversations took place, I attend closely to the educational models the teachers followed and the instructional materials that they used before I turn to the actual content of the lessons. After analyzing the approaches of each catechetical team, I address the three main focal points of instruction —the Eucharist, the Mass, and the basic tenets of Catholicism— and how the children seemed to interpret each of them within the context of their Faith Formation classes. Ideally, each area of study influenced the others: As the children learned more about the Mass, they came to realize what the priest was doing as he consecrated the Host for the Eucharist, what was happening when they watched other parishioners receive the Sacrament each week. Now each child used everything that he or she learned to develop his or her unique understanding of the Sacrament.

First Communion History and Ritual Practice

Many of these communicants had been waiting for years to receive the consecrated bread and wine with the rest of their congregation. Melissa, a nine-year-old Latina American girl, told me, for instance, that her First Communion was special because "I got to taste the bread and wine 'cause I never got to taste it. I just got blessed by the priest when my mom received Communion."[2] For the priest to offer Melissa the consecrated Host rather than a blessing, she had to attend Faith Formation classes and demonstrate that she knew that in Communion the bread and wine turned into something greater than these common elements. Her desire to receive the consecrated bread seemed to evidence that she already knew that Communion, or the Eucharist, was a religiously important event.

The Eucharist is the primary ritual of the Catholic Church's seven sacraments—Baptism, Confirmation, Reconciliation, the Eucharist, Marriage, Holy Orders, and the Anointing of the Sick. In simple terms, a sacrament is a "sign addressed to the senses, a 'symbol' of a spiritual reality, a reality essentially divine."[3] Through these rituals, Christ "infuses his grace into the soul(s)" of those people who have been prepared to receive them.[4] By definition, then, the term "sacrament" implies Christ's immediate presence. Christ's presence makes all sacraments of the Catholic Church important, just as Christ's immediate and real presence in Communion sets it apart from other rituals. In Communion, a Catholic receives the body and blood of Christ. As the *Catechism of the Catholic Church* states, "The other sacraments, and indeed all ecclesiastical ministries and works of the apostolate, are bound up with the Eucharist and are oriented towards it. For in the blessed Eucharist is contained the whole spiritual good of the church, namely Christ himself."[5] Mary Key, the director of religious education at Blessed Sacrament, explained: "Christ comes to us in that very intimate personal way as food, and we ingest him. He becomes physically a part of us —who we are."[6] The emphasis on the centrality of the Eucharist has a long history. As Thomas Aquinas suggested, "In this Sacrament Christ Himself is contained substantially, while in the other sacraments only Christ's power and his momentary act are contained."[7]

When God infuses the Holy Spirit in the bread and the wine through the process of transubstantiation, it changes the substance of the bread into Jesus' flesh. The *New Catholic Encyclopedia* provides a description of the complexity of the process: "On the level on which the senses can attain reality nothing has changed; but on the level on which the believing intellect grasps reality, the bread and the wine become the savior's body and blood, without altering their empirical properties."[8] Thus, when Catholics eat the bread, they ingest Christ into their bodies in the Host, strengthening their bond with the Lord, for with this act he actually dwells in them. Within the Eucharistic liturgy, as Father David Barry, Holy Cross's pastor, explained to the children, the priest consecrates the bread, asking God to place the power of his blessing on the bread so that it might become for the Church the body of Christ.[9] Thus, while Protestant communion memorializes and celebrates the Last Supper, Catholics take Jesus' words as recorded in the Gospel according to John more literally: "I am the living bread that came down from heaven. Whoever eats of this bread will live forever; and the bread that I will give for the life of the world is my flesh" (Jn 6:51). As Paul writes in Galatians, "It is now no longer I who live, but Christ who lives in me" (Gal 2:20). The Eucharist's special ability to join the believer with Christ separates it from all other sacraments. For the children, like Michael, an eight-year-old African American from Holy Cross, the Eucharist offered "an opportunity to get closer to Jesus, God, and Mary."[10] Although the adults would agree with Michael's assessment, many of them also hoped the children would comprehend that the Eucharist allowed them actually to become one with Jesus. But would the children be able to grasp these complexities of this union, and if so, how?

The mystery and complexities of the doctrine of transubstantiation has led to many arguments about how much Catholics need to know before they receive the Sacrament and when young Catholics should begin to receive Communion. In the early centuries of the Church, babies sucked the wine from the fingers of the priests after their baptism. In the *Quam Singulari*, Pope Pius X decreed in 1910 that the "Eucharist [was] done at baptism until the 13th century, but to avoid all danger lest the children should spit out the consecrated Host the custom was obtained from the beginning that the Eucharist should be given under the species of wine alone."[11] Because of this concern with reception and the more pressing worry of the child's preparedness for the ritual, the Fourth Lateran Council in 1215 decided that children should not receive the Eucharist until they had reached the age of reason (a moment that the council failed to define) and had some understanding that the consecrated Host in the Sacrament differed in kind from ordinary bread.[12] Three centuries later, the Council of Trent, held in response to the Protestant Reformation, reaffirmed this position. At this time, many communities moved First Eucharist from the time of Baptism to the child's twelfth, and some as old as the fourteenth, birthday—about the same age that Protestant children were being accepted as adult members in their religious communities through confirmation.[13]

Pope Pius X, however, believed that children younger than twelve could make the necessary conceptual distinctions and that this union with Christ was too important to postpone. In 1910, Pius X put an end to many of the long-standing debates surrounding first reception of the Eucharist when he issued the encyclical *Quam Singulari*, which decreed: "The knowledge of religion which is required in a child in order to be properly prepared to receive First Communion is such that ... he can distinguish between the bread of the Eucharist and ordinary, material bread, and thus he may receive Holy Communion with a devotion becoming his years."[14] Pius X called the time when the child could make this distinction "the age of reason," which he declared to be approximately seven years old.[15]

Therefore, since 1910, seven- and eight-year-old children, like those at Holy Cross and Blessed Sacrament, have participated in First Communion, the second of three rites in the Catholic Church's tripartite structure of initiation. This initiation begins in infancy with Baptism, when the child is purified of original sin and welcomed into God's family. It then moves through First Communion, when the seven- or eight-year-old child becomes part of the mystical body of Christ through his or her reception of the Eucharist, and ends with Confirmation, when the child (at age sixteen in the Raleigh Diocese) takes personal responsibility for his or her faith. Therefore, in parishes around the world parents bring their children to Faith Formation classes and First Communion Masses to ensure that they take what many Catholics feel is the inevitable second step on the path of Catholic initiation. Britney referenced the natural progression of faith development, explaining, "Everybody has to do it [First Communion] eventually."[16] Without receiving First Communion, after all, the children could not take personal responsibility for their faith in Confirmation.

To be eligible to continue their progression through the sacraments by partaking in the Eucharist, the children had to fulfill the diocesan requirements for participation. The diocese required that the children have: "(a) Knowledge of Jesus and some of the main events in his life. (b) An awareness of Jesus' love and that he is someone very special in the children's life. (c) Awareness of the Eucharist as Jesus' special presence different from ordinary bread. (d) A basic understanding of the liturgy in keeping with the child[ren]'s mental maturity. (e) Formation of a desire to receive the Eucharist. (f) An understanding of the manner of receiving Christ's Body and Blood."[17] The catechists and priests at these parishes worked hard to teach the children the required elements; however, they also believed it was important to go further than the diocese suggested. They wanted to teach the children that belonging to the Church meant more than understanding doctrine: it also meant learning the defining characteristics and traditions of their parish. They wanted, as did the parents, to instill a general sense of Catholic identity in the communicants, which focused to a large degree on their own parish culture. This doctrinal and cultural information became the building blocks with which the communicants formed their interpretations of First Communion.

Teaching Principles, Practice, and Participation

Even though many children did not like to spend each Sunday in class, many, like Cara, recognized that to receive First Communion, "we had lots to learn."[18] The teachers too felt a great deal of pressure to ensure that this next generation of Catholics was well prepared. They sought to help the children discern the difference between ordinary bread and the consecrated Host, and to ensure that they did understood the Eucharist's meaning required many hours of Faith Formation classes as well as time spent learning alongside their parents at Mass and at home. In concert with the Church, Ms. Fabuel and the other catechists often emphasized that the parents were the children's primary catechists. As Ms. Fabuel remarked, "I'm an assistant to the parent, and it's the parents' job to make sure they [the children] know the stuff. It's up to the parents to go over the lesson with them. It's really a team effort, and we have a good team."[19] In their discussions about responsibility, neither the catechists nor the parents ever talked seriously about the children's responsibility in their own sacramental preparations.

As the adults prepared the children for the Sacrament, they continually looked forward to the communicants' future life as Catholics. As I noted earlier, many adults believed that the children at seven or eight years old could not comprehend fully what they were being taught. This belief that the second-graders, although they may have learned a great deal during the year, could not think deeply about the connections that they were making seemed common in both parishes, although the belief did not seem to be universally held by all adults in the parishes. Even if the children might not have been old enough to understand Church doctrine fully, however, the "little sponges," as Ms. Fister, the assistant catechist in Ms. Fabuel's class, and others referred to the children, could absorb a great deal.[20] Few adults believed, however, that these young children evaluated this information as they absorbed it. Reflecting on the communicants' age, Ms. Lauffer, mother of one of the Holy Cross communicants, said, for instance, "I guess Confirmation . . . is a full acceptance by the child, or by the young adult, in a very conscious way of joining the Church. Whereas I think in First Communion it's more of a 'they're just along for the ride.'"[21] With this statement, Ms. Lauffer expressed many adults' belief that in receiving First Communion, the children were simply conforming to adult expectations and prescriptions, whereas during Confirmation, young people made informed choices about their faith.

This focus on the children's inability to interpret their faith and on the adults' role in the religious formation of the child seemed to assume that the children were not active in their own faith development. In the face of the great resistance some children displayed to learning their lessons and the great amount of reflection displayed by others, the adults seemed to maintain a belief that the children in general were passive learners who were molded, as so many modern parenting experts claimed, by the behaviors and beliefs that adults taught them and displayed in their actions. Rarely did any adult mention that the children interpreted for themselves what adults taught them either formally or informally. My work clearly shows, however, that the communicants utilized information from all areas of their lives to develop their own understandings of the Sacrament.

Only Mr. Thomas made any reference to this reality: as a catechist, he explained, he had to "walk a straight line, so that the curves that the children's minds would inevitably create would not take them too far from the true essence of the Church."[22] In this comment, Mr. Thomas did not seem to believe that the turns taken by the children's minds would lead them in directions that might threaten the state of their souls, as his own catechists would have. Instead, as he gives the children some agency in their own faith formation, he seems to highlight only that their agency will be counterproductive to the teaching efforts of the adults because the "curves" in the minds of the children would detract from their efforts at understanding the Church and almost necessarily lead them away from its "true essence." Thus, while he perceived no inherent danger in letting the children talk about each week's lesson, he believed that the parents and teachers continually needed to direct the children's interpretations of Catholic teachings toward what the adults believed was the truth. (Of course, what the adults taught in the classroom and elsewhere were their own interpretations of what they had learned in catechism.)

Given that the adults had to be persistent in their guidance, the catechists believed that, since the children spent a great deal of time with their parents each week while the catechists spent only one hour in Faith Formation class, the parents needed to see themselves as the primary catechists. Only the parents could demonstrate the importance of Catholicism to their children each day by praying with them, modeling for them behavior in keeping with the beliefs of the Church, and talking about the Sacrament with them in the time between classes. Only they could model what it meant to be a good Catholic for their children. Even those parents who made only minimal efforts demonstrated some degree of commitment to their role as catechists, however, by at least bringing their children to participate in the Sacrament. The parents of fifty-eight children at Holy Cross and Blessed Sacrament wanted their children to participate in First Communion, even if these parents did not all remember their own First Communion. The catechists also had no doubt that some parents and children could barely remember the last time they went to Mass. A strong desire that their children receive the Sacrament brought many parents back to the Catholic Church after a long absence. Because of this, First Eucharist was also promoted by the parish leaders as a moment for adult faith formation. To ensure that all the parents knew the meaning behind the Sacrament, each parent meeting included some element of adult catechesis and reflection. Some parents seemed particularly annoyed by these efforts, while others told me that they "learned a lot of things."[23] Britney's mother also seemed to learn a bit (her daughter revealed) when Britney brought her corrected workbook home with her each week. "My mom has been helping me, and I say, 'Mom, I got it wrong,' and she says, 'Well, it's my fault.'"[24] Even though some of Britney's answers may not have been correct, the willingness of her mother to help her daughter with her homework, like those parents who attended class each week, showed a greater degree of commitment to the program than was evidenced by some parents. Most parents seemed simply to be going through the motions, as many of their children did each Sunday morning, because the meetings were a required part of First Communion preparation.

Given this great variety of both prior knowledge of Church doctrine and interest in it among the families in each class, at neither parish could the catechists assume, as they prepared lessons for their fifty-minute classes, that the children would know anything about Church practice or belief. Although some children learned about Jesus at home, for many children this sacramental year marked their first formal religious education. For instance, when I asked Britney, who said she had been coming to Sunday school at Blessed Sacrament for only one year, if she had recently moved to Burlington, she replied, "No, I've been here; and then my mom said, 'Britney, next year you have to go to Sunday school.' And I was like, 'huh?'"[25] Many children had this experience, while others, particularly many Hispanics, moved too frequently to join any parish's faith development program. The religious education staff realized that many children had not attended Faith Formation classes before and that, given post-Sacrament Faith Formation attrition rates, many might not return after they had received the Eucharist. Yet some of these children may have stopped going to Faith Formation classes but have continued going to Mass. The relationship that these children had with the Sacrament, then, may have remained unchanged or grown stronger but not disappeared as the attrition rates might lead one to assume.

Approximately 40 percent of the Holy Cross's 1997 First Communion class, 75 percent of the Mexican portion of Blessed Sacrament's 2001 class, and 30 percent of the white portion did not return after First Communion.[26] The tremendous drop in Faith Formation participation indicates that First Eucharist may fail as a ritual of initiation for most children if their initiation into the universal Catholic Church is supposed to be marked by their continued participation in their local parish. For, on the surface, it seems that the connection that the Eucharist creates between the children and the Church is not strong enough to keep the children interested in maintaining their commitment to the Church—a commitment that should lead a child to participate in the third step of faith development, Confirmation. Of course, the level of a communicant's participation in Faith Formation classes may not reflect the extent of his or her actual interest level in the Church at all: if the communicant is interested, his or her absence may not be the child's fault, since the child can get to Faith Formation class only if driven by a parent; similarly, if a communicant is not interested, then he or she may still be in attendance at Faith Formation class because he or she was dragged out of bed each Sunday morning and forced to attend. Given these constraints, the exact level of a communicant's commitment to the Church is hard to gauge, but it is clear from the substantial decrease in attendance after First Communion that the Sacrament was not universally successful in ensuring the children's continued attachment to the Catholic Church.

Having taught First Communion classes for a number of years, many of the catechists planned their curriculum with the understanding that the Sacrament might likely fail in getting the children (and their parents) to honor their obligation to the Catholic Church by attending Mass regularly and furthering their faith development. Moreover, they knew that the children would not be focused solely on their faith development while they attended Faith Formation classes. Thus, the teachers tried to remain undistracted by all the noise, glue, and movement in the classrooms each week and attempted to teach the communicants "the basics."

This sacramental preparation marked the first time that the Church systematically introduced the children not only to its symbols and its tastes but also to its moral and ethical codes. Many adults hoped that knowing these fundamentals would enable the children to have an active Church life, see themselves as a follower of Jesus, and create a lifelong relationship with the Catholic Church. The catechists worked with the children to give them a firm, universally Christian, and particularly Catholic religious foundation. The classes with broader Christian messages took various forms.

The catechists showed up each Sunday morning after the earliest Mass to teach religious education for a variety of reasons, from trying to ensure that the children have as meaningful a First Communion as they did, to just wanting to make sure that communicants were properly prepared for the Sacrament. The Church's notion of proper preparation had changed a great deal between when these children were receiving their First Communion and when their parents had. The dioceses had long been offering these religious education classes, formerly known as the Confraternity of Christian Doctrine (CCD) classes, to public school children for approximately one hour a week.[27] Before Vatican II (1962–65), these classes, like all Catholic religious education, primarily stressed memorizing prayers as well as the answers to questions posed in one of a variety of catechisms. The most poplar manual was the *Baltimore Cate-. chism*, created by the Plenary Council of Baltimore in 1864. Cardinal James Gibbons declared it the official text for Catholic education in the United States twenty-one years later. From that point until the late 1950s and early 1960s, catechists taught Catholic children their faith's doctrine and theology primarily through memorization of that text.[28] Although there were some efforts to move the children away from memorization as early as the 1930s, most children continued to learn the catechism. As Katie's mom said of her First Communion preparation: "We had to memorize a book. If we didn't memorize it, we couldn't make our First Communion."[29] Through these catechisms, the Church hoped to impose uniformity on its religious education program. Although there were some efforts at more child-centered learning as early as the 1940s, the process of rote learning and the widespread use of the *Baltimore Catechism* did not end until Vatican II, after which concern with active learning supplanted worries about catechetical uniformity.[30] With this shift away from memorization, Katie's First Communion preparation would necessarily be different from her mother's: the concepts her mother learned through repeated drills, Katie was to be taught through activities.

After Vatican II, the Church fully embraced the tenets of progressive education that were being developed by Thomas Edwin Shields within the world of Catholic education, just as G. Stanley Hall and John Dewey were promoting it in America's public schools.[31] As early as 1906, Shields, a professor in the Department of Education at the Catholic University of America, argued that Catholic schools needed to move beyond strict memorization to a child-centered approach to education. "It is true," he wrote, "that we were done with the old fallacy which led many well meaning teachers to feed their children's souls on words and word drills at a time when their imaginations and hearts were famished for want of real food."[32] Although Shields pushed for Catholic schools to adopt progressive education reforms at the beginning of the twentieth century, most Catholic educators continued to use more traditional methods for the next forty years or more. In 1965, however, Pope Paul VI declared, "Children and young people must be helped with the aid of the latest advances in psychology and the arts and science of teaching."[33] Thus, the religious education classroom, like many secular educational facilities, was transformed from a place where children came to absorb facts passively into a site where students actively gained information for themselves. As the Catholic religious educational system began this shift, many parishes opted for interactive workbooks and later included even more hands-on activities in their lessons. Ms. Key explained: "We don't do *Baltimore Catechism*–style teaching, which used to be memorized. We're more in tune with the way teaching is done now. It's more of a facilitation of the learning and not focusing so much on the memorizing but trying to put experience and knowledge together. That's why we do more activity-based things in conjunction with the material that's in a book, so that it's experiential knowledge."[34] This kind of teaching, based on experiential knowledge, permitted the kinds of deviations that Mr. Thomas had told me about, deviations that the *Baltimore Catechism* did not allow, since that pre–Vatican II teaching style sought to preclude the children's interpretations, which could endanger the state of the children's souls.

Although Blessed Sacrament and Holy Cross tried to stop using the *Baltimore Catechism* style of teaching, many catechists relied on drills or lecture to ensure the children knew the facts required to participate in the Sacrament. In weekly drills, the children at Holy Cross learned how the ritual components of the Mass fit together. Mr. Thomas, for instance, opened one class by saying, "Let's review the mechanics of the Mass to understand what Communion is all about." I sat at the back of the U-shaped group of tables that were surrounded by the twenty children who answered Mr. Thomas's rapid-fire questions:

> Mr. Thomas: "First reading?"
> Ryan: "Old Testament."
> Mr. Thomas: "Second reading?"
> Ryan: "New Testament."
> Mr. Thomas: "Penance?"
> Jim: "Take all your sins back."
> Mr. Thomas: "Eucharist?"
> Maureen: "The Table."
> Mr. Thomas: "Nope."
> Ryan: "The Body and Blood."[35]

This review was one way that the catechists stressed the organization, gestures, vestments, and symbols of the Mass. Teaching well after Vatican II, the catechists now were told to move away from the more familiar drills to teach the communicants in a language and style that was quite different from how the catechists and the parents had been taught. *Trends in Catechesis of Children in the United States*, published in 1976, shows that the Church tried to address this problem early on: "The most recent revisions of the text and program materials reflect efforts to address the difficulty in communicating with parents by including more traditional statements of doctrine in the books and other materials used in religious instruction. It is hoping that this will have the added advantage of acquainting children with the religious language and thinking of their parents, thus fostering dialogue at home."[36]

In reaction to this problem of translation, both parishes had workshops with the parents in which they offered a refresher course on the sacraments as well as an explanation of how the Church's teachings had changed since the parents learned them. At Blessed Sacrament, for instance, Ms. Tackitt offered an extended discussion about why the Church had changed the term "Confession" to "Penance" and finally to "Reconciliation." In part, it seems Ms. Tackitt offered this explanation to calm parents' fears that their children might have the same feelings of sinfulness that they themselves might have had during their own First Confession decades ago. Through this change, Ms. Tackitt emphasized, the Church refocused the rite from one of confession of sin to one concerned with atonement and finally to one concerned with the individual's relationship with Christ and community.[37] This shift toward seeing the Sacrament as communal and relational was but one aspect of the Vatican II focus on the humanity of Jesus and on seeing the members of the Church as the people of God. These two Vatican II ideas affected the children's First Communion experience in more ways than just the name and style of confession. Centering on Jesus' humanity, for example, meant that the teachers worked to show the children that Jesus was their friend, as I discuss in Chapter 4. Preparing the communicants to be part of the Church, the people of God, also meant that the children needed to learn how to participate in the Mass, rather than be passive observers of the priest's actions.

Classes after Vatican II tended to emphasize using activities "to reinforce . . . understanding of the doctrine."[38] By the 1990s, the most popular model for these interactive lessons came from the Italian scholar Sofia Cavalletti. First fully outlined in *The Religious Potential of the Child*, Cavalletti's theory of teaching religion was modeled after Maria Montessori's ideas on education.[39] Like Montessori, Cavalletti believed that children learned best through engaging their senses in ways that matched their stage of development and their desires.[40] In creating her approach, Cavalletti began from the assumption developed by the Romantics that children were naturally spiritual. She argued that "far from imposing something that is foreign to him [the child], we [religious educators] are responding to the child's silent request: 'Help me to come to God by myself.'"[41] Neither parish in my study used Cavalletti's hands-on program of religious instruction, *Catechesis of the Good Shepherd*. Ms. Key from Blessed Sacrament, however, spoke of Cavalletti's work often, and Cavalletti's principles seemed to guide both parishes' Faith Formation classes.[42] For example, the guidelines for the child's readiness in Holy Cross's First Communion handbook reflected Cavalletti's goals for religious education: "It is important that both the parent and the catechist *assist* the child in coming to know Jesus for himself, not in a [second]hand relationship, which the adult might try to give the child."[43] Although there was still a great deal of memorizing to be done, the catechists at both parishes also created situations through which they hoped the children would discover their own relationship with Jesus.

Rather than a rapid-fire "call-and-response" drill to learn the Ten Commandments, for instance, the communicants at both parishes engaged in a series of discussions and activities through which their teachers hoped they would learn the commandments and the benefits of following them. The catechists at Blessed Sacrament, for instance, reminded the communicants that to live in accordance with God's will, they had to both behave properly and reach out to others in their community. As Britney explained, we "made cards to old people . . . because we were going to show that we cared and we were praying for them."[44] The class hoped, she continued, to make these older adults feel better. Using rubber stamps of church symbols, markers, and stickers, the adults hoped to teach the children to love others by having them write letters to the parish shut-ins, the elderly parishioners who could not physically make it to Mass. Having heard stories about two homebound parishioners the week before, the children worked diligently on their Easter cards that second Sunday in March. The silence that enveloped the classroom as the students grabbed crayons and stickers to decorate their construction paper evidenced their collective interest in the project. Although this interest may not have extended to the tenets the catechists hoped to teach the children, the teachers believed that through participating in the project the children might learn this lesson to "love thy neighbor" without even realizing it. Perhaps they were correct, for the only sounds above faint whispers came from some of the Spanish-speaking students who needed help spelling "bunny," "how are you?" and "Easter" in English. Of course, for a few children the silence was more a sign of resignation than of interest. Dean, for instance, attracted Ms. Fabuel's attention not because he was talking but because he had decided to put only stickers on his paper. She stood by his desk, imploring him to draw a picture for these parishioners, who all needed some cheering up. As she walked away, Dean slowly picked up a marker and mumbled under his breath, "I wish there were no Sundays!" "Why?" I asked, having just barely heard this comment. "Because then I wouldn't have to come here," he replied as he turned back to his work.[45] Here Dean spoke clearly for all of those children who hated Faith Formation classes. And, like his classmates, he did it in a way that would not get him into trouble with his teachers. The mumbling of his comment, however, did not diminish the strength of Dean's feelings. Nor did his comment mean, as I discuss in Chapter 4, that Dean did not want to participate in First Communion.

First Communion would not be Dean's only reward; along with receiving the Sacrament, the parishioner who received Dean's card sent him a thank-you note with a penny in it for good luck during his First Reconciliation and First Communion. The smile that swept across Dean's face as he placed the penny in his pocket may indeed have taught him something about how good it can be to do something nice for someone else.[46] This ongoing project did, in fact, help the children to remember others at various times throughout the year. Many communicants mentioned these letters in our conversations, especially those, like Dean, who received replies. Through these responses, the children seemed to learn how much little acts, like making a card, could mean, even to a stranger. The catechists used the conversation, the video, and the letter-writing project to help the children to realize that they had the power to make good choices and that their choices—good and bad—had consequences. They could enact God's commandment to "love thy neighbor," or they could disappoint God and their parents by ignoring such opportunities. By encouraging the children to actively engage in and contribute to the lesson, the catechists wanted them to feel its impact and consequences directly, something that an exercise in rote memorization could never do.

Similarly, through her lessons at Holy Cross and her conversations with her mother and her friends, Maureen learned that "Catholics have to have a certain way to live your life—not just a free life. There are rules."[47] She learned some of these rules from Mr. Thomas's evocative storytelling. Rather than asking the children to use their markers to illustrate how they could please God, Mr. Thomas asked the children at Holy Cross to use their imaginations. As he told the story of Jesus' walk to Calvary, he implored the children to model their behavior after Jesus' life. Banging his hands on the table to get the class's attention after an outbreak of laughter, he began his lesson with the cadence and spirit of a Protestant preacher exhorting his congregation to follow God: "This is where we have to make a difference. Let's talk about Jesus as a peacemaker. . . . Imagine, imagine, imagine." The class, sitting on the outside of a U-shaped table, had their eyes fixed on Mr. Thomas, who stood near the table in the middle of the "U." He implored them to let their imaginations bring them further into his story. "Walk with me. Walk with me! . . . He's carrying a big heavy cross up the street and up the hill. . . . People are *spitting* on him. . . . You hear what I'm saying? They're *spitting* on him." The previously silent class erupted into laughter, but Mr. Thomas continued quickly, regaining their attention: "He could have wiped out all those people, the very ones spitting on him and throwing rocks at him. He could have [Mr. Thomas snaps his fingers] just that easy. Now, what did he do? Listen, he's strung up on the cross, and what did he do? He looked up in the sky, and he said, 'Forgive them Father for they know not what they do.' *Peacemaker*." After a dramatic pause, he continued, "I bop you on the nose." Again the class laughed. "As hard as it is. As hard as it is, you say: 'Stop. I know I can beat you. . . . But I'm going to walk away. The peace of Jesus be with you.'"[48] Although class ended before the children discussed how they could act as "peacemakers," many of them seemed to have been listening to Mr. Thomas's lesson.

The children's talk of Jesus' and their own behavior often reflected this lesson. For example, when Ms. Williams asked the children what the Holy Spirit had done for them in the "What Catholics Believe" lesson, Michael answered, "He said 'Stop, instead of getting back at people.'" [49] Similarly, during the First Communion retreat, Maureen asked, "What was he [Jesus] like?" Paris had a one-word reply: "Peacemaker." [50] Like Michael and Paris, many children seemed to have connected with Mr. Thomas's retelling. They could envision themselves on that street, watching Jesus, or carrying the cross. Mr. Thomas's choice to put them along the route to Calvary facilitated the connection between the children and Jesus, the Peacemaker, increasing the likelihood that the students would remember it. And it seemed to have been quite effective.

Through storytelling, role-playing, and card making, the catechists strove to create environments in which the children felt God's love and explored his commandments. These children did much more than memorize catechetical statements about the Sacrament: they enacted their understanding either in arts and crafts projects or through placing themselves on the road to Calvary. Using these lessons, the catechists reinforced the underpinnings of the children's religious lives and the importance of the Christian tenet of love for others.

Blessed Sacrament's Faith Formation classes seemed to be influenced more by creative projects than were Holy Cross's weekly lessons, which emphasized the children's explorations through discussions such as the one that opened this chapter. Each week, Blessed Sacrament's catechists used art and community-involvement projects that highlighted the lesson's main objective. Ms. Fabuel described their Faith Formation strategy, saying that they always tried to "come up with a project to illustrate this week's main theme." [51] These projects ranged from finger painting images of heaven using shaving cream (one of the communicants' favorite activities) to writing letters to the parish shut-ins (an activity enjoyed by many). While Holy Cross's monthly parent/child workshops were centered on hands-on activities, the weekly classes were not, although they sometimes ended with a short project, including drawing pictures of Jesus washing each child's feet on Holy Thursday.

The two parishes not only employed different instructional techniques but they also used different materials. Ms. Wright-Jukes at Holy Cross chose to write her own lessons each week, and although they followed the basic outline of many textbooks, she tailored them to her specific class. Thus she could make her lessons relevant to her class of African American Catholics by including saints who are important to African and African American Catholics such as St. Peter Claver and St. Martin de Porres. Blessed Sacrament's catechists, on the other hand, found materials that suited their class's unique needs in Sadlier's bilingual *Coming to Jesus* workbook.[52] The book is divided into four sections, beginning with "Our Catholic Faith," which focuses on general Catholic doctrine. The middle two units offer more in-depth instruction on Reconciliation and the Eucharist, while the final portion highlights First Holy Communion and the children's new relationship with Jesus. Each chapter follows the same structure, with the first page or two offering thought questions that relate to the children's lives, the next few pages telling a Bible story, and the final pages providing a summary and review test. Unlike Blessed Sacrament, Holy Cross had no homework or review tests. The children demonstrated their knowledge in their classroom conversations. From these chapters (or outlines, in the case of Holy Cross) the catechists had to create a class that would be informative, effective in negotiating differences in the children's prior knowledge, and interesting enough to hold the children's attention.

Whatever materials they used, when the catechists brought these lesson plans into the classroom, they often were altered, even thwarted, by the class's attitude that Sunday (Figure 7). Teaching two dozen seven-year-olds, the catechists had to be ready for surprising responses to their questions as well as interesting inquiries, such as Maureen's "Why was Jesus a boy?" Along with unexpected questions, the children also attempted to shift their class's direction through their behavior. Some children left their seats to wander through the classroom. Some communicants passed time in class taunting their neighbors. And the communicants' constant chatter some Sundays overwhelmed the discussion. These bored children sought distraction in whatever ways were available to them.

While the children often did receive the attention and entertain-

FIGURE 7. *Communicants making a craft project*

ment they sought through making noise or refusing to participate in other ways, the din often made it difficult for the teachers to stay focused and for the children who were trying to pay attention to hear that day's lesson. Ms. Richards, who began teaching the communicants at Blessed Sacrament after Christmas, explained some of their behavior, saying, "I think the hardest thing is for second-graders to sit still for any length of time. And, of course, you have the boys who are into the roughhousing kind of thing. Just trying to keep control of the class is something I think that I need to maybe do some studying on."[53] This was not just a problem for Ms. Richards or the teachers at Blessed Sacrament; on my first visit to Holy Cross, seven of the eighteen children went back and forth to the bathroom in thirty minutes. For all the teachers, veterans or novices, getting through a day's lesson could be difficult. They never knew how it would go until they were well into teaching that day's lesson.[54] As the children roughhoused, strained to hear, or left to go to the bathroom or get a drink, the catechists tried to engage them in projects or stories that would introduce them to important aspects of their traditions and keep them interested. Through talking to their neighbors, wandering around the classroom, or daydreaming, children who did not like Sunday school or were just bored used the means available to protest their forced presence in class each week and to keep themselves entertained. Similarly, other children did what they were told so as to make it through each class, just as many of their parents sat through the parents' meeting. Thus, although the communicants' parents brought them to class each week, many children registered their displeasure with particular projects or generally resisted the catechists' lessons in any way they could. Therefore, often the catechists' efforts to keep the class interested failed at least for some children, which meant that those communicants did not learn parts, or perhaps all, of that day's lesson.

In many ways, these children who did not like Sunday school were the catechists' biggest challenge. The children's lack of desire to learn about Jesus and the Church has plagued catechists for years, and it is not the result of too many video games or any other modern distraction. In 1941 Louis LaRavoire Morrow, D.D., wrote a First Communion primer that he began by lamenting: "Too many children are bought to look on the catechism lesson as an onerous penance, to be avoided as much as possible, and endured only upon inducement of bribes in the form of candy, toys, holy pictures, [etc.]."[55] At Holy Cross and Blessed Sacrament, the children did not receive "bribes," but they were given time to color and cookies to eat when it fit with the day's lesson. Through a variety of discussions, art projects, and workshops, the catechists attempted to pass on these beliefs and sensibilities to the children. Through the ongoing conversation between the adults' teachings, which varied in their own unique ways from official Church doctrine, and the communicants' understanding of them, the children seemed to struggle to create a workable interpretation of the upcoming event from the information they were being taught. At least one idea, however, seemed to come naturally to the classes—the desire to receive the Eucharist.

Receiving the Eucharist

Most of the children wanted to become members of their parish, but not through the abstract information that the adults were discussing with them in Faith Formation class. Rather, they wanted the sensorial knowledge that members had. They wanted to be able to touch what other parishioners touched and to taste what other parishioners tasted. While some of the children had not been to Sunday school before, most, if not all, had been to Mass, where they had been excluded from receiving the Sacrament. Just knowing that they would soon be able to participate in this once forbidden ritual seemed to mark the true start of the children's First Communion experience. From the beginning of their sacramental preparation, many children were excited about the prospect of receiving the Eucharist. As nine-year-old Lily told me six weeks before she would receive the Eucharist, "I can't wait to taste the bread and wine."[56] It seems, then, that the rite of initiation began long before the children reached the sanctuary door on the day of the event. It began in the moments when the children realized that they would soon join the rest of the parish in the Eucharist—when the idea of receiving the Eucharist started to become a reality and the children's distant desire for inclusion turned into excitement for participation. The adults immediately recognized this excitement. As Ms. Wright-Jukes said of her son, four months before he received the Sacrament, "He's pumped. He just wants to get the bread."[57]

A Theology of Taste

The adults' understanding of the children's anticipation, however, could never reach the fevered pitch of many of the children's desire to be a part of this ritual. Remembering how she felt before First Communion, Samantha, an enthusiastic nine-year-old from Blessed Sacrament, exclaimed, "I just wanted to get the bread; that's all I wanted to do."[58] Although the communicants rarely made mention of their excitement to the degree that Samantha did before they received the Sacrament, it came through strongly both in their discussions with me and with their classmates about how the Eucharist might taste and in the contrast between their drawings of First Communion before and after the event. In our pre-Communion conversations, the children's eagerness was often palpable. Only three children, however, talked specifically about their feelings of anticipation, which had been building at least since the beginning of Faith Formation classes. Rather, in our conversations, many communicants discussed their expectations for receiving the Sacrament. When I asked Justin (who drew a picture of himself reaching out at Holy Cross's altar saying "Amen") if he was excited about First Communion, he smiled and said, "Yes, mostly [for] when I get to have the bread and wine for the first time" (Figure 8).[59] His responses—both verbal and pictorial—implied a sense of anticipation that Kim and Paris stated more directly. When Kim, a Brazilian American from Blessed Sacrament, and I began putting the crayons back into the box at the end of her interview, I asked her if there was anything else she thought I should know about First Communion. "I don't know," she said as she handed me her picture, "but that you have to wait a long time."[60] Though we had talked extensively about praying, dresses, and the Eucharist, she wanted to make sure that I knew that for communicants such as herself, First Communion was about waiting. Paris, her counterpart from Holy Cross, suggested that she had been waiting *too* long for the Sacrament. At Communion, she explained, you "*finally* get to taste the body and blood."[61] Her emphasis on "finally" underlined the feeling of expectation that hung over our table as we talked of First Communion.[62] In this waiting the children remained separated from the adult congregation that received the Eucharist each week. In depicting themselves as people apart, the children also seemed to render themselves inactive, perhaps even passive, in their separation. Standing before the priest initially, they needed an adult to act, to give them permission either through word or action, and they had to behave appropriately in response, in order to join in this central ritual. With the next gesture—by the priest in offering the Host and by the children in receiving it—that invisible barrier between the children and the adult congregation would disappear.

In emphasizing the moment just before they would participate in the Eucharist in their pre-Communion drawings, many children captured visually the anticipation I heard in their voices and saw on their faces. As Dean, his mother, and I waited to order breakfast at a local restaurant, he used the crayons to draw a picture of himself "getting ready to get [the] bread first" (Figure 9). He drew himself, mouth wide open, as the first stick-figure communicant in

FIGURE 8. *Justin reaches out to receive the Sacrament*

line. Dean's depiction of himself, the center of attention, waiting open-mouthed before the priest reinforced his comment that the best part of First Communion was that "you finally get to eat something during Mass."[63] In describing the event, other children did not depict themselves first in line in their drawings; however, many communicants expressed their eagerness to receive the Eucharist through their drawings in slightly more subtle ways.

FIGURE 9. *Dean leads a line of smiling communicants*

In their pre-Communion pictures, all the communicants who drew themselves inside the church portrayed themselves as frozen in the moment of anticipation just before the priest gave them the consecrated Host. While they could have drawn themselves eating the Host, returning to their pew after receiving the Sacrament, or in a variety of other ways, all these children used the crayons to show themselves standing at the altar waiting to taste the bread. Often, they depicted themselves standing before the priest's, or the Eucharistic minister's, outstretched hands, as in Britney's (Figure 10), José's (Figure 5), and Justin's (Figure 8) pictures. Like José, Roxanna also positioned herself next to the priest, although, unlike any of the other children, Roxanna drew herself standing in the center aisle of the sanctuary waiting to receive both the bread and the wine (Figure 11). Though her picture shows progression, as the viewer follows the stick figure down the aisle, she does not show herself having received the bread and waiting to take the wine. Instead, she depicts herself waiting to receive each element. The words Roxanna chose to describe her picture also imply this sense of anticipation. "It is me," she explained, "when I am going to eat the *cuerpo de Christo y sangre de Christo.*" [64] Here, like so many of her peers, she responded to my request, "Would you please draw me a picture of First Communion?" by illustrating her waiting. Alison went one step further in her drawing and allowed the viewer to see the Sacrament through her eyes (Figure 12). She does not appear in her drawing; instead, the viewer seems to be standing in her shoes. Looking at her picture, we all stand before the altar waiting for the priest to hand us the bread.

FIGURE 10. *A priest dressed in purple reaches out to Britney*

These illustrations of waiting stress that the children's understandings of their separation from the adult congregation center on
action as much as on *belief*. It was not primarily the lack of doctrinal
understanding that caused the children to feel separated from the
adults; the children recognized that they were excluded from participating in the central ritual of the Church because they could not
perform the necessary movement. Here in these pictures, the children depict themselves anticipating the moment when the priest
places the consecrated Host in their hands or when they placed
the Host in their mouths. Having seen family members receive the
Eucharist at Mass and even practicing it themselves, it seems that

FIGURE 11. *Roxanna awaits the bread and wine in the center aisle of the sanctuary*

the children could easily have drawn different pictures. The post-Communion pictures drawn by the children were often very different, as I discuss below. However, in highlighting the moment of waiting before First Communion, the drawings emphasize that the children knew they had not yet joined the larger congregation, had not yet "tasted Jesus."

Reinforcing their separation, even when they had other choices,

FIGURE 12. *Alison invites the viewer to see First Communion through her eyes*

the children emphasized their position as apart from the adult parishioners, a position that they also remembered in the months after receiving the Sacrament. As we sat on the floor in the vestibule of Holy Cross's Activity Center nine months after she had made her First Communion, Cara explained her desire for the Eucharist: "I was grateful that I had the body and blood of Christ 'cause all my brothers and sisters got some and I wasn't happy 'cause I didn't have any. . . . I always wanted to get it. . . . My mommy said, 'You can't. You have to wait until your First Communion.' . . . I didn't want to wait." [65] After participation in the Eucharist, her classmate Ferris spoke similarly about the waiting. He said in a frustrated tone that he "used to hate standing in the pew while my grandmother and my mom went up to get the bread and the wine 'cause my mom would always say, 'That day [will] come.'" [66] In this waiting, the children wanted to belong to this special group of people that included their parents, their grandparents, and their older brothers and sisters, who went to the altar each Sunday, and they also wanted to have the special, adult, and sacred knowledge of how the consecrated bread and wine tasted.

By contrast, the parents, priests, and catechists never referred to the sensual experiences that were a part of the ritual when they described their expectations for how receiving this Sacrament would change the communicants' understanding of their relationship to Jesus, their parish, and the Catholic Church. The adults hoped that children would learn about Jesus, feel closer to him, and come to understand that the consecrated Host contained his "special presence."[67] Their teachers wanted this knowledge, both intellectual and experiential, to bring the communicants into the larger Catholic Church and to help them form spiritual relationships on which they could depend throughout their lives. Despite their different approaches, however, the children did feel they were transitioning into a knowledgeable group through the Eucharist, as the Church dictated. For the children, however, their initiation happened, in large part, through taste and participation in the ritual, and the group they were joining was limited to those persons whom they had seen receiving the Sacrament—parents, grandparents, initiated parishioners—and did not extend to a sense of participation in the larger Catholic Church, which they never mentioned in our many discussions. Thus, as a rite of passage, First Communion worked differently for the children from what the Church dictated: receiving the Eucharist remained a personal and immediate experience, rather than a broader doctrinal commitment to the universal Catholic Church. The children anticipated the taste of the wine and the Host, the one great secret of the Catholic Church that they could not learn until the instant they received their First Communion.

The communicants' discussions of the flavor and texture of the Host demonstrated the centrality of taste in their expectations, anxieties, and interpretations of the event. Concerns about taste seemed to tie together many of the children's interpretations of First Communion by grounding them in sensual experience.[68] At Holy Cross, Ryan said it most succinctly when he explained that First Communion was "about tasting and learning about Jesus and when he's suffering."[69] Similarly, Elizabeth from Blessed Sacrament explained that in First Communion "you're eating something very special from a very long time ago."[70] Britney reinforced the importance of eating in her comment that First Communion "makes you feel proud and you get to eat stuff and you get to come closer to God."[71] The children, it seemed, understood that this bread was different from other bread, for it connected them with God in a new way. It allowed some of them to cross the expanse of time to the Last Supper, others to taste Jesus, and still others to obtain physical evidence of a more personal relationship with Jesus. Again, from a doctrinal perspective, it was this personal relationship with God and Jesus that was important to the children, not their relationship with the wider Catholic Church.

For many children, this concern with taste arose from the desire to participate in the Eucharist with the rest of the congregation, as well as from curiosity about the flavor of the consecrated bread. For Paris, as for all the children with whom I talked, Communion was important because "we got to taste the Body and Blood."[72] Melissa, like most of the children, "really [did] want to eat the bread a lot."[73] In the moments before they received the bread and wine, but even in practice, some children seemed to change their minds. Although Michael had told me earlier that he was excited about receiving Communion, sitting next to his mother during the final rehearsal he turned to her, face frozen in determination, and stated, "I'm not going to eat that nasty stuff."[74] He was the only child to state publicly that he would not eat the Host; however, many of them were quite vocal about not wanting to drink the wine. Many children, especially those at Blessed Sacrament, did not want the wine. A few of them stated flatly, "I won't have wine."[75] Other children, like Maureen, wanted to "finally find out if they used real wine or grape juice."[76] The communicants soon discovered that the chalice did, in fact, contain real wine—a new and somewhat unpleasant experience for most of them. During Holy Cross's final Faith Formation class, the week after First Communion, the children sat around the statue of Mary in the gazebo behind the church talking loudly and emphatically about how much they hated the wine. Hunter, a vivacious eight-year-old African American boy, firmly expressed the opinion of many of Holy Cross's First Communicants: "When I received the wine, it didn't taste good to me."[77] The wine was universally anticipated with fear and received with much dislike. The children's discussion of the wine centered around its status as an "adult" drink that had been off-limits to them previously. A few weeks after they had their First Communion, the children's concern with taste remained, although the focus shifted from the wine to the bread (perhaps because the communicants thought they had expressed their negative feelings about the wine clearly enough).

Unlike the wine's ability to mark the Eucharist's space as "adult," finally tasting the body of Christ allowed the children to experience the lessons of blessing, union, and transubstantiation that they had learned in class. As I discuss below, eating the consecrated Host apparently allowed at least one child to experience the doctrine of transubstantiation concretely through her sense of taste—just as talking about taste had permitted other children to express their expectations before receiving the Sacrament. Some adults, however, wondered whether "second grade, or eight years old, may be a little young for a true understanding of . . . what's going on."[78] A few of the children's answers may have exceeded the adults' expectations, showing that at least some of the children did understand this mystery in some way. Yet these children and their classmates used words and media differently from those words and media employed by the adults. Cara, for instance, expressed her experience of transubstantiation through her description of how the Host's taste changed from the practice to the First Communion Mass. Nine months after her First Communion, she noted that while the practice bread tasted "like plastic," the "real one" tasted "good, very good." Why? "Because it's the real one, and the one we took in practice wasn't real. It wasn't made."[79] Thus, Cara experienced transubstantiation through her sense of taste and expressed her experience in the most concrete way available to her. Although she could not explain the bread's transformation from the practice to First Communion, neither could many adult Catholics. Even the definitions of transubstantiation offered by Catholic scholars, like the one I recounted in Chapter 3 seem vague and awkward. Cara knew, however, that the bread she tasted on Communion Saturday was not the same as the unconsecrated practice Hosts.

Nonetheless, Cara's sensual understanding of transubstantiation may not have translated into a firm belief that she actually ingested Jesus' body and blood, as Katie's question, "Will it taste like a real body?" which began the introduction to this book implied that Katie might believe.[80] Some of her classmates, in fact, reacted adversely to the suggestion that the bread and wine did more than represent Christ's sacrifice. Ryan, for example, drew a picture of the Host to represent his First Communion experience because he said that receiving the Host made him feel special. Ryan's picture (Figure 6) demonstrated the close attention he gave the Sacrament by including the Greek symbol for Christ that appears on each Host. According to his explanation, this intense focus on the Sacrament did not translate into a belief in "real presence." At the suggestion that the bread became Jesus' body, Ryan said: "It's really like bread, but I wouldn't eat anyone's skin or drink anyone's blood. That's nasty."[81] Perhaps the concreteness of Ryan's vision would have made transubstantiation implausible to Cara and the other children, or perhaps Cara and Ryan represented the differing viewpoints on transubstantiation held by Catholics of all ages. Father Barry, for instance, estimated that approximately one-third of all Catholics believe that the Eucharist symbolically represents Jesus' sacrifice, rather than actually reenacting it in blood-less form.[82] Thus, although Chris, a rambunctious seven-year-old African American, successfully answered the rapid-fire questioning in his Faith Formation classes at Holy Cross by explaining that the body and blood of Christ was "the real thing," this response does not necessarily mean that on First Communion day he believed he was actually ingesting Christ's body.[83] His response could mean only that he wanted to demonstrate his mastery of what he had learned in class and please the catechists, priests, and parents who wanted him to learn it. He may just have wanted to give the "right" answer, or perhaps it meant something more: from our conversation, it is difficult to know. Whatever meaning he intended, this response, as well as similar responses made by some of his classmates, demonstrated that the lessons the communicants were learning were causing them to think about the meaning of the bread and to apply this newly learned vocabulary to their experiences.

This preoccupation with taste, whether pleasant or unpleasant, led to comparisons of the bread and wine with "a jelly sandwich," along with other analogies and explanations that the communicants used to help themselves and me understand the consecrated bread's taste both before and after they had tasted it themselves.[84] Paul, a seven-year-old African American boy from Holy Cross, liked the Host because "it tasted good." He continued, "It looks like paper, but it's not. It tastes good."[85] Other children, like Hunter, were disappointed. "I thought the body would taste like something. It just tasted like cardboard."[86] Far from tasting sacred, the Eucharist tasted ordinary. Reflecting back on this comment as I talked with children at Blessed Sacrament who seemed to hope that in some way the Host would taste like Christ's body, I wondered if they too would be disappointed when they received the Host. While none of my post-Communion interviews revealed that the children were disillusioned with the Sacrament, neither do they reveal extreme expectations for how the Sacrament might change their lives. Rather, the children seemed to have relatively practical interests in receiving the Eucharist—learning the meaning of the objects they saw each Mass, teaching their bodies to move as the adults moved during the liturgy, and discovering the consecrated Hosts' taste. They did not want to be excluded any longer. They wanted to belong, just as the adults had hoped they would.

The Meaning of Consecration

In contrast to these memories and illustrations of waiting, the communicants' drawings sketched after they had tasted the Eucharist put action at the center of their interpretations.[87] In their post-Sacrament pictures, children such as Melissa drew themselves holding the bread and wine (Figure 13). Some communicants illustrated a different moment in the liturgy: Hunter's picture (Figure 21) shows him lighting his candle, and José (Figure 20) depicts himself speaking before the congregation, as I will discuss in Chapter 4.[88] Here, the children shift from drawing themselves frozen, arms open in anticipation, to depicting themselves as actors taking hold of the Eucharist or performing another prescribed ritual gesture in front of the congregation. With this move to performance

FIGURE 13. *Melissa holds the chalice and Host with the pews behind her*

the children did two things: first, they joined the adult congregation and, second, they stood as agents in their own religious lives. In these drawings and in the liturgies themselves, the congregation watches as each child reads texts, holds candles, and receives the Host. No longer were the children members of an unrecognized congregation apart; having acted appropriately before their families and friends, they now saw themselves as integral members with significant contributions to make to their parish. To make this transition, however, the children had to "get Jesus."

After encountering these many pleas to "get the bread" each week, Ms. Wright-Jukes and many other adults recognized the children's eagerness to receive the Sacrament. The parents and catechists knew that the children were impatiently awaiting the time when they could go to the altar with their grandmothers and grandfathers, mothers and fathers, sisters and brothers. For instance, when Mr. Dwyer and I talked in the parish house, he leaned back in his chair as he tried to explain to me, a Protestant researcher, why his children and his students were so excited to receive the Sacrament: "They see all these people going up and receiving the body of

Christ every week—the bread and the wine. For years they've had to sit there on the sidelines and watch. And now they get to participate in that."[89] Like Mr. Dwyer, Father Barry understood that Faith Formation classes were much less interesting to the communicants than finally getting to taste the consecrated Host and the wine. "The kids," he said, "just want to walk in line with everyone and get Jesus."[90] The children's anticipation of receiving the Eucharist seemed to intensify the weight they placed on having their First Communion and to guide their interpretations of the event. Though much of the children's and the adults' attention may have been focused on "getting Jesus," both groups also realized, although to different degrees, that it was the effect of this reception that made it so important.

The priests and catechists spoke often about teaching the children the Eucharist's meaning and helping them feel an intimate union with God and the Church. Father Briant and Father Barry, for instance, concerned themselves primarily with instructing the communicants about the doctrine of transubstantiation. Father Briant explained that he wanted the communicants to know "that it is special bread and that Christ is present."[91] Father Barry echoed this statement: "We firmly believe that the bread and wine actually become the body and blood of Christ himself, which is what I want the children to understand."[92]

Father Barry's goal, like the goals of many adults, stressed the beliefs that supported the mysterious transformation of the Eucharist. It seems that having long since become accustomed to receiving the Sacrament and performing the movements that accompany it (and, perhaps being more inclined to talk about doctrinal issues in an interview), these adults did not discuss the importance of the sensuous aspects of the ritual in our conversations, but the communicants did. The catechists' first goal, like the priests', was to have the children grasp the Eucharist's importance. Ms. Fabuel, for instance, explained that she hoped the children would comprehend "that this [transubstantiation] happens through the power of the Holy Spirit and the words the priest [says], and that ... when they get Communion they get Jesus in their hearts."[93] While Ms. Fabuel's interpretation of the effects of the Eucharist resonates with the Protestant culture in which she lives, others' beliefs seemed closer to official Church doctrine. With a voice full of wonderment, for instance, Ms. Richards said that she hoped that "if nothing else, they can just appreciate the wondrous gift we have in the Sacrament of Eucharist. You know, it truly is Jesus."[94] Thus, as the children moved through this rite of initiation, the religious educators hoped to introduce them to the mysteries of their faith as each catechist understood them.

While no Faith Formation lesson could teach the children all the mysteries, the priests and catechists worked to point them in the right direction through art projects and role-playing. Almost every Sunday, the teachers reinforced the idea that in the Mass the bread and wine became the body and blood of Christ. They did more than talk about this transformation: during one parent/child workshop at Holy Cross, for instance, Father Barry tried to bring this understanding to life by taking the children into the sanctuary to show them the difference between the consecrated and unconsecrated Host. The sound of the children heading to the pews was reminiscent of a hard rain on a tin roof. In a moment, they stood in their pews saying, "Girls here," and "This is the boys' row." Once the shouting had quieted, Father Barry asked them, "Where does God live in the church?" Julie, a shy white girl, answered, "In our hearts." A great answer, he acknowledged, but not the one he sought for this lesson. So he made his way to the right of the altar to give the children a hint. Then he posed the question for a second time, as he pretended to lean against the gold tabernacle that hung to the right of the altar. Amid a bunch of high-pitched giggles, Father Barry invited the children to see if Jesus was home. They gathered in close around the golden door of the tabernacle, as he took the brass ciborium (the vessel that holds the consecrated Hosts not consumed during the last Mass) out of the tabernacle that holds it and said, "Now we'll see Jesus." He opened the lid. Little brown and white hands immediately reached for the bread, but he quickly warned their owners against touching the consecrated Host. This bread, he told them, was special. Unlike the bread he would give them before they left the church that day, the bread within the ciborium had been touched by the Holy Spirit and transformed into the actual body of Christ. This act of God, he told them, made Christ present. At the end of his explanation, Father Barry asked the children to form a straight line down the sanctuary's center aisle to practice receiving the Eucharist. He told the children how to "make a throne for Jesus," by placing their left hand over their right hand, so that the priest could place the Host into their left palm. He told the children that they should then pick up the Host with their right hand and place it in their mouth. After practicing this motion, the children and I lined up to receive an unconsecrated Host. As he placed the Host in each child's hands, he reminded him or her that this bread was unconsecrated, that "Jesus could not be in this bread because the priest had not called for God's blessing."[95] Father Barry quietly encouraged a few children who seemed hesitant to eat their first Host (a feeling I soon understood as he put an unconsecrated Host in the "throne" I had made with my own hands). In this activity, Father Barry translated the theology that unites and defines the Catholic Church into words that he hoped the young communicants could understand. In so doing, he tried to create a lesson that would shape the children's understanding of First Communion.

Although it is difficult to measure the exact impact of this lesson, many of the children from Holy Cross seemed to realize that blessing the bread made a difference. Hunter emphasized the point to me when he stressed, "If it isn't blessed, it isn't the body."[96] Similarly, for Paris the special part of First Communion was that "we get to eat the bread when it's blessed instead of when it is just plain."[97] The children's decision to highlight the importance of the priest's blessing demonstrated that Father Barry's church tour, in conjunction with other classroom exercises and parental instruction, taught many children what the diocese required: that the consecrated Host "differed from ordinary bread."

While Father Barry attempted to teach the children at Holy Cross the difference between consecrated and unconsecrated Hosts through physically showing the children the Hosts and explaining Jesus' movements, Blessed Sacrament's First Communicants created pictures to represent this change. Ms. Fabuel and Ms. Richards gave each of their students a half sheet of yellow paper and a whole sheet of white paper, while Ms. Jeffries and I handed out scissors and glue. The catechists then asked the children to draw a free-form chalice underneath a Host on the yellow piece of paper. Once almost everyone had finished, the catechists showed the children how to cut out the chalice and Host carefully, so that they left the cutting in one long piece. When the communicants had each piece cut out, their teachers told them to paste the circle and the chalice on one side of the white paper, and the yellow paper outline facing it on the other side. Once the children had completed all the cutting and pasting, Ms. Fabuel and Ms. Richards asked them to label the yellow circle "bread" and the yellow chalice "wine." When the class had finished this task, the catechists asked the children to write "Body" next to the circle created from cutting out its yellow counterpart, and to label the outline of the chalice "Blood." This project offered the communicants something concrete to help them remember what happens during the consecration. For some children, like Shannon, who reminded the class that the bread and wine wasn't the body and blood "until the priest makes them that," creating a construction paper chalice may have cemented the idea of a difference between the consecrated and unconsecrated Host.[98]

Although none of the children talked about transubstantiation in any more detail than saying that the bread and wine become the body and blood, these lessons, as well as what the children learned at home and at Mass, clearly helped some communicants understand this difficult concept. The children primarily expressed a deeper knowledge of this concept when they discussed the Eucharist's taste. While the diocese required that the children learn that the bread they received in Communion was categorically different than ordinary bread, the catechists and the priests hoped that the children would learn more about the Eucharist than the material effects of transubstantiation. They also wanted the communicants to know that Jesus joined them in a real, physical way when they ate the Host. The priests spoke often with the children about the divine union that occurs when they receive Eucharist. "God is love," Father Briant said to me. "That's the whole thing of it, and he doesn't want to be separated. . . . It's this union, it's this intimacy with our God that we're trying to get children to understand. . . . He is with them, not in some figurative, not intimate way but in the very core of their being."[99] As the conduits through which God's grace flows into the sacraments, Father Barry and Father Briant, not surprisingly, spent most of their time with the children trying to help them understand the "union of heaven and earth" that occurred inside them each time they received the Eucharist. In the Eucharist, the children belonged to God in a substantial and real way. The priests conveyed these beliefs to the children in their retreats, church tours, and First Communion sermons.

Father Barry also designed a role-playing activity to help the children at Holy Cross understand their position as Jesus' followers as it simultaneously taught them about the Sacrament. During the First Communion retreat, Father Barry re-created the Last Supper with the class to help the children understand its sanctity. While the parents ordered the communicants' ties and veils, Father Barry took the children into the adjacent room that had been set up for their role-play. He asked them to sit around the outside of a square of tables clad in white tablecloths. Father Barry then sat in the center of the front table. He told the communicants that, like Jesus' friends at the Last Supper, they needed to listen to him reverently. Then, he began the role-play, saying, "This is the last time that I'll have this kind of meal with you. I'm going away, and you can't follow yet. But I'm going to leave something behind." After describing the way the children needed to act to ensure that they could join Jesus one day, he continued this sacred role-play, stating, "I will leave something behind to help you remember me when you come together. When you eat bread and wine you will be united." Father Barry then tore off big pieces of the bread. "This is not like when you're in church; this represents, but is *not*," he reminded the children, "the body of Christ. So be on your best behavior." The children solemnly took the bread that Father brought them as he broke character and said, "I feel like a waiter." Once all the children had a piece of bread, he explained to them, "When you eat this bread you get closer to Jesus, and God the Father, and each other." The solemnity around the table was broken when someone said, "It's like a picnic." Then Michael, a seven-year-old African American boy, returned to the sacred role-play, asking, "When you're gone, who will take your place, Father Barry?" "You will. That's why you're here learning to be closer to God." Then he asked them, "What does Communion do for you?" Paris responded, "So we can be united in peace." Someone else added, "So we can go to church and get the body and blood any time we want." Finally, Maureen shifted the conversation by commenting, "So we can be like Jesus. What was he like?"[100] This workshop served both to educate the children about the Last Supper and the meaning of the Eucharist and to increase the children's excitement for when they would finally partake of the consecrated bread. More than preparing them to receive the Eucharist, it allowed them to be part of the elite group of Jesus' followers through the roleplay. With only weeks to go before First Communion, Father Barry hoped that they would realize that soon they would be like the disciples. They would belong to an elite spiritual group. Father Barry, it seemed, wanted that group to be followers of Jesus, while the children seemed to be focused on the idea that soon they could have the body and blood any time they wanted, like the adults in the parish. Returning to their parents after the Last Supper reenactment, all the children reported excitedly to their mothers that they had gotten to be disciples.[101]

For the children, then, intellectually grasping the Eucharist seemed far less important than what they learned through their senses. While the adults, whose memories of their own initiation had faded, focused on Church doctrine and abstract concepts, the children, who were experiencing the Sacrament through their senses of taste, touch, and sight, talked much more of the sensuous and concrete aspects of the Sacrament.[102] It was this knowledge through the senses that the communicants had desired for so long, and it was their lack of it before First Communion—as well as their inability to perform the ritual gestures and understand the church symbols—that seemed to keep them from feeling like true members of their parishes. Although the parents and the priests would have included them among the parish's flock and understood each of them to be Jesus' child, the children did not feel like they truly belonged. They were a congregation apart. So on that First Communion Saturday, when the parents and teachers watched to see if the communicants performed the gestures correctly, the children awaited the moment of initiation into the parish: only as the children took the consecrated Host from their left hands, placed it on their tongues, and tasted the Host for the first time did they see themselves as truly belonging to their parish.

Decoding the Symbols

The experience the children seemed to want most was to eat what the other parishioners ate and to move as the other parishioners moved. Before the children could feel that they belonged to their parish and be united with Jesus in the Eucharist, however, they had to learn the "Catholic way," as eight-year-old Ferris put it.[103] In gaining this knowledge and correctly participating in this "adult" ritual, the communicants came to see themselves as more than the children they had been when they entered Communion classes. They demonstrated that they belonged as members in the adult congregation by proving they knew the parish's practices, both verbal and visual, by decoding the Church's symbols and performing its gestures. While teachers and priests did not say that instructing the children about the meaning of the chasuble (the priest's outer vestment), paten (the plate used to hold the Eucharist), and tabernacle (the ornamental container that houses the reserve Communion Hosts) was essential to the communicants' development as Catholics, they did attempt to familiarize the children with the vessels and vestments used in the Mass. During sanctuary tours, for instance, the priests and catechists allowed the children to touch the different objects used in the Mass, stand at the lectern, and walk behind the altar table as the priest does each Sunday. The children interested in Faith Formation wanted not only to taste the Eucharist but also to understand the vestments, colors, and ritual objects that they saw used during Mass each week.

While the teachers exposed the children to most aspects of the liturgy, some parts of the communicants' preparation did not appear prominently in their First Communion interpretations. For instance, although the children at Holy Cross did a quick review of the parts of the Mass each morning, the communicants rarely mentioned it in our discussions.[104] The children generally referred to their knowledge of the Mass's structure in broad terms. Maureen's comment was typical; she said that they "learned about the Mass and what happens and stuff."[105] Similarly, at Blessed Sacrament, where the children spent only one week on the Mass, the communicants did not mention anything but the Eucharist.

In contrast, learning about the objects used in the Mass and the movements performed by the congregation each Sunday captured the children's attention and became a primary means through which they interpreted the Sacrament's meaning. The children put heavy emphasis on the importance of this knowledge of the Church's objects and gestures in their interviews and drawings. In their conversation and artwork, the children often used the information they gleaned on the church tour, through completing a few worksheets about objects in the church, and perhaps through parental instruction.[106] The detailed pictures the children drew both after the church tours before First Communion and after First Communion demonstrated that they understood the significance of objects of the Catholic Church—its ritual vessels and liturgical colors—which they had not understood before the process began and which those children younger than them still could not grasp.[107] Anthropologist Zdzislaw Mach argues that "symbols are often regarded as something mysterious, the interpretation of which requires special initiation, preparation, or even sacred and secret knowledge."[108] This characterization of symbols reflects the communicants' perception that learning the secret knowledge of the Church's objects and ritual cycle would initiate them as capable and informed members. Through knowing the secrets, the children moved out of the group of the uninitiated, out of the group of children who "won't understand until they get older," and into the adult membership of their parish. Paris, a bright and serious seven-year-old African American girl from Holy Cross, for example, included a detailed altar table in her picture and dressed the priest in purple, the liturgical color that Father Barry had emphasized during his Lenten church tour (Figure 14). She explained the significance of the priest's vestments as I sat with her in the workroom beside her classroom in Holy Cross's Activity Center. Having just told me that she would be a dancer in next Saturday's First Communion ceremony, Paris leaned over the table as if she were telling me a secret and added, "Sometimes he [Father Barry] wears purple." "When?"

FIGURE 14. *Paris in her white dress stands before the priest in his purple vestments*

I asked. "When people are being blessed or baptized—at special times."[109] Likewise, Britney and Katie at Blessed Sacrament tried to put the priest in the right color for the season (Figure 10). Britney, like Paris, decided that purple would be the best color, and after a long discussion, Katie, a bubbly and bright seven-year-old Mexican American, chose gray. Through their drawings and our conversations, it appeared that as these children struggled with the color of the priest's vestments, they were demonstrating both to me and to themselves that they now knew the meaning behind some of what they saw when they went to Mass.

Like Paris, the children also demonstrated their increased understanding of the Church through their detailed drawings of the altar table and sometimes through their interpretations of drawings. Many of the children with whom I talked identified, but did not discuss, these symbols. However, they worked diligently to make the objects in their drawings exact replicas of the ones they saw at Mass, even when they did not put as much effort into other aspects of their pictures. Ferris's post-Communion picture, on which he spent little time adorning the priest, himself, or his godfather, includes a colorful carafe of wine on a bright red altar cloth with a

FIGURE 15. *Ferris with his uncle walking to the brightly colored altar table*

design on it, much like the ceramic carafe and African-style *kinte* cloth that covers Holy Cross's altar table (Figure 15). In this way, he highlighted the sacramental elements (although he included the carafe rather than the chalice that most of his classmates drew) as the most important part of First Communion. Simultaneously, he conveyed the message that he attended closely to the objects used in his church: he knew the vessels needed for the Sacrament he would soon receive. Although all the children I interviewed before or after their First Communion drew these objects, only Brian, an eight-year-old white boy, mentioned learning about these objects when we talked just before his final First Communion practice. At Faith Formation classes, he explained, "we learn about Jesus and God and his symbols and things like that."[110] As the children I interviewed drew as many of these symbols as they could remember seeing on the altar table in response to my request for a drawing of First Communion, they identified them, an act that they seemed to believe would have been impossible before the church tour and First Communion classes.

Elizabeth's image demonstrated most poignantly the importance of knowing about these items and their meanings within the context of the First Communion ritual (Figure 16). When asked after First Communion to "draw a picture of First Communion," she did not include either herself or the priest. She sketched grapes, a stole, a chalice, a Host, an Easter candle, and wheat—the objects that appeared on the banner she made during the First Communion workshop. These were the items that the Blessed Sacrament communicants brought down the aisle to "set the table." She described the picture: "I have the candle [that] someone lit during Reconciliation—I mean First Communion. The grapes are there because they were there at the Last Supper. Wheat, because you use wheat to make bread, and I drew the bread and the wine and the priest's little thingy that I can't remember the name of [the stole]."[111]

Her classmate Alison, a quiet and friendly seven-year-old white girl, also worked to display her knowledge of the Church by adding great detail to her illustration of the altar. In drawing the altar in her pre–First Communion picture (in an almost imperceptible lemon yellow), she included as many ritual objects as she could—the "cloth" under the chalice, the tablecloth, the chalice, and the Host—describing the different elements as she worked (Figure 17). It appeared that learning the articles on the altar in her Faith Formation class and receiving the Eucharist gave her new status as something more than a child. When I asked her after First Communion what it was like to take Communion now, she replied, "It's like a

FIGURE 16. Elizabeth draws the Church's symbols

memory to me . . . of when I was a kid." Surprised by this answer, I inquired further, "So you're not so much of a kid now?" "Well, kind of," she said hesitatingly, as if she was unsure how to put what she felt into words. So I tried one more question: "How do you think you're different now?" "I used to not know a lot of stuff about the Church, but I do now," she explained.[112] Thus, Alison seemed to connect her post-Sacrament standing within her parish, and perhaps outside, with her knowledge of her Church. Ferris echoed her emphasis on this knowledge when he explained that through his preparation for the Sacrament, he now "underst[ood] the Catholic way."[113]

Only by "understanding the Catholic way" could Ferris and his classmates participate in their First Communion Mass as their parents and teachers hoped that they would in all Masses. The children learned about being involved in the Church not only through their classes and weekly Masses but also through the First Communion liturgies. While they were most excited about receiving the Eucharist, the communicants also presented the gifts at the offering, acted as lectors, and stood before the congregation as they fulfilled the other responsibilities of the First Communion liturgy. By assigning the children these duties, the catechists told the children that they believed they were ready to participate in the Mass as the adults did. Many children were, to use Maureen's word, "overjoyed" about receiving their assignments: one shy little girl exclaimed when she was assigned her task for the liturgy, "Daddy, daddy, I'm a reader."[114] The pride she seemed to feel at being assigned this chance to talk before the congregation was matched by Britney's pride over getting to speak in front of the church for the first time.[115] Other children were embarrassed to have to dance or speak before their parents and friends. However the communicants felt about their particular jobs, the fact that they had tasks at all demonstrated to the children that they were ready to participate in the Mass in a way that the children believed was significant.

The children, as Ms. Fabuel explained, had been participating in the Mass since they began attending the church, but as First Communion approached, this participation had to become more active: "The Mass is something that if they are going to get something out of, they're going to have to participate in . . . singing the songs and, when they have the handshake of peace, actually doing the handshake of peace. When we say the Our Father grasping a hold of the hands on either side of them to make the people see that that is community—that is their community. This is part of their community. [Their community] is all these people. We're all one in Christ."[116] The children, given their drawings, would most likely disagree with Ms. Fabuel. They did not seem to equate holding hands and singing during Mass with participation. Rather, they said that with First Communion they could finally do something during Mass. From their perspective, then, the First Communion liturgy marked the first time they could really participate in the Mass. Many children, like Maureen, embraced this opportunity, telling me that after First Communion she got "to look forward to something that [she would] get to actually do."[117] Furthermore, like many of her counterparts, she took this responsibility to do something seriously. They had to pay more attention during Mass and think about Jesus, as I will discuss in Chapter 4.

Conclusion Interpreting the Eucharist

For both the adults and the children, receiving First Communion marked the moment when the children participated in the central ritual of their faith. The adults hoped that this moment would tell the children to do what they should have been doing all along—participate. When I asked Ms. Cement after First Communion, for instance, what she had most wanted her son to learn through his participation in First Communion, she responded, "It wasn't a thing that was most important for him to learn, but for him to understand, you know, that he had to participate fully."[118] While she focused on her son's participation in the Mass, Katie's mother, a Mexican immigrant who had been attending Blessed Sacrament for more than two decades, looked beyond the Mass. "I want [Katie] to participate in church and grow up with a big heart," she said to me in halting but self-assured English. "I want her to participate not just [in] First Communion, but *participate*."[119] Like many other parents at the parishes, Ms. Hernandez hoped her daughter would have a vibrant Catholic faith.

As they came to understand the ways of the Catholic Church, to gain the knowledge of what was once mysterious and secret, the communicants finally saw themselves as able to participate in the Mass. Through tasting the Eucharist and decoding the colors and symbols they saw each week, the communicants seemed to believe that they were leaving the world of unknowing children and becoming people who could stand as individuals in front of their parish, rather than as part of a family or as someone's child. From the children's perspective, then, First Communion allowed them to become members of their own parish, rather than the universal Catholic Church, while to the adults it appeared that preparing for and receiving the Sacrament was an essential step in the communicants' Catholic development.

Far from understanding themselves as developing Catholics, the children seemed to view themselves as full participants in the Sacrament. For the children, understanding some of the mysteries of their faith had an automatic effect on their position in their parish: they shifted from beings frozen in anticipation apart from their community to dynamic individuals acting within their parish. Thus, the communicants did not look forward to their future participation in the Catholic Church (only Britney mentioned Confirmation). They did not focus on their new membership as First Communicants in the universal Church; rather, the children emphasized the new sense of importance they each felt as individuals and the change they each sensed in their own relationships and their status both in their parish and in their families. They gained this feeling of belonging to their families and their parishes through the celebrations that the adults and Jesus had for them when they successfully demonstrated that they had learned, and could perform, the secret knowledge and rituals of their parish. It is to those celebrations of the children, both heavenly and earthly, that I now turn.

The church suddenly became unusually quiet for a sanctuary filled with more than three dozen seven- and eight-year-old children. I turned in the pew toward the back of the church and immediately understood the reason for the sudden hush. Father Briant, who was carrying the brightly colored vestments of the Catholic Church, was walking down the aisle to the altar. Within moments he stood in front of the children, who were squeezed into the first three pews on the right side of the sanctuary, where Ms. Fabuel had asked them to sit after they had finished practicing genuflecting. Father Briant asked the class, "How many people celebrate Thanksgiving?" I watched as white and brown hands flew into the air. "How many have turkey?" he continued with a warm smile. All the hands went up again. "How many celebrate birthdays?" Many communicants now started to giggle as they raised their hands once more. "How many have cakes?" The giggling grew louder as some communicants decided to keep their hands in the air. "How many have big Christmas dinners?" Those communicants who had put their hands down now raised them again. Just when many children seemed to think they had figured out the game, Father Briant asked, "Do they come from McDonalds?" "No," the children shouted. "Very important things," he explained, "always happen with a meal. Special things also happen around a table. Where is the table in the church?" The communicants excitedly pointed to the altar table. Father continued, "It's a simple wooden table like the one on which Jesus had the Last Supper."

"Who was at the Last Supper?" Father Briant asked the children. Unlike in response to easier questions, this time only four or five hands went up. He called on one little girl who said "Jesus." Another little boy self-assuredly added "Mary" to the guest list. Father Briant smiled and laughed a little as he said, "Well, we debate that." After a few more responses, he continued: "That's right. You can't have a party alone. If Jesus were alone it wouldn't be special, so who does he invite to the table?" Voices came from all sides of the pews saying, "Grandma and grandpa . . . friends . . . us . . . everyone." "They're such theologians," Father Briant commented to the adults in the room. Then, he shifted the discussion to another part of the celebration.

"What's the special food that we have?" he inquired. "The bread and the wine," one child replied confidently. "Just bread and wine we could buy at the Food Lion?" Father asked, raising his voice at the end to emphasize the question. "No," the class responded in unison. "What is it?" "The body and blood," the children answered. "We see the bread and the wine with our eyes," Father explained, "but we see the body and blood with the gift of faith. We come because we want to be with the Lord, who talks to us, feeds us, and lets us know that we're loved."

Then the conversation changed again to examine the Bible and the special clothes that the priest wears when he is working. Father Briant called for three volunteers to come and stand next to him. When the three boys reached the front of the sanctuary, the priest handed them each a different color vestment as he explained the colors' meaning: "Purple we wear during Lent and Advent, marking special times of sacrifice; red we wear when a saint shed his blood; green for most Sundays because it's the color of life." Father Briant went on to tell the children about the "underwear of Jesus' time [the alb]" that he wore underneath the vestments and the stole that he wore around his neck to symbolize that he was "ready to go to work" when he was "going to make Jesus present here." He then gave the children a chance to ask questions before the "field trip" ended.

As I listened to Father Briant and the children talk about the Last Supper, parties, and what makes a celebration, I was struck by how effectively this lesson seemed to address aspects of this rite of initiation that are ignored when one sees it only as the reception of the Eucharist. Analyzing First Communion in context reveals that for most of the children and many adults, it is a celebration in which the Eucharist is the "special food" eaten by the special guests dressed in sacred attire, a celebration in which the children are joined by Jesus, their priests, their catechists, and their families.[1]

This chapter focuses in large part on celebration and the impact of celebration on the children. The children celebrated not only through the First Communion liturgies but also with the parties that followed it. The adults put much energy into creating these celebrations. Parish and family parties (and the extensive preparation for those parties) showed the children that the Sacrament was important both to their Church and to their families. The attention that the children received in all these activities emphasized the significance of the Sacrament to the children's family as well as the communicants' importance to their parishes and their loved ones. As they prepared for the Sacrament through Faith Formation class and secular preparation, most children seemed to gain a greater sense of their significance as individuals to both parish and family. Finally, the communicants' drawings and conversations displayed their conviction that in learning the movements and mysteries of the Church through practicing gestures and receiving the Eucharist, the children earned their family's, teacher's, and Jesus' respect, which allowed them to claim their own position within the central congregation in their parish.

Both the children and the adults also understood that receiving the Sacrament of First Communion fundamentally altered the children's relationship with Jesus. In Faith Formation classes and in home preparations, all the participants shared the belief that First Communion both strengthened the children's relationship to Jesus and marked a significant moment in each child's family history. The adults focused on the effect of the Sacrament on the children's standing within the universal Catholic Church, for the adults understood that this ritual was a rite of passage that would formally introduce the children to their faith for the first time. When children interpreted receiving the Sacrament of First Communion for me, however, their interpretations showed they believed that the event allowed their *parish* to see them as individuals and as capable members of the *parish*, a belief that the adults never mentioned to me in their discussions of the rite.

In the last chapter, I focused in a corporate sense on the First Communicants' initiation *as a group* into their Church and their parish. In this chapter, I examine how this rite and the celebrations that accompanied it significantly influenced each child's feelings of importance and personal connectedness to Jesus, as well as to his or her parish and family. While the children may have understood the shifts in their transcendent relationships through the celebration of the Eucharist, the paraliturgical celebrations allowed them to realize more fully their new bonds to their parishes and families. These bonds developed as each child saw himself or herself being valued as an individual initiated into full participation in the parish, not simply as someone's child or as part of a group of initiates. And, perhaps more important, the children believed (as they participated in the celebratory events) that their parents and teachers saw them this way as well.

The communicants' perceptions of the power of this celebration began to take shape long before First Communion Saturday. The children's interpretations started when they talked with their parents about First Communion, and they evolved further as the children were given more opportunities to interact with other parishioners in celebratory preparation. To understand how the children's and the adults' actions and conversations worked together to form the communicants' interpretations, I not only look at their interactions in the sanctuary, but through my conversations with the children, I also follow their progression from department stores through the liturgy to the parish hall and family barbeques. In all these spaces, the children responded to the adults' energy by emphasizing that they were the center of attention. More than that, the children felt that they were being seen by both the adults and by Jesus as fellow parishioners, as members of the adult parish.

I begin by discussing the importance to the children of gaining Jesus' individual attention. They garnered the attention of Jesus and of the members of their parish by performing the actions needed to receive the Eucharist. Having the congregation watch them display their knowledge of the Church, performing the gestures of the ritual correctly, and finally tasting the body and blood of Jesus all led to parish and family celebrations, and these celebrations, in turn, reinforced the significance of both the rites and the children. These celebrations, as Father Briant emphasized, need guests, and just as the priest wore his vestments, the guests and the children also wore appropriate clothing for the ritual. The final parts of this chapter, therefore, focus on the parties (both in the children's homes and in the church), which served to strengthen the children's bonds to their families and to their fellow Catholics and the traditional clothing that marked them as First Communicants. These celebratory elements also strengthened a broader, intergenerational understanding: First Communion became a celebration of love, respect, and belonging that emphasized the children's inclusion at the table, both with their families and with Jesus. Given the children's broad understanding of First Communion, designating one of these celebrations as secular and the other as sacred was an artificial distinction, for the children seemed to see each of these as essential to understanding the importance of receiving the Sacrament. One was no more holy or special than the other; each supported the central moment when the communicants would finally get to taste the consecrated bread and wine.

Learning Jesus' Love

Although the adults recognized the children's yearning to "get Jesus" in the Eucharist, the priests and religious educators as well as many of the parents hoped that when the communicants received the Eucharist, they would also remember that the Sacrament is God's ultimate gift to his followers, the gift of Jesus' body and blood. Communion, many adults hoped, would bring the children intellectually and physically closer to Jesus as it taught them about his unending love and allowed them to partake of his body and blood. In our conversations, the children also seemed to suggest, however, that they saw this closeness in a personal, individual way. This sense of individuality played a large role in the communicants' interpretations of the Sacrament. In the moment that they correctly placed the consecrated Host in their mouths, it seemed that many communicants sensed that God loved them deeply and personally. During the preparation for the Sacrament, the catechists and the priests, in particular, told the children that Jesus saw each child as important and that he loved each of them. It is "important for young people to see themselves as belonging to the family of God," Ms. Key explained. She wanted them to comprehend "how important even one person is. . . . How precious we all are and how God . . . will come looking for us."[2] Although I cannot know what the children thought when they stood before the altar, in their conceptions of Jesus' love that they shared with me, the children fulfilled one of the adults' major goals for First Communion—that, as the diocesan guidelines outlined, they become aware "of Jesus' love and that he is someone very special in the child's life."[3] The catechists wanted the children to know that through the Eucharist, Jesus expressed his constant love for each of his followers, not just his sacrifice for the Church universal. The communicants' interpretation of such teachings seemed to reflect their comprehension of the message that God loves each of his children—both young and old—unconditionally and uniquely. Although the adults may have wished that the children also believed that they had *always* been important to Jesus as individuals, the communicants and the adults seemed to focus on Jesus' relationship with the children with more intensity during their First Communion preparation than during their previous efforts at faith formation (if there were any).

Given the emphases in Faith Formation programs on experience and participation rather than memorization, the children focused on Jesus' presence in their lives almost to the exclusion of any study of the events in his life or his historical place in the Bible and the Catholic Church. By and large, the children said nothing about, and showed no interest in, the life of Christ. Only Christopher, from Blessed Sacrament, referred to Jesus' life directly when he quoted, perhaps unknowingly, the Apostles' Creed, while explaining what he learned in Faith Formation class: Jesus "died on the cross and on the third day he rose again."[4] The only other child to mention any details about Jesus' life, Ryan, from Holy Cross, said, "The most important thing to me [about having First Communion] is learning about Jesus and his body and blood and how he suffered."[5] Instead of focusing on particular aspects of Jesus' life, the communicants—reflecting the religious educators' emphases—talked more about the bread and the wine and about their new understanding of Jesus' and God's love for them. Many of Ryan's and Christopher's classmates, for instance, said only that they "learned about Jesus." Learning about Jesus was, for Paris, however, an essential step in receiving the Sacrament. She explained that communicants received the Sacrament only "after learning about him [Jesus]."[6] Given the communicants' responses, when the children spoke of learning about Jesus, they did not mean that they had memorized biographical details. Ms. Patricia Matterson, the director of Blessed Sacrament's Hispanic ministry, who prepared the older Latino children for First Communion, wanted the communicants "to hear about Jesus and to know Jesus."[7] But rather than impart the events of Jesus' life to their classes, the religious educators at both churches created many exercises to encourage the children both to believe that Jesus was always with them and to form a "friendship" with him.

In this emphasis on Jesus as friend and mentor, the catechists moved away from older understandings of Jesus as a judge to whom children must submit without question. The catechetical team at Blessed Sacrament, for instance, designed a short lesson in which they asked the children to act as Jesus' disciples. One Sunday morning in September, Ms. Fabuel led the combined second grade class out the school's back door and onto the lawn. There, she divided the children into groups of three or four, with some rebellion from those whom she did not place with their friends. Once all the children were in place, Mr. Dwyer walked from group to group, asking the students to follow him. Luckily for the teachers, all the communicants said "I will," for this exercise did give each child a chance to say "no." Once the children agreed, they then joined the line behind him as it slowly grew to encompass the whole class. As they moved from cluster to cluster, Ms. Fabuel reminded the students that Mr. Dwyer was gathering them together as Jesus gathered his disciples.[8] As the children fell into line behind their teacher, they accepted, even if only in a role-play, responsibility for their status as Christians. Here Jesus, played by Mr. Dwyer, asked each communicant to follow him, stressing the importance of the children as individuals. When he did so, Mr. Dwyer trusted that they would say "yes," rather than using this moment to express their dislike of Sunday school or their indifference to Jesus.

This lesson had little effect on some children; for others, however, it taught them that they were now capable of choosing their own relationship with Jesus and that in this space they could join his closest group of followers. In so doing, the children became one of Jesus' friends, and he became their leader. Britney believed, for example, that she could now be "closer to God."[9] Even those children who were not interested in these kinds of exercises seemed to understand that having been dropped off at class by their parents, they had to participate a little bit in the exercises, and if they wanted to know the Host's taste, they had to attend Faith Formation. The catechetical mission of bringing the children into relationship with Jesus drew the many adult volunteers to teach the children to embrace their relationship with Jesus.

The catechists and priests all spoke passionately about their desire for the children to understand that they belonged to God and that God loved them. As they taught the communicants of his sacrifice, the catechists and priests facilitated the development of the children's relationship with God and Jesus; they tried to make the communicants feel his divine presence in their lives. As I sat across from Ms. Wright-Jukes in the basement of Holy Cross's Activity Center, for instance, her eyes grew wide and her words came more quickly and forcefully as she told me that she wanted the children to leave her class "seeing God as their Father, [because it would] help them to understand that no matter what you do, someone is there that loves you. Whenever you feel alone, God is there." She went on to explain, "I often think that they know that their parents and relatives love them, but it's harder to understand that someone you can't see loves you."[10] To help them understand God's intangible but ever-present love, Ms. Wright-Jukes held a First Communion workshop in which she and Father Barry presented the children with the Lord's Prayer. During the ceremony, the catechists and Father Barry prayed that God would count the communicants among his adopted children. Everyone present prayed that the communicants might truly learn what it meant "to call God, Father."[11] The message was that God, as their parent, would always love each one of them. While the children participated in the ceremony attentively, however, when they talked with me and drew pictures, none of them referred to God as parentlike or as "Father."

Similarly to the adults at Holy Cross, the catechists and priests at Blessed Sacrament also hoped the children would feel this divine love. Each time Father Briant spoke to the children, from the pulpit or in the classroom, he emphasized that God saw each of them as unique and important. Like Ms. Wright-Jukes, Father Briant felt that the only way children could come to understand God's unconditional love was to see it as akin to parental love. When I asked him what he hoped the communicants would learn through First Communion, he replied that, in part, he wanted them to understand "how special they are and not only in their parents' eyes, but also in God's eyes. And their [parents'] love [for them] is a reflection of his."[12] While Father Briant primarily directed his message to the adults at parent meetings, not the children, his goals helped set the tone for Blessed Sacrament's Faith Development program.

Ms. Fabuel brought the comparison Father Briant made between parents' unconditional love for their children and God's unconditional love for his children into her classroom through a simple group exercise. She brought God's abstract love to the children through an action that they could understand: a hug. Almost every week, she asked the children to stand and give themselves a "bear hug." When the communicants grew especially rowdy, Ms. Fabuel stopped talking, raised her hands over her head to make a half circle, and said, "What is this?" "A circle," the class answered almost in unison. "What does it represent?" she continued. "Jesus," they answered even louder. On some days, this response marked the first time in the lesson when all the children (even those inclined to wander around the room or hit their neighbor) listened to what Ms. Fabuel was saying and doing. "And when you bring it down . . ." "Jesus is giving you a bear hug!" the children would shout before she could finish the question. Then Mrs. Fabuel asked, "Why is it a circle?" "Because Jesus' love is never-ending," the children quickly replied. She would follow this response with, "Why is that important?" The crowd usually yelled a wide variety of answers. Each week I listened to these responses, trying to distinguish one child's answer from that of another. In the end, a Latino boy's state-ment seemed to encapsulate the majority of his classmates' senti-ments: "Because it tells us that Jesus is there when we're lonely."[13] Ms. Fabuel did this exercise so often, she said, because she wanted the children to realize that "Jesus loves them always. That's why we have the big circle and the big hug, so that whenever they do feel alone and feel like they need help . . . they can get it just by closing their eyes and feeling Jesus' presence around them."[14] Here they learned that Jesus' love did not stop at the sanctuary door but stayed with them throughout the week. His love came not only through re-ceiving the Eucharist but also through an invisible hug when they felt alone.

The students found this exercise so memorable that even those communicants who only attended Faith Formation classes sporadi-cally included it in our conversations. Christy, an endearing seven-year-old Latina who usually attended class only once every two to three weeks, explained that "God is always with us, that's why I don't have to be afraid of thunder anymore."[15] Through this lesson the children were taught, and came to understand, that God was not a distant historical or spiritual figure but was an active presence in their lives. He knew when each of them was scared and lonely. He was always ready to show each of them his love by giving them a big bear hug.[16]

In emphasizing the children's personal relationship with Jesus, especially his unconditional love for them, the catechists taught the children that even though they were just coming to know Jesus, he already knew them. While the communicants at Blessed Sacrament learned that Jesus knew when they were sad, at Holy Cross the chil-dren envisioned Jesus being with them even when they played with their friends.[17] During Holy Cross's First Communion workshop, the catechists asked the children to draw pictures of Jesus playing with them and their best friend. Most of the communicants' draw-ings depicted Jesus as another person playing baseball with them or holding their hands. Only one child drew the kind of picture one might expect of a child who believed Jesus was an omniscient critic: Jesus looking down on him and his friend, observing their behav-ior.[18] The teachers wanted the children to learn that Jesus was not a distant deity who came to judge their sins or one who cared for them only on Sunday. They hoped that performing these exercises would teach the children that Jesus was present in all their activities, protecting them and loving them. On the whole, the children's pictures illustrated that they were comfortable with Jesus and perhaps that they even saw him as a friend. Even those who may not have been as interested in Faith Formation class seemed to come to believe that Jesus was with each of them in their daily lives.

Like the children at Blessed Sacrament, the communicants at Holy Cross also came to see Jesus as a friend, rather than as a father. Jesus supported the children, listened to their troubles, and joined them on the playground. This Jesus stood in stark contrast to the Jesus that many of their parents and teachers encountered in their own First Communion preparation. Unlike older Catholics' memories that tend to cast Jesus'/God's ever-present watchful eye as a negative, leading them to speak often of their fear of God, these children seemed to see Jesus' watchfulness as positive and loving. In part this focus on Jesus as friend stems from the Church's increasing emphasis on Jesus' humanity. The parishes' location in the Protestant South also may have influenced this understanding. Here, the children and the adults were living, working, and going to school with Protestant Christians who often expressed their concern about their own, as well as Catholics', personal relationship with Christ. Finally, the Catholic focus on Jesus as friend may follow a larger American (Protestant) cultural trend outlined by Stephen Prothero, in *American Jesus*, in which Jesus was transformed from the Christ of the Trinity to the Jesus of "What a Friend We Have in Jesus." The children's vision of a Jesus that played soccer with them certainly reflected the modern American understanding of him as a friend. For instance, although the children wanted to make Jesus proud of them during First Communion, none of them spoke about disappointing him.

The emphasis on Jesus' love for the children as individuals was expressed in Holy Cross's First Communion Mass through the story of Jesus as the good shepherd. The teachers had focused throughout the preparation for First Communion on how Jesus cared for the children, instead of Scripture; rather than tell a Bible story, the catechists and parents created visual aids and activities to demonstrate Jesus' love. To highlight the individual importance of each communicant, for instance, the catechists and some parent volunteers created a First Communion banner made of felt that depicted Jesus with a shepherd's crook walking among the sheep. Below each sheep in his flock, Ms. Lauffer and Ms. Wright-Jukes wrote a child's name in black paint. By assigning each child a sheep, they reflected that year's First Communion theme, taken from the Bible verse: "The sheep hear his voice, and *he calls them by name*" (Jn 10:3).[19] Looking at this banner, each communicant could see Jesus right there walking with the sheep, including the sheep with his or her name on it. There was nothing abstract about Jesus' presence among his flock. Each child was also given a small porcelain sheep, each in a different pose emphasizing the sheep's individuality, to commemorate First Communion. As the Sacrament approached, members of the class sometimes spoke about their sheep on the banner, and Maureen included hers in her drawing. Having Jesus call each of their names seemed to communicate effectively that not only were the children coming to know Jesus in a new way but also that he knew them and valued them personally as individuals. Thus, though Jesus came to all the initiates through the Eucharist, the children's interpretations emphasized that he came to them as individuals, not as a group.

The children returned Jesus' interest in them with their own desire to come to know him. Many of the children explained the purpose of First Communion as Hunter did: First Communion "felt like an opportunity to get closer to Jesus."[20] While Hunter seemed to view the change in his relationship with Jesus as occurring in only one direction—him moving toward Jesus—Maureen imagined a more reciprocal relationship. "When you have your First Communion," Maureen explained, "it's special because it's special for God and for yourself. It's special for God because God is having a little *celebration* for you because you're seven, in the second grade. And you get to eat a little bit from the Last Supper, from Jesus. And Jesus is happy for you."[21] Thus, just as First Communion offered a chance for the children to receive Jesus in the Eucharist, it also provided God and Jesus a chance to celebrate each boy and girl who came to the altar. In receiving Jesus, the children were the focus of his attention, just as he was the focus of theirs.

The Center of Attention

While the children appeared to feel a growing closeness with Jesus as a result of their Sunday school projects and other discussions, the communicants did not feel as if they fully belonged to their parishes until they demonstrated their understanding of the "Catholic way," as Ferris called it, through their ability to perform the gestures they saw in church each week. This membership was something they had to earn through their adultlike behavior. Just as many children realized that Jesus gave them his love unconditionally, they also seemed to understand that their membership in their parish, and their position at his table, was not given to them unconditionally. They had to show that they could behave like the adults around the table to earn a place of their own. Throughout the liturgy, the children said they felt that Jesus and their parents would be watching to see if they deserved that place. That knowledge was both intimidating and exhilarating to the communicants. The communicants knew that they were stepping out from the pews in a new capacity for the first time, by themselves, and at that moment, when the Host was placed in their hands, they were being seen in this new context by their parents and by Jesus. The adults understood that the rite of initiation occurred on the level of the universal Church as the children took their place at the table with all other Catholics, thus joining the children to their historic religious heritage. But the children focused much of their interpretation on their initiation into the parish and family. While belonging to the Church and the community of Catholics may be primarily a matter of receiving the Eucharist with all its theological significance, belonging to a particular parish demands attention to, and a demonstration of, the specific traditions and customs of *that* group: it was this group—the parish members and their families—that the children wanted to please.

While I cannot know how each child understood his or her desire to get the ritual's movements correct, the intensity with which each child approached learning these gestures supported John J. Mac-Aloon's understanding of performance: "Whatever performances do, or are supposed to do, they do by creating conditions for and by coercing participants into paying attention."[22] As MacAloon stressed, observers cannot impose meaning on this attention. Lily, for instance, looked forward to First Communion with some trepidation since she knew she would be "embarrassed because there are a lot of people there when you get it." This worry caused her to practice the litany of bending and straightening intently, for she despaired that "sometimes [she] fe[lt] like I am never going to get this stuff."[23] Although much of my conversation with Lily lead me to believe that she was extremely excited about receiving "a gift from God" through the Eucharist, her fear of embarrassment demonstrated that the communicants' motivations for acting correctly could not be easily deciphered. Some children practiced these movements as a means to protect themselves from public ridicule in addition to or rather than as a way to demonstrate their devotion to the Church or their respect for God or to garner the praise of their parents.

Just as enacting these movements with care did not necessarily evidence any particular religious conviction, neither did the children's focus on gestures denote a lack of concern with meaning. As ritualist Catherine Bell has convincingly argued, thought and action are not two distinct categories; rather, thinking and acting cannot be separated.[24] The children's need to demonstrate these movements did not mean that this ritual was primarily an external experience for them. "Gestures," as Ruel W. Tyson Jr. and James L. Peacock have argued, "are not secondary means to other primary ends" but an integral and inseparable aspect of First Communion.[25] Meaning for the communicants, as for many ritual participants, came as they learned to train their bodies in accordance with the requirements of the ritual, as well as when they came to a greater understanding of the significance of their movements. Yet performance and understanding did not always go hand in hand.

The communicants saw Catholic gestures—the sign of the cross, genuflecting, and the appropriate reception of the Eucharist—whenever they went to Mass, and they learned the specific movements each week in Faith Formation class. Although the catechists did not mention wanting to teach the children these sacred motions, they spent a great deal of class time trying to ensure that the children got them right, especially the sign of the cross. At both churches, class began with the sign of the cross and a prayer. One Sunday I joined the prayer circle at Blessed Sacrament standing between a seven-year-old white girl and a seven-year-old Mexican girl. A few moments later, Ms. Fabuel, the lead catechist, moved into the center of the circle and asked the children to raise their right hands. Once they differentiated their right from their left—not always easy at seven—she offered the class a baseball mnemonic to remember how to make this all-important gesture. "Home plate," Ms. Fabuel said as she touched her head. "Pitcher's mound," she said moving her hand to the center of her chest. Next she moved her hand over to her left shoulder, saying "third base," then "first base," as she touched her right shoulder. Even with this helpful model, many children remained confused. At times during opening or closing prayer, or when they practiced receiving the Host, various teachers and assistants had to take the children's hands to guide them in performing the sign of the cross. Likewise, at Holy Cross, the children practiced this gesture every Sunday in class, so that it might come as naturally to them as nodding their heads to indicate "yes." Ms. Fabuel's mnemonic helped some children get the gestures and movement correctly, and performing the gestures correctly would avoid embarrassment for the children (and perhaps Ms. Fabuel as their teacher) in front of the parish members who would see an unblemished ritual.

For the First Communicants, learning how and when to cross themselves was not the only thing they had to master. They also had to learn how to hold their hands when they received the Eucharist. Then they had to remember to genuflect—right knee touching the ground, not left—when entering the pews. Many children were quite overwhelmed by this list. Britney, for instance, catalogued all these movements when I asked her about her First Communion: "I had to bow, do the sign of the cross after I took the bread" (and in a previous interview she had mentioned that she had learned how to genuflect, but had forgotten).[26] For other children, such as

Kim (who lamented under her breath during practice, "I don't even know what's going on here"), trying to practice these movements with the class led to complete exasperation.[27]

During Holy Cross's church tour, Father Barry turned learning to genuflect into a game. He called the children to the front of the church and showed them how to genuflect before they entered the pew. The children huddled around him, slowly touching their right knee to the carpet, mimicking the priest's actions. Once everyone had practiced, Father said, "Simon says, 'genuflect.'" From the back of the sanctuary I saw the fifteen heads of the first communicants that came to class that Sunday going up and down as they knelt and stood again and again in response to Father's (Simon's) directions. After they finished playing "Simon Says," Father Barry asked the children to sit down. Later, the teachers also spent much time and energy trying to help the children perfect these movements.

With only one hour a week and so much to learn, the catechists also suggested that the parents help the children practice the gestures during Mass and at home.[28] Practice appeared to be essential. Although the teachers may have hoped that receiving the Eucharist would be a wholly sacred experience, the demands of First Communion kept much of the children's attention on their physical bodies, for the children had to receive the Body of Jesus in the correct way, which necessitated much practicing of the sign of the cross, genuflecting, and making "thrones for Jesus." By having the children practice these movements at home, in Mass, and during Faith Formation classes, many adults desired that these Catholic gestures would become ingrained, forever linking the children to their Church. The teachers and many parents hoped that the children would make a habit of crossing themselves each time they prayed, just as they would naturally drop to their knee before they entered a pew. Turning gestures into habits, as the social and political scientist Paul Connerton and others have argued, has great power: "Habit is a knowledge and a remembering in the hands and in the body; and in the cultivation of a habit it is our body which understands."[29] It seemed that from the children's perspective, they were not cultivating a habit that would inscribe the markings of Catholicism onto their bodies and memories. Rather, they were learning the gestures of membership into their parish's adult communities, as distinct from the universal Catholic Church. These gestures differentiated them from the parish's "children," who still ran carelessly into the pews and went to Communion with their hands crossed over their chest to receive only the sign of the cross on their forehead as a blessing.

All of the practicing increased the children's anxiety, as they realized the importance of moving correctly throughout the ceremony, particularly during the Eucharist. Their hyperattention to movement seemed to make the catechists' and priests' spiritual, prayerful goal for the Sacrament impossible to achieve.

The communicants evidenced their focus on embodied gestures of the Church's rites through their concern with performing these new movements correctly, which they believed would solidify their new identity within their parish community. The children expressed the link between performing these gestures and being viewed as autonomous members of the parish through the intensity with which they practiced, their descriptions of the gestures in our interviews, and their concern to "get it right" in front of the congregation. As Maureen from Holy Cross explained after she received her First Communion, "You have to put your hands in a certain shape." "Was it hard to remember what you were supposed to do?" I asked. "I was really panicked," she replied.[30] This panic seemed to stem primarily from her concern with performing the gestures in front of the congregation and perhaps making a mistake, a concern that many children shared. Through enacting these motions by themselves at the altar, Maureen and the other children gave up the protective comfort of blending into a group in order to claim their own unique places in the parish.

As anthropologist Barbara Myerhoff argues about her work with older adults, "Rituals create a setting in which persons can *appear* . . . by devising a reality in which they can stand apart."[31] In "standing apart" from the uninitiated children, however, the communicants also seemed to understand themselves as each standing *within* their parish communities. Yet the children realized that everyone would be watching to see if they knew the identifiable Catholic gestures needed to receive the Sacrament in that moment that they stood apart from their fellow communicants.

In her interview after First Communion, Melissa, from Blessed Sacrament, barely discussed the party she had excitedly described to me a few months earlier.[32] Instead, she focused on her anxiety about performing all the required gestures correctly and on how happy she felt when she was receiving the consecrated bread and wine. Although she clearly enjoyed being the center of attention in many ways, when she received the Eucharist that attention also took on a more scrutinizing and agonizing spin: "I was nervous because it was my first time. . . . My mom was there, and I didn't want to mess up because I would make a little fool of myself. I was happy when I sat down after Communion because . . . it was like the people were waiting for me to make a mistake on my moves."[33] The presence of Melissa's parents increased her anxiety because she hoped to make her family proud, and she wanted her parents to see perfection in this special moment in her life. Other children expressed similar opinions; the majority of the children I observed but did not interview also seemed concerned to get it right for both their audience and themselves. They rehearsed the gestures over and over before the ceremony. This last-minute cramming, which was done by all the children, was especially noticeable at Blessed Sacrament, where the pre-ceremony waiting period was much more structured than that at Holy Cross. At Blessed Sacrament's 12 May 2001 ceremony, for instance, Molly, a seven-year-old white girl in a white dress and veil, rehearsed the sign of the cross again and again. When I tried to reassure her that she was doing it correctly and that everything would be okay, she replied, "Yeah, but I'm just practicing."[34] Then, reinforcing Molly's impulse to practice, one of the assistant catechists walked down the line checking to make sure that all the children knew how to hold their hands when they received the Eucharist. This last "check" resulted in all but the most resistant children practicing different gestures. Some children began trying to coordinate their genuflecting with crossing themselves, while others worked on mastering the many different hand positions—from the palms together stance of the opening procession to the hand signs used in the closing song. Soon the moment would arrive when they would be able to demonstrate their ability to perform these actions just like the adults did each weekend at Mass. Balancing the pressures of the day, the religion teacher from Blessed Sacrament school repeated, "It's a prayer, not a performance," a meditative mantra to calm both the children and the catechists as they made adjustments. But no one was convinced. Despite the effort to slow racing hearts and lower rising blood pressures, the communicants seemed to think (and later confirmed) that a mistake would not only be embarrassing but might also prove in some way that they were still "children," not ready to move out of this stage.

Within moments, however, the children would be receiving the bread and the wine they had coveted for so long. Finally, they felt they would come to know what, for them, was the greatest ecclesiastical secret: the taste of consecrated bread and wine. Many other secrets of the Catholic faith and their theological significance would have to wait. Many children feared this part of the ritual the most. Some of the concern about the wine and the bread, like the concern with ritual gesture, was that its unfamiliar taste would cause the child to "mess up" or, worse, throw up. As Elizabeth, from Blessed Sacrament, said, "I was furious [nervous?] because at practice the wine was a new taste. It made a sour taste in my mouth. I thought I might get sick on my stomach." [35] Elizabeth was not alone in her worries about being sick: one boy at Blessed Sacrament could not bring himself to swallow the Host at practice or during First Communion. However, Cara, a nine-year-old African American girl from Holy Cross, was proud of her performance: "I didn't spit it out [during practice]. A lot of other people spit it out." [36] (I did not notice anyone spitting out the Host at practice.) Cara's account vividly expressed her concern about being able to swallow the bread, a ritual act that would allow her to join the adults.

In providing the children with an opportunity to display their newfound competency, First Communion became the ultimate moment of visibility; the children were no longer the ignorant kids hidden back in the pews while their families went to the altar. Each communicant sensed the congregation watching him or her as that communicant placed the Host in his or her mouth, and the parents and teachers craned their necks to get a clear view of that child's performance. The catechists and parents hoped that the communicants would remember what they had been taught—to take the Host with their right hand, to be careful with the chalice, to say "Amen," and to cross themselves. The adults waited to see the instant when the children would be united with Christ. For them, the children would become part of the Body of Christ: having ingested the bread, they would become part of the one Body with all the Catholics who had received the Sacrament before them. For the communicants, however, when they received the Sacrament, they would taste what all those older parishioners tasted each Sunday, and the children felt a great deal of pressure to drink the wine and eat the bread in the same way the other parishioners did.

For Holy Cross's First Communicants who went to the altar with their godparents, the role of the congregation as examiners was ameliorated in some way by the comfort of the hands of these trusted adults on their shoulders. When the adults' role changed from audience members to participants, some of the children's anxiety decreased. This supportive presence appeared in a few of the First Communicants' drawings and words. Although Maureen had said earlier that she was panicked, she also explained that having her godfather there "helped me to not be so nervous."[37] The congregation's presence, then, did more than represent the eyes she felt on her that morning; it also seemed to stand for those who supported her passage into her new standing in the Church. Sitting on the back stairs of the church, Maureen tried to help me understand this shift from anonymity to visibility and from outsider to insider. Maureen's post-Communion picture, drawn eight months after First Communion, attracts the viewer's eye to the central ritual, to the priest's smiling face as he hands her the bread and the wine. In contrast to her pre-Communion picture (Figure 18), in which Maureen stands as the focal point and the congregation is barely visible, in the post-Communion picture (Figure 19) she seems almost anonymous. In this later drawing, she shows the viewer only the back of her white dress.[38] The audience also plays a much larger role in this illustration than do the small stick fig-

FIGURE 18. *Maureen's pre-Communion drawing shows a stick-figure congregation watching Maureen and her godfather*

ures in the right-hand margin of the earlier picture. In this later rendition, the audience members come alive, their personalities evidenced through their various hairstyles and skin colors. As she showed herself to be part of the congregation, Maureen talked about the individual attention she received from those in the pews at the moment she depicted. When I asked her whether the man with the top hat worried that people would notice him, she replied,

FIGURE 19. *Maureen's post-Communion picture highlights the audience*

"No, they're all looking at me."[39] Using my crayons and her own gestures as aids, she told me that First Communion made her "feel like . . . I'm really part of the church."[40]

Like Maureen's, many children's post-Communion interviews at both Holy Cross and Blessed Sacrament demonstrated that they now saw themselves as part of their parish; they focused less on themselves and their roles in the ritual. The inclusion of the congregation, or reference to it, simultaneously focused the viewer's at-

FIGURE 20. *José speaks from the lectern*

tention on the child, as in Melissa's drawing, and allowed the viewer
to see that the child and the priest were not the only participants
in this event. After First Communion, the congregation played a
substantial role in the interpretations of the event by the children.
In nine-year-old José's post-Communion drawing of himself speaking before the congregation (during the dressing of the altar before
First Communion Mass at Blessed Sacrament), the pews suggest
the presence of the audience, just as his inclusion of three micro-
phones illustrates how important it was for his voice to be heard
by his audience (Figure 20). Describing his picture, this enthusiastic Mexican boy exclaimed, "[It's] me speaking on the speaker
and the people listening to me." [41] Children like José who included
the congregation in their discussions of First Communion seemed
to view the people in the pews as fulfilling a dual role. They were
family members and friends offering support while simultaneously
inspecting the children's actions to ensure that they had done them
correctly. In part because they received the parish's approval, the
First Communicants reported a change in their relationship with

FIGURE 21. *Hunter lights his candle*

their church. Hunter, who did not include the congregation in his post-Communion drawing but drew a moment when he stood alone facing the viewer and by implication the pews, commented that for him First Communion was "fun . . . because I was getting more attention and I was more welcome in the church" (Figure 21).[42]

Perhaps because of Holy Cross's focus on the children's new admission into Jesus' flock, Hunter and his classmates echoed this feeling of belonging in our conversations to a greater extent than did the communicants at Blessed Sacrament. Those children displayed their feelings of belonging primarily through their drawings. In their pre-Communion pictures, many children at Blessed Sacrament with whom I talked before Communion chose to place themselves outside the church building in their drawings. This external placement seemed to highlight their sense that they did not belong in the Church. In contrast, the majority of their post-Communion pictures placed them in the center of the congregation or at the altar with the congregation looking on. Only Alison, however, directly addressed this feeling of belonging when she explained that First Communion was important "because I'm part of the church. . . . It's my church," a sentiment she did not express in her pre-Communion interview.[43]

As they learned how to genuflect and which shoulder to touch first when making the sign of the cross, the children seemed to be aware that their identity within the parish was changing, a shift that meant they would have new responsibilities to Jesus and to their parish. After performing the ritual gestures and receiving the Eucharist, Maureen said, "Most grown-ups think you have a right, that you should probably listen to Mass instead of doing something else."[44] She believed that she would be seen by grown-ups as having a right to sit in the pews, to listen like the adults, and to perform adult tasks (such as collecting the offering) only when she could shift the placement of her arms during the Eucharist from the child-like position, crossed over her chest in preparation for a blessing, to the adult position of outstretched hands prepared to receive the Sacrament. With these children, as with other religious adherents, "members live their religion by doing it, acting its rites, restating its memories . . . thus gaining an identity and a world to live in."[45]

Along with performing gestures such as the sign of the cross that united them with the Catholic Church, the children also learned to move in accordance with their parish's unique identities, particularly at Holy Cross. Holy Cross's communicants, for instance, learned to walk to the beat of a drum for the First Communion liturgy, while six of the children demonstrated their proficiency at African dance. Although the children could not articulate the connection between this performance and the parish's racial identity, virtually all of them included it in their discussion of First Communion. Their comments centered on either their excitement about doing the dance or the embarrassment that dancing in front of the congregation caused, rather than on how it highlighted their heritage or distinguished their parish from those that surrounded it. Ryan said, for example, "I liked when they were dancing in the dance routine because it was something new in the church and not just saying all this prayer."[46] Ryan talked of differences, but he did not label these differences in racial terms. Paul, on the other hand, whispered to me across the table, "I didn't like the dancing part because I think I was embarrassed."[47] But Paul, like his shy counterparts at Blessed Sacrament and Holy Cross, performed the required gestures in spite of his embarrassment, perhaps because he had little choice and possibly because he wanted to show the congregation he was one of them.

As the communicants discussed their desire to belong, they expressed no sense that the beliefs and gestures which they were taught linked them and their parish to other Catholic parishes in Durham, Burlington, or elsewhere. However, the children's lack of understanding about the universal Church did not necessarily evidence their inability to conceive of something beyond their immediate experience. This absence of understanding likely reflected, in part, the lack of instruction they received about their membership in the larger body of Christ. At Holy Cross I never heard the teachers mention the universal Church. At Blessed Sacrament the children had only one lesson on ecclesiastical structure.

Membership and Its Responsibilities

In performing the required gestures, the children seemed to feel that they had passed the test for membership in their parish. For the communicants, belonging to the Church had a meaning that their parents and teachers did not entirely share. The children's feelings of belonging to their parish evolved from their view of their status before and after First Communion. The children's drawings and comments evidence a transition in the children's feelings toward the parish community from suspicion and anxiety before the ritual to comfort and support from this community afterward. The children recognized that belonging to the parish carried with it both rights of participation and duties to act responsibly as attentive church members. These aspects of "belonging" that I discuss gave the children a new sense of importance and status in their parish.

Scale seemed to be the biggest difference between the adults' understanding of the children becoming members of the Church and the children's interpretation. The parents discussed the universal Catholic Church, whereas the children spoke of membership in a more local context. Although the communicants did not demonstrate that they understood their parish as part of a wider Catholic community, some children did perceive that certain differences in practice separated the Catholic Church from others attended either by them or by another family member.[48] When I asked the children what it meant to be Catholic, they had a variety of answers, all centering on what people at other churches did (or did not do) on Sundays. Ryan, for example, who had non-Catholic relatives, explained, "I have cousins who don't eat pork."[49] From listening to the children and interpreting their drawings with them, they appeared to have little understanding of the diversity of Catholic expression or the uniqueness of their own ceremony. This lack of knowledge likely resulted from their limited experience outside the Mass they attended; very few of these children went to Masses at other churches or even to Mass at different times in their own parish (although some Hispanic children occasionally attended an English-language Mass). Although the children did not understand the ritual of the Eucharist in the wider context of the universal Church or highlight the distinctive characteristics of a Catholic identity, they did focus intently on how they felt about being included in their parish as they walked up with the adults, hands outstretched, to receive the Eucharist at each Mass.

At Holy Cross, where the 1997 catechetical team centered the celebration on the theme of belonging to Jesus' flock, the children spoke often of feeling welcome and of belonging in their parish. However, at Blessed Sacrament, the classes and the First Communion liturgy focused on God's forgiveness through the story of the forgiving father (formerly the story of the prodigal son), which may have made the communicants at Blessed Sacrament more likely to speak of God's love. Having not emphasized the sense of belonging in their classes or liturgy, the communicants at Blessed Sacrament did not discuss belonging with me directly in our conversations. Rather, the children articulated their feelings of belonging primarily through their drawings and discussions of receiving the Eucharist with their parish. Children in both parishes illustrated these feelings of belonging with crayons and paper.

Although the communicants in each parish emphasized different aspects of what it meant to be individual members of their parish, separate from their parents, they all expressed feelings of inclusion in their post-Communion drawings and conversations. Before First Communion, most of the children's drawings pictured themselves outside the church. While some of them did include other children from the class, at least one child, Dean, seems to have included them only because they were part of his class, not because they were central to the moment in which he received the Eucharist in front of the congregation (Figure 9). When I asked him who was standing behind him in his drawing, he mentioned some of the other boys from class and then said, "Yeah, but you can't see them." "Can you see you?" I inquired. "*Yeah*, right there," he answered incredulously, pointing to the first stick figure in line.[50] Before First Communion, only a few other children, such as Maureen (Figure 18) and Britney (Figure 10), included members of the congregation (and in Maureen's case, her godfather) in their drawings. Further, they barely mentioned them in our conversations. Before the event, the children's attention rested where that of the adults did—on the communicants: together the children and adults picked out First Communion outfits, memorized prayers, and perfected the children's gestures. This increase in attention and the mounting anxiety seemed to preclude them from thinking too much about the supporting cast of friends and family who would partake in the Sacrament with them.

Highlighting their excitement in the weeks leading up to the celebration, the communicants seemed not to think about the role the congregation would play. Most children who included members of the congregation in their pictures and conversations before First Communion included them as anonymous onlookers. Only Maureen, who, according to her mother, had already received some encouragement from the parishioners at Holy Cross, mentioned anything about the congregation before First Communion. With a big smile on her face, she explained that at First Communion, "you get to eat a little bit from the Last Supper from Jesus and Jesus is happy for you. Then you get blessed from God and from Jesus and from the priest and all the people in the church, even if you don't know their names. That's the best part."[51] Most of the children did not appreciate this "best part" of First Communion until after the ritual. Even for Maureen, this link to the parish became clearer after she received the Eucharist. Through the intensity of their practicing, their detailed conversation about ritual gestures, and their anxiety about the public performance, the children seemed to convey a connection between performing these gestures and achieving a place of their own, rather than being in their parents' shadows in their parish.

Through their pre-Communion drawings the children expressed this sense that after First Communion they would understand themselves to be individual members of their parishes and thought that the adults in their parish would too. In these drawings they stood by themselves before the altar. All the communicants reported the feeling that "everyone was looking at me" when they walked up to the priest.[52] This notion of being seen by the congregation comes through starkly in Melissa's pictures before and after her First Communion at Blessed Sacrament. Her first picture shows her clothed in a white dress, with pink roses on her head, standing in front of the church with one of the boys from class (Figure 22). After she drew her picture, we talked mostly about her expectations for the Sacrament and the party she would have afterward, a party about which her mother also talked a great deal. Seven months after First Communion, her drawing depicted her standing in the church wearing her bejeweled dress and tiara, which she and her mother bought in New York City, holding the chalice and the Host. Unlike the first drawing, this one includes the pews, which both imply the presence of the congregation and draw the viewer's eye to Melissa (Figure 13). Melissa's choice to move herself from outside the church building in the first drawing to inside the sanctuary in the midst of the congregation in the second one illustrates her new sense of belonging in her congregation. Having had her First

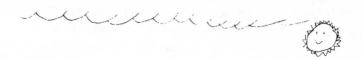

FIGURE 22. *Melissa stands outside the church in her dress*

Communion, she moved from being an outsider, unknowledgeable about the ways of her parish and unrecognized, to a valuable insider worthy of the congregation's attention.

With this new sense of ecclesiastical belonging also came new responsibilities for all the communicants. After First Communion, José said that he liked going to the Spanish Masses now because he got to "set up the table and go back there and show the people, like, where to take the bread and the wine."[53] While the Anglo children at Blessed Sacrament had to wait until they were in the fifth grade to assist at the Mass, the First Communicants at Holy Cross, like those children who attended Blessed Sacrament's Spanish Mass, could become altar servers immediately after receiving the Sacrament, perhaps because the larger Anglo parish had more children who could be altar servers and the smaller parish and congregation needed altar servers.[54] For these First Communicants, the celebration marked the time when, as Hunter told me enthusiastically, "I got to be an altar server and do other things."[55] The ability to assist in the Mass seemed to augment Hunter's and other children's new sense of welcome in the parish and at the Mass. From Maureen's comment mentioned earlier about her new "rights," it appears that her mother, like some other parents, communicated to her daughter that she "had a right" to pay attention during Mass by no longer bringing childish activities with her to church.

The Catholic Church's rules reinforced her mother's suggestion that Maureen had moved out of childhood and away from childish activities by allowing the First Communicants to be altar servers and participants in the Mass in new ways. These new roles and obligations conveyed a sense of belonging, purpose, and importance that many of the children had not felt before. After First Communion all the children emphatically expressed this sense of inclusion with the excitement and seriousness with which they described their expectations for, and experience of, receiving the Eucharist.

Joining the Family

Attention in the church and from the parish was not all that mattered to the children: the communicants also commented on the presence of their extended families. Britney, for instance, cried as she walked down the aisle because only her mother had made it to the church on time. The rest of her family, however, arrived by the time she made her speech, in which she explained some of what her classmates were doing as they "dressed the altar" before the liturgy.[56] According to Britney, the presence of her family to see her speak before the congregation and receive the Eucharist gave the Sacrament much of its meaning.

Although the two generations, children and parents, interpreted many of the finer points of the First Communion celebration differently, they seemed to agree that it allowed the children to feel God's love and to belong to their parish (if not their Church) in an important, familial way. Among the adults, some emphasized one aspect of this ritual interpretation more than others. The differences arose primarily between religious educators and parents. The religious educators focused principally on fulfilling their vocation to foster the children's sense of belonging to God and the Church. Many parents, on the other hand, also used this ritual as an opportunity to show children their connection to their family, so that they might perpetuate family traditions.[57] For both the parents and the religious educators, one of the central goals of the celebration was, as catechist Anne Fister said, to "make it memorable," just as it had been for many of the adults.[58] Ms. Fister was referring not only to the children receiving the consecrated Host in the sanctuary but also to extra-ecclesiastical practices of family celebrations. By making it memorable, the parents would hopefully make the children want to experience the Eucharist again, and to that end, they would tell the children just how important the Sacrament was to the Church and to their families.

The adults, like the children, understood First Communion's importance in differing ways, some of which centered more on the family and some of which stressed the Church's doctrine. Ms. Jeffries spoke the most enthusiastically about its religious aspects: "All the time I used to say to my mom, 'I'm going to become a nun.' . . . I loved the church. I loved it!" Ms. Jeffries said of her First Communion, "At the time my feeling for God and for the church was so wonderful. . . . I didn't have a white dress for my First Communion, but that was the most beautiful day I ever had."[59] She, like all the catechists, put great effort into making it a special day for the communicants by teaching them how close they could be to God. She hoped that the children learned these lessons well.

Through the Faith Formation classes, she and her colleagues at both Blessed Sacrament and Holy Cross wanted the children to learn the significance of receiving Jesus. The catechists realized that First Communion was more than receiving the Sacrament, however; it was also a time for celebration to mark the children's progression in the Church. Just as family celebration was an important part of most adults' First Communion experience, so too the adults ensured that it would be a part of the children's experience. As he reminisced about his First Communion, Brian's father, Mr. Jones, seemed to express much about how both the adults and the children interpreted these celebratory parties. Cocking his head slightly to the right and allowing the beginnings of what would become an all-encompassing smile to wash over his face, he said: "After [Mass] we went to my cousins', and they had a big party up there. But, I remember, you know, it was fun . . . just to hav[e] a party.

I was a young kid. I was about nine years old."[60] Like Mr. Jones, some adults seemed to want the communicants to feel as special as they had felt when, years before, their families gathered to watch them receive the Host in church and celebrated with them afterward at home. Ms. Fabuel (who put a tremendous amount of energy into preparing the children for participation in the Sacrament) said, with just a touch of embarrassment, that she did not remember receiving the Eucharist at all: "My cousin made his the same day at a different church so we had our party together. It was one day of great big parties all day long. . . . [T]he actual receiving of the First Communion, I don't remember that. I remember the parties."[61] Although Ms. Fabuel hoped her students would remember the Eucharist more than the cake from the family celebration, she also knew that both kinds of nourishment were important. While the teachers sought to create the feeling of importance by designing special First Communion liturgies for the children, they also prepared a parish post-Communion party. The parents did the same at home by making sure their children attended Faith Formation classes and by giving their children a family party and new First Communion clothes. Although some mothers and daughters may have put more emphasis on their dresses than they may have on the Sacrament, the adults' activities reinforced the Sacrament's significance and the children's sense of importance and belonging.

Each parish celebrated its new members at the altar table by setting up tables of its own in the parish halls and filling them with cake and other goodies. These parties (along with those given by the children's families) emphasized the importance of successfully performing all the necessary gestures by showing the children that receiving the Sacrament merited the adults' time and attention. And it offered the children a great sense of accomplishment and relief. While not all the children mentioned these celebrations either before or after First Communion, some children reported that the parties added to their excitement and anticipation of the Sacrament. When I asked Melissa if she wanted to have First Communion, for instance, she seemed to ignore my question altogether and answered excitedly, "And then I get to have a party at my house."[62] In imagining her First Communion during our First

Communion interview, Melissa demonstrated that for her, receiving the Eucharist and attending her party were closely tied, just as some of the adults remembered their First Communions. Like all the children, she seemed quite excited that friends and family were coming to see her receive Communion and that they would then celebrate that milestone with her at a nearby inn.

Although Melissa's celebration was uncharacteristically elaborate for the children in this study, many communicants at both parishes had a similar enthusiasm for their post-Communion festivities. Virginia, a shy seven-year-old Mexican girl whose older sister was also celebrating First Communion, spoke animatedly about what her family had planned for their post-Communion party, which coincided with her brother's birthday. She smiled, made a big circle with her hands, and said, "My mother says we're going to make three cakes. We're going to have the biggest cakes."[63] As her face brightened and her smile grew, it seemed that the size of the cakes somehow reflected her excitement for First Communion and her own sense of importance. For other children (especially many other Latinos, whose parents had little disposable income or time), eating at a restaurant supplanted the homemade desserts and rented party rooms. José, for example, spoke with great anticipation of the pizza he had chosen for his celebratory meal; Roxanna said enthusiastically that after the Mass, her family was going out to a restaurant. Similarly, Elizabeth, an eight-year-old white child who described receiving the Sacrament in great detail, beamed as she told me her favorite part of First Communion was "the celebration at the end. . . . My mom and dad took us out to my favorite restaurant."[64] Although Alison liked "going up there" and receiving the Eucharist the best, she too noted that she got to choose her favorite restaurant for her post-Communion meal. These diverse celebrations marked First Communion as an especially important event.[65] These discussions, like many others, demonstrated that the children included the entire celebration, from their preparation to receive the Eucharist to their family parties afterward, as part of the Sacrament. Even though the anticipation for the reception of the Eucharist set that moment apart from the rest, it did not render the other aspects of their experience profane.

Those children who talked about their parties, the cakes they would eat, or the restaurants where they would gather with family seemed to feel some of what Brian's father, Mr. Jones, remembered about his First Communion and the importance of being recognized and celebrated when you are eight or nine years old.[66] "Just having a party" or getting to choose the restaurant where their families would eat after Mass seemed, for some communicants, to solidify their perception of the event's importance to their families, to increase their excitement, and thus to highlight the event's and their own significance.

While special family celebrations stood out in some children's minds, other children expressed much less interest in them. Seven months after his First Communion, for instance, Paul, could not remember what his family did after Mass, perhaps because he was just so "happy, happy it was over."[67] Hunter also seemed unimpressed by the post-Communion festivities. He simply commented rather unenthusiastically, "We went out to eat and we, like, had a party."[68] While Hunter's and Paul's lackluster responses to the party were unusual, it does reflect both that for some children parties were of little importance and that for others the party was, perhaps, another source of anxiety in an already stressful day. In our conversations and in what I overheard in and out of class, even children who relished the celebrations, such as Melissa and Elizabeth, did not let the parties eclipse their excitement about receiving the Eucharist. Of course, the focus of the children's conversations might have shifted to the party when they left the confines of the church, but in our conversations the party seemed only to be a piece of a much greater whole. They, like Father Briant, understood that the celebrations necessitated food, friends, and special clothing, because First Communion was a special event.

As Father Briant emphasized when talking about the Last Supper, you cannot have a party alone. According to the children you have to invite "grandparents, friends, everyone," and many parents and children did just that. As Ms. Fister commented, "What makes it memorable, I think . . . is how something like their First Communion grows into everybody coming and supporting them."[69] Unlike birthday parties, for this occasion family members came not only from down the street but also from across state borders to watch the children participate in the parish celebration. Paris, for instance, told me excitedly about how her "dad's family [was] gonna fly from Florida" to come to the Mass.[70] Maureen also had relatives fly in to see her, while others had grandparents and godparents drive long distances. All family members—those who traveled from near and far—carved out time to celebrate the children and their accomplishments. For many children, their family's presence made a great impact on their interpretations of First Communion. Maureen, for instance, who talked enthusiastically about her new relationship with Jesus, said that her favorite part of First Communion was her "family being there."[71] As Ms. Fister explained, to celebrate the Eucharist, "people fly in from California to see a seven-year-old receive their First Communion."[72] Both aspects of Ms. Fister's statement seemed to be important to the children—that family members were coming and that they were coming to see *them*. First Communion "becomes a family reunion . . . [with] as many family members as they can squeeze into the parish."[73] For Britney, even the space that the parish provided for her family was not large enough: "I'm mad because I want lots of people to come see me have my First Communion, but they said you can only have one pew. But [Alison's] mom said that we could use some of her pew because there's only going to be the three of them."[74] While Britney emphasized how her many relatives might not be able to squeeze into the pew, many children, especially the Latinos, focused on the relatives who would not be able to see them receive the Sacrament. Virginia, for example, said excitedly that her uncle, who lived with her family, would come to the Mass, but she added sadly that his twin sons could not come because they lived with their mother in Mexico.[75] Sitting on the back stairs of Blessed Sacrament School drawing bright flowers around a cross, Lily's eyes glistened with tears as she quietly said, "I wish my grandma could come, but she's in Mexico so she can't come."[76] This girl's sadness extended beyond wanting her family to see her receive the consecrated bread; she, like many others, also seemed to realize that her participation in First Communion was important to her grandmother and other family members. First Communion was something to be shared.

These events seemed to go beyond simply having a party; they were efforts at social communion that united the child to the family just as the Catholic Church believed that the Eucharist united the child with the universal Church.

At least one family from Holy Cross (and I surmise many others at both parishes) closed the distance between their son and his extended family by making phone calls. Ferris expressed his frustration with this practice, saying, "I went home and my mom kept on talking on the phone with my relatives and everything, how I did all this good job."[77] Through phone calls, visits, and perhaps cards and letters, this family interaction during First Communion showed the communicants how highly their families valued both them and the Sacrament. Thus what the Catholic Church might consider secular activities did, in fact, shape the children's interpretations, highlighting the significance of their religious experiences. From the children's perspective and perhaps that of their parents, party clothes became as sacred as the priest's vestment during First Communion.

Dressing the Part

Along with Faith Formation classes and party preparations, clothing played an important part in the children's celebration of the Eucharist. For some children, such as Christy, who were barely interested in the Eucharist, First Communion was special because to receive the Sacrament meant "you get to wear those pretty white dresses and pretty white shoes."[78] Like the parties, the dress clothes hanging in the communicants' closets also reminded them of First Communion's importance in the weeks before and after the Mass. The children and their parents wove multiple meanings into the prescribed clothing. The adults viewed the clothes as an important element in the carrying on of traditions, while many children seemed to associate their clothes with being important, grown-up, and the center of attention. For both groups, clothes marked the day's significance, showed respect for the Sacrament, and maintained important connections within their families. The adults and the children, both boys and girls, spoke of the white First Communion dress and veil as sacred and traditional—almost to the exclusion of comments about the boys' new "Sunday" clothes. The boys and girls, as well as their parents, agreed that these white dresses set the girls apart as communicants, just as the priest's purple, red, and green vestments signified that the priest was officiating at the Mass.

While the adults focused on the dresses' uniformity and the message it sent about the children's purity, the children's comments revealed that these clothes did more than just emphasize their role as initiates and the clean state of their souls. Like many adults, sociologist Gary Wray McDonough, for instance, only briefly mentions the Communion dress, asserting a single meaning for it. He states that "all the girls wore white party dresses, symbolizing their purity."[79] While this interpretation has some validity, it does not reveal much about what these dresses mean to their wearers and their purchasers. The children, for instance, talked of holiness, queens, and brides, but never of purity. Even for adults, white does not always signify purity. The meaning of white, like the meaning of the First Communion dress, depends on context, on who is reflecting on its meaning and when they are doing it. After all, Martha Manning points out in her memoir, *Chasing Grace*, that the nuns warned her and her female classmates that white made "boys think of bed sheets."[80] In the case of the First Communion dress, formerly Catholic women, older women still affiliated with the Church, Catholic children, and their parents all seemed to weave multiple meanings into the prescribed clothing. Some adults saw the white dress as representing the purity of the girls' souls. For these children and parents who were in the midst of preparing for and celebrating this rite, the clothes marked the day's importance, showed respect for the Sacrament, and made connections within their families.

Virtually all First Communion dresses are white, and most girls, across generations and around the world, also wear white veils. Its uniformity allowed the dress to connect the girls in the 1997 and 2001 classes with other Catholic girls and women—past, present, and future. As Kathleen Hage asked in her essay *The Communion Dress*, "Could this dress, purchased . . . before Vatican II still be relevant to the current First Communion celebration?" "The 1998 class of communicants," she explains, "will process down the aisle and look much like that 1961 procession" for which the dress was originally purchased.[81] The Communion dress's ability to bring the Catholic world together, along with the importance of this tradition, was suggested in the 1954 First Communion dress drive organized by the National Council of Catholic Women to ensure that needy "young girls in Europe may be suitably clothed for their First Communion."[82] The council wished for girls to be suitably clothed in white dresses and veils even though the Catholic Church had no prescription for First Communion clothes.

The concept of "suitable dress" had much more to do with vernacular tradition than with ecclesiastical guidelines. Although acceptable attire equaled white dresses and veils for virtually all female First Communicants across the globe, Ms. Dalton, who organized the council drive, recognized regional differences. She noted that American girls' dresses are generally short sleeved, knee length, and made of white silk or cotton. However, "in most countries," she said, "the dresses are worn ankle-length with sleeves to the wrists and necks high enough to reach the base of the throat."[83] These differences in style are as important to analyze as are the similarities. The differences emphasize the girls' connection to their ethnic groups as well as the girls' own tastes, as Ms. Dalton implied and the girls' dresses at Holy Cross and Blessed Sacrament displayed.

Despite these differences, First Communion garments, like wedding gowns and other ceremonial attire, carry multiple meanings in part because of their fundamental uniformity through time and across geographic space. In contrast to normal Sunday dress, these ritualized and traditional clothes set the communicants apart from the rest of the parishioners. As clothing used in a rite of initiation, the Communion dress serves, as anthropologist Penny Storm explains, to differentiate "the wearer(s), in [their] consecration from the profane."[84] The parishioners could easily identify the initiates, just as the initiates could recognize their classmates. To maintain this uniformity, parishes often restrict the family's choice of First Communion attire. Holy Cross mandated the First Communicants' dress: the boys were required to wear dark pants, white shirts, and red neckties, and the girls, traditional white First Communion dresses and veils (although Maureen wore a headband of white silk flowers).[85] Most of the girls wore simple dresses that fell just below their knees.

Blessed Sacrament, on the other hand, had no fixed dress code to avoid placing a financial burden on the families. Ms. Key asked only that the children wear their "Sunday best." She elaborated on this decision before the 2001 First Communion: "I don't know people's financial situation, and I don't want this to be a burden. Most of the boys come in blazers. Ties are optional but strongly encouraged. Some will wear the bow [on their arm]—whatever they like—but no jeans. For the girls, all the girls will wear white dresses. I don't know why, but they always do."[86] Thus, even when the individual church allowed families greater freedom to select the children's clothing, tradition for the girls seemed to constrain the parents' and the children's choices. Ms. Key was right. All the girls came in white dresses. The cotton or silk dresses worn by the Anglo and African American children at both churches usually had short sleeves and fell just below the knee; the Latinas at Blessed Sacrament, in contrast, wore floor-length taffeta dresses, often embellished with the image of Our Lady of Guadalupe on the front panel (Figure 23). Most of the Latinas' dresses also had layers of lace or decorative bows that set them apart from the standard Sunday attire of jeans or casual skirts and cotton tops. The idea of donning this elaborate outfit made Virginia's eyes light up as she spoke of her newly purchased dress. As she drew her First Communion self-portrait, she said, "On my First Communion day, my sister and I are going to be dressed like queens" (Figure 24).[87] For Virginia, then, and perhaps for many other Hispanic First Communicants who wore crowns, the dress's magic came from its ability to transform the wearer into adult royalty (note that she was a queen, not a princess) rather than a bride or a pure little girl.

While most girls drew detailed representations of themselves in their dresses, only a few boys focused on dress: Hunter talked about a gray tuxedo that he did not wear for First Communion, and Eric sketched himself in a "big blue suit with black shoes"

FIGURE 23. A Latina communicant in traditional Communion dress

FIGURE 24. *Virginia looks like a queen in her Communion dress and veil*

(Figure 25).[88] Although only those two boys described their clothing in detail, all the boys drew themselves in "suitable dress," ranging from tuxedos to suits to brown slacks. It seemed that the boys' clothing—ties, dark pants or khakis, and white shirts—did not distinguish this sacred day from others with as much clarity as the girls' dresses did. Ferris, for instance, drew himself at First Communion in just an outline, giving no indication of his clothing's significance (Figure 15). He explained: "I really don't like getting dressed

FIGURE 25. *Eric in his big blue Communion suit*

up. The only reason I did it was because my mom wanted me to . . . look nice." [89] Like Ferris, Ryan said he would have preferred to wear "baggy clothes" but that he wanted to "respect Jesus." [90] In emphasizing the reasons they wore "nice" clothes for First Communion, the boys agreed with many adults, who felt that this attire positively influenced the children's experiences. For example, Ms. Cement, whose son was a communicant at Holy Cross, stated: "I . . . like the idea that the kids feel that this is important enough [to dress up for]. This is sort of a symbol of its importance: We're going to look really nice for this." [91] Father Barry went further in his explanation of the role of new clothes, or "suitable dress," in the ceremony. "If we have an experience of our interior sense, taste, touch, and so on ... how do you objectify that?" he said. "How do you let that sensate world express the interior senses? I think that's what they're doing. New clothes are always a sign of joy." [92]

Not all the children, however, interpreted the dress that way. Perhaps the children who helped to choose their clothing understood it as being more significant than those communicants who did not. Whereas the majority of boys wore clothes already in their closets, the girls either went on special shopping trips or were given their dresses by older family members. The special circumstances that surrounded the selection of their dresses seemed to make the details more vivid to the girls.

For the girls, the clothing may have accrued more importance because they heard older women's stories of *their* dresses, which connected the girls to these previous generations. The dress created an important symbolic link between these and other generations of Catholic girls and women. To emphasize these links, many Catholic girls wore their mother's or sister's dress. Alison from Blessed Sacrament, for instance, explained that wearing her older sister's Communion dress was special because "she wore it and it's really pretty." [93] Even those girls who did not wear a family member's dress had a sense of familial continuity. The girls frequently volunteered, for instance, "to pass [their dress] down to the next person in line." [94] Or, as Cara said, "My mom will probably keep it in the closet until I have a grandchild." [95] Paris focused on a spiritual relationship in describing the connections. She said that she had to wear the white dress she drew, "because we have to act like Mary in all white Communion clothes." [96] Paris often mentioned Mary and her apparitions in class, so this opportunity to "act like Mary" likely highlighted the importance of the ritual and, perhaps, simultaneously increased the pressure to act piously and correctly carry out all gestures learned in class. Though adults may associate Mary with the Immaculate Conception and "purity," it is not clear whether Paris had this image of Mary in mind. Perhaps Paris was reflecting one of her parents' explanations of the dress. Or perhaps Paris, like some of the other children, believed that white was a holy color and thus that wearing white would aid her in acting holy. What "holy" meant for Paris I cannot be sure about, but her reference to Mary clearly identified First Communion and her Communion dress as something sacred that connected her with the Mother of the Church.

Although Paris was alone in connecting the dress with Mary, almost all the girls commented on the stylistic similarities between their dresses (old or new) and those worn by past communicants, which helped to unite the generations. As Ms. Wright-Jukes said, "It's tradition. I wore the same dress thirty years ago." [97] The fact that all the parents at Blessed Sacrament bought their daughters traditional dresses even when they were not required to also demonstrated the importance of this generational bond, which seemed to remind the Catholic women of their tie to the Church as well as the familial connection between the girls and their older female relatives. Aside from Paris's statement about Mary, however, the girls did not seem to extend this connection to the universal Church, as some of their mothers had hoped. Nor did the boys express a sense of connection with the ritual clothing worn by their male relatives. Thus, although the clothing helped to highlight the day's importance, its sacredness, it was not as effective a tangible marker of the children's belonging to the Catholic Church as the adults had assumed it was. The children knew that their classmates and their family members had similar First Communion clothes; they did not realize, however, that Catholics outside their immediate experience had worn this attire. Nonetheless, the wearing of "suitable dress" by the communicants evidenced their connection to Catholic family members, which was important within their own world, further strengthening their membership within their family and their parish.

Conclusion Focusing on Present Relationships

Contrary to the presuppositions of many priests and catechists, the communicants did not talk about the post-Communion parties and clothing as being more important than receiving the Eucharist. In fact, the secular/sacred distinction makes little sense because the parties and the clothes seemed to be part and parcel of the Sacrament for the children. Although what adults might have called "externals" may have diverted some attention from the more traditionally religious aspects of the Sacrament, these aspects apparently enriched both the children's and the adults' interpretations of First Communion. Attending to these celebratory aspects reveals that the communicants' interpretations of the Sacrament were not developed exclusively in the church. The parties that the adults planned, along with the extended family members who attended those parties, seemed to increase the children's sense of the Sacrament's importance. These guests came to see *them*, to watch them receive the consecrated bread and wine. Through their words and gestures, the children demonstrated how important it was for these loved ones to be present and how disappointed they were when family members could not attend. The children wanted all of their family to join with their parish in seeing them receive the Sacrament. Although the communicants did not perceive these Catholic relatives as representatives of the universal Church they were now entering, they did relish their attention and support.

Although the communicants did not invoke the concept of the universal Catholic Church, when they discussed dress they seemed to sense a broader significance of First Communion beyond their immediate surroundings. Not limiting their discussions of dress to themselves, they spoke of their families and their relationship with the divine. Through their dresses, the girls also made connections with other women in their families — past, present, and future. These ties, however, did not seem to go beyond the family tree and extend to the broader Catholic community. When older girls at Holy Cross talked about their First Communion, they did mention that the dress linked them to the 1997 female communicants. (Ryan's ten-year-old sister, for example, noted that "we had kinda the same dresses as the girls in Ryan's First Communion.")[98] Yet even these older girls localized this connection to particular classes, not universalizing it as the grown-ups did with such words as "Catholic tradition."

While all the children seemed to understand First Communion in its broader parish context, each child added his or her own concerns and emphasis to his or her interpretations. Some communicants, for instance, felt forced to attend the classes regularly. They said they hated the classes because they had to sit still or awaken early. Sunday school, Dean said, "burns my butt."[99] Other children's concerns centered primarily on the actual reception of the Eucharist, as well as the gestures they would perform. They worried about whether they would be able to swallow the Host, since they had not liked its taste or texture during practice. Thus, although the vast majority of the children expressed a belief that First Communion welcomed them into their parish as capable individuals, they all had unique concerns and perspectives. Some communicants feared drinking the wine, whereas others did not. Some wanted the Communion Mass to be over before it began so they did not have to stand in front of the congregation, while others felt nervous only when they walked down the aisle. But all the children—African American, Euro-American, Mexican, Mexican American, and Filipino—could not wait to "get Jesus."[100]

Listening to the children, analyzing their drawings, and participating in their classes allowed me to understand the differences in the communicants' interpretations and interests. These differences stand in marked contrast to the monolithic presentation of "the initiates" that most studies of rites of passage present. In his seminal work *The Ritual Process*, for instance, Victor Turner described initiates, stating: "The neophytes are merely entities in transition, as yet without place or position."[101] The initiates with whom I worked, however, could not be reduced to mere entities without a place, for they were vibrant individuals actively participating in this transition by continually readjusting their understanding of their place within the parish as they incorporated some of the new information that they were learning from the adults. When the adults planned the communicants' parties, taught them a movement, or told them a story, the communicants moved closer to membership in their parish. It was in these moments that the secrets of the Church began to reveal themselves and the children felt individually important to their parents and teachers. Finally, when they learned the secret of the Eucharist, they believed that Jesus too valued them individually and that they had at last gained a place at the altar. As the children performed the gestures they were being taught, tasted the Eucharist, and received praise from the adults, they made the transition from one of the many youngsters who attended Mass to a young person who participated in Mass. They saw themselves as members of the parish.

conclusion

"Hey, Miss Susan," a voice called as I headed into a local department store. I turned to see two middle-school boys in sweatshirts and jeans walking on the other side of the mall. It took me a moment to realize who the boys were: Ferris and Ryan from Holy Cross Catholic Church. Ferris, perhaps having sensed my initial confusion, asked, "Do you know who we are?" "Yes," I replied, "of course." I began to ask them about school and church when Ferris jumped in and said, "You don't have your notebook." "No, Ferris," I smiled and said, "I don't carry it everywhere, just church." He flashed a quick smile in return and said, "So are we in a book yet?" "No," I replied, "but you will be soon, I hope." With that, the boys were swept up in a group of friends from school. We waved to each other as they turned into the candy store. They were at the mall on a field trip with Immaculata Catholic School, and both geographically and chronologically a long way from our former days together in Faith Formation class. In the boys' now twelve-year-old faces, I saw signs of the eight-year-olds that I had played with before Faith Formation class. Given their physical and mental growth, as well as their subsequent religious training, I was sure that their perceptions of First Communion would be very different from those they had had five years earlier. These past perceptions, however, were now my present challenge as I struggled to analyze their interviews and organize them into that book in which Ferris had hoped to find himself by now.

I wondered how Ryan's and Ferris's interpretations may have changed over time. However, I had decided years before to concentrate on their perceptions as First Communicants as they prepared for and interpreted First Communion at the time of the event. In so doing I wanted to highlight the children's role as thoughtful participants in this ritual. Thus, I chose to do an intensive ethnographic study of First Communion preparation, reception, and immediate reflection, rather than a longitudinal study, which would have revealed more about how Catholics continually reshape and reinterpret their memories of First Communion. Had I interviewed the children only after they had received the Sacrament, even if just a few months afterward, I would have heard little about their anxieties over taste. At best, I would have been offered only comments about the disgusting taste of the wine and disappointment over the blandness of the Host like those I received in the post-Communion interviews I conducted. I would also have missed the intense concerns the children had about their abilities to perform the gestures of the ritual, or their change in focus from themselves to their parish as evidenced in their pre- and post-Communion pictures.

When taken alone, the post-Communion comments of the children about the taste of the wine may be the kind of interpretations that lead adult researchers to believe that children are incapable of truly understanding an event. But when placed in the context of the entire event and not just the end result, these remarks serve to enhance the children's analysis of the event. Hearing these comments as pieces of a whole allows a researcher to realize that while children saying they hated wine may be an expected statement, in context it has a strong correlation to their concerns about behaving like an adult during the liturgy. Wine is an acquired adult taste, and a child's difficulty with that taste may mirror the difficulty that the child senses in attempting to participate as an adult in the Sacrament. Similarly, a child saying that the Host tasted like cardboard when taken out of context might be viewed as another example of a "kids say the darnedest things" moment. When put in the context of the great degree of anticipation that the child had about how *consecrated* bread would taste, however, the comment might be understood to express unfulfilled expectation and tremendous disappointment that Jesus' body did not taste like something more delicious and magical—the child approaching transubstantiation as a sensual rather than an intellectual experience. This analysis can raise important questions. For example, if the child's expectations for the taste of consecrated bread and wine are not fulfilled, does this negative experience in any way detract from the goal of the Church to have its young people embrace transubstantiation as an important concept in their spiritual development?

The Ritual in Time and Scope

The results of my research represent a snapshot in time. While it is impossible to give a definitive interpretation of each drawing and conversation that formed the basis of my research, my work with these children demonstrates that many of their comments and drawings expressed their effort at an important moment in their lives to incorporate new knowledge of their parish into their developing understanding of the Catholic Church and their role in it. As these children continue to grow, gain knowledge, and receive the Eucharist (if they do), their perceptions of their First Communion experience will continue to change, just as they were changing before, during, and after they received their First Communion. These future perceptions, or interpretations, may tell researchers more about how people perceived their relationship to the Catholic Church over time, to evolving prescribed gender roles, or to something else; they will not, however, reveal how the communicants interpreted their participation in the ritual when they were First Communicants. Without understanding this perspective of the ritual, the ritual from the inside and at the time it occurs, scholars will miss a critical set of interpretations.

Investigating rituals from the participants' perspectives is important to understanding all types of rituals. As I stated earlier, although much work is being done to illuminate the perceptions of adults, almost no work is being done to interpret the understandings of children. With this book I hope to have offered scholars a methodology by which children's perceptions of other religious events may be studied in the future and a glimpse into what such a study may reveal.

Age as a Fourth Category of Analysis

In its broadest sense, this study has explored a rite of passage. For both the children and their parents, First Communion encapsulated more than just the reception of the Sacrament. Like other studies that have applied performance theory to understand ritual, this ethnographic study of First Communion supports the precept that religiously significant events are influenced by factors occurring both inside and outside the sanctuary. After hearing children's stories about receiving Jesus' body at the altar and conversations about entertaining out-of-town relatives, it became clear to me that "First Communion" for these children referred to what happened not only in the church but also in their Sunday school classroom, on their dress-buying trips to the department stores, and during their family celebrations. For the participants in this study, First Communion began with Faith Formation classes and shopping trips, built to the reception of the consecrated bread and wine, and continued with post-Communion festivities. The children seemed to weave the class projects, the party dresses, and the many other elements of these para-Communion events into their interpretations of the ritual.

My fieldwork led me to the conclusion that labeling First Communion a rite of passage is only the first step in analyzing the ritual. While this label signifies the specific ritual's form and function from the institutional Church's viewpoint, it says little about the expectations and interpretations of those who are participating in it. How the children defined the event differed significantly from the definition found in encyclopedias and the *Catechism of the Catholic Church*, in part because the actual rite itself is much longer than scholars who focus only on the hour-long liturgy suspect; many scholars and Church officials in the past have often described First Communion referring only to the Mass at which the children receive the Eucharist for the first time. By attending to the words and actions of the children and the adults interpreting this ritual, I have tried to show that the functional definition of First Eucharist obscures the dynamic, multivalent meanings of this rite of passage.

Analyzing the entire ritual event, as the participants themselves view it, provides a rich perspective from which to observe the many nuances in interpretation and understanding experienced by both the children and the adults. Although neither the adults nor the children understood this ritual exactly as the Church defined it, in this book I focus on the most invisible participants in the celebration from a scholarly perspective—the communicants themselves.

Learning Ritual

Often when scholars investigate ritual, they do so by analyzing the actions and interpretations of well-practiced ritual participants. The participants with whom I worked, however, were not seasoned ritual experts; they were novices in terms of both their understanding of official Catholic doctrine and the facility with which they could perform the Eucharist. As I stood with the children as they hesitatingly responded to Father Barry's direction, "Simon says, genuflect," I realized that, in this and many similar moments, I was witnessing one aspect of ritual that rarely appears in ritual studies—how ritual is learned. The catechists sought to train the children's bodies to be Catholic just as they provided Catholic doctrine for the communicants to absorb intellectually. Even though the catechists did not discuss with me their role in teaching the children how to move appropriately, many times I left Faith Formation classes wondering if Cara or José could truly be a Catholic if they could not cross themselves correctly. Given the amount of practicing that the children did before First Communion Mass and the children's apprehension over whether they would achieve successful performance, perhaps they wondered this too.

Learning in this case meant more than rehearsing gestures; it also meant, for example, decoding symbols, encountering doctrine, and tasting sacred food. To whatever extent and in whatever way these forms of knowledge came together to inform the children's interpretations, they did so simultaneously. Thus, although scholars often tend to promote the intellectual over the sensuous, the children made no such distinction. What the children understood came together as a result of the lessons that they learned through lecture, participation, movement, sight, and taste, as well as through the impact of family, tradition, and parish culture both inside and outside the classroom. The intellectual understanding that the bread was Jesus' body, for instance, seemed to blossom for some children when they tasted, or imagined they tasted, it for themselves. Yet for other children, their anticipation of the event and concentration on performance overshadowed all other aspects of the ritual. For virtually all the children, however, their knowledge of the ritual and of its importance to their families and their parish provided them with a new sense of comfort and confidence immediately after their participation in the Sacrament. Through this education and experience, as well as their knowledge of parish traditions and Jesus' presence, most of the children came to sense the invisible but omnipresent love of Jesus and to understand that their families and parishioners saw them as vital members of a lineage that shared their Catholic faith.

Of course, as I discussed in Chapter 4, not all the children committed themselves to participating in the Eucharist to the same degree. Although virtually all the children expressed great excitement about receiving the bread and wine, some children walked to the altar and made a "throne for Jesus" largely because their parents forced them to do so. In his work arguing for the importance of the body in religion, Ruel W. Tyson Jr. asserts that "gestures are pivotal for they are at once public and personal. They are articulations of tacit beliefs and explicit feelings."[1] Investigating children's religious lives challenges the notion that performing certain movements evidences particular beliefs, first because as novices the children often did not know the beliefs that the congregation may have thought the children were "articulating," and second because many of the coerced participants performed actions that reflected little personal faith conviction. For many children, family pride in their performance and acceptance into the adult community of the parish were more effective motivations for their participation in the ritual than was any opportunity to express their Catholic beliefs.

(In)Voluntary Participation

Researchers of American religious history often apply the concept of voluntaryism in the legal and political context established by the First Amendment to the Constitution. But the concept of voluntaryism was infused with important new complexities in my study. Children seldom have a choice about their participation in religion. Although some children may cajole their parents into taking them to church so they can enjoy the liturgy, sing, and see friends, children often find themselves at Mass against their will. Many children, such as Britney and Dean, would have preferred sleeping late or playing soccer to sitting in Faith Formation class, but they did not get to choose how or where to spend their Sunday mornings. As with many other activities, these reluctant participants came each Sunday because their parents made them come. Although they were free to express their dismay by nodding off or causing disruptions, if their parents brought them to Faith Formation, the children had to attend class. And in the case of Blessed Sacrament, they had to attend a joint Anglo and Latino class. These examples suggest that studying children blurs the boundary between voluntary and mandated participation. For the parents, the decision may be voluntary. For their children, this is often not the case. The important inducement to faith development that voluntaryism provides to adults is at best obscured and often absent in childhood faith development.

In the context of parish life, the concept of voluntaryism when applied to adults and children can have an entirely different and unexpected significance. At Blessed Sacrament, the religious educators used the children's participation to create both the next generation of Catholics and a parish that reflected its racially and ethnically inclusive mission. Religious studies scholar Paul Numrich has argued that in churches which have both immigrant and native Euro-American populations, those populations often form "parallel congregations," divided primarily along the lines of language and, to a lesser extent, by ethnicity. In these parishes, the parishioners use the same facilities but rarely meet together.[2] Since the leadership at Blessed Sacrament could not require its adult members to go to integrated events or Masses, it relied on the one area of participation where they did have control to facilitate integration — children's religious education. As Ms. Barbara Pegg, the director of religious education (DRE) from another Durham Catholic Church, Immaculate Conception, stated, "We mostly work at integration through the children because usually the children can speak both Spanish and English, while the parents speak only Spanish."[3] In this sense, then, the children became the parish leadership's tool to facilitate cultural integration, which was difficult to cultivate directly through voluntary adult participation.

The children's function as ethnic integrators and cultural translators extended far beyond their own childhood friendships and education. Blessed Sacrament, along with many other parishes in the South, hoped that the children would also bring their white and Latino parents together into one community. At Blessed Sacrament, the First Communion workshop had all the parents working side-by-side to help the children make banners, bake bread, and learn songs.[4] As the parents worked together in the workshop, Ms. Key, Blessed Sacrament's DRE, hoped that they would get to know one another and begin to interact at nonscheduled times and that through their socialization the Latino parents would begin to feel comfortable becoming involved in parish activities with their new Anglo friends.[5] Although this kind of broader exchange had not yet developed at the time of my research, children of different ethnic and cultural backgrounds from Guadalajara, Pittsburgh, and Burlington, with whom I stood in the prayer circle at Blessed Sacrament each Sunday, voluntarily began to stand next to each other, hold one another's hands, and call each other "friend." In this small way, perhaps, the children, by becoming one class instead of two parallel groups within the same classroom, were becoming teachers themselves, and the boundary between the voluntary and the mandated took on new complexities in this multicultural setting. For while the parents had a choice about whether to come to Faith Formation, the children did not, yet the children were voluntarily establishing relationships with their teachers and classmates of various ethnicities that their parents had not. Still, the parents voluntarily supported their children's faith formation and in doing so began to participate with other like-minded parents of different ethnicities. Furthermore, though the adults had forced many of the children to be in class, the communicants chose the extent to which they would participate and how open they would be to creating new relationships with their classmates, fellow parishioners, and Jesus.

Children's Congregations

The adults at Blessed Sacrament looked to the children to bridge two distinct adult congregations in a parish of which the children did not feel a significant part before First Communion. While the adults may have assumed that the communicants saw themselves as integral to their parish, the communicants perceived a clear difference in knowledge, capability, and responsibility between themselves and the adults whom they saw each week receiving the Eucharist. The children at Holy Cross and Blessed Sacrament told me in various ways—through their words, actions, and art—that First Communion marked their journey from immature, nameless bystanders in their congregations to informed, capable members. At First Communion, their parents acknowledged the children's ability to participate in the most sacred ritual of the Church and, particularly at Blessed Sacrament, to perform adult duties during the Mass. However, the children's emphasis on their own sense of belonging as newly formed, capable parish members differed from the adults' sense that these young people were still children. This difference in generational interpretations demonstrates, in part, that First Communion succeeded as a rite of passage more from the children's, than from the adults', point of view. The children understood themselves as moving from their position of anonymity to adultlike belonging, whereas the adults focused on the communicants as persons beginning to embody and carry on traditions of the Catholic faith, but still as children.

From the children's viewpoint, they did constitute a separate group within the parish before First Communion. However, since the children and adults clearly came into contact often in their church and in religious education classes, treating them as parallel congregations (of the type that Numrich in a different context describes) is too severe. As the Faith Formation classes at both parishes evidenced, the adults continually interacted with the children, teaching them, celebrating with them, and coercing them to participate in various activities. Thus, however distinct the children may have perceived themselves to be from those who knew the mysteries of the Church, the two groups were far from two separate, but coexisting, congregations that rarely meet. Rather, the communicants' perceptions suggest that different age groups within a congregation may sense that differences in age, or knowledge of the faith or other distinctions, may, in some contexts, create sub-congregations within the larger parish. The children were under adult supervision and also at their parents' sides during Mass, yet they still understood themselves to be separate from and even invisible to the parish before First Communion.

Both Holy Cross and Blessed Sacrament made distinctions between children and adults, and I argue that the children incorporated certain distinctions into their own interpretations of their religious experiences. The children with whom I worked focused on the differences between their own pre-Communion gestures and knowledge and the gestures and knowledge of those parishioners who had already received First Communion. Considering their own distinctive practices and values, to what extent do First Communicants constitute a distinct subgroup with its own interpretation of congregational identity? And to what extent is this distinction important in parish life? In my research the children reported that they did not belong to their parish's congregation until they received the Sacrament, belonging instead to an ill-defined category of uninitiated parish children. Although I did not study the parish life of pre-communicants, my research would suggest that these children saw themselves as having a distinctly different relationship with their parish from the relationship experienced by those children and adults who had received the Sacrament. The intensity of the feeling of separation, however, may increase as the children come closer to receiving the Eucharist because they are then focusing their attention on this divide.

Children's Interpretations

Talking with children (and the adults who supported them) as they prepared for and received the Sacrament, I found that the two generations' interpretations of the event and its importance converged in their understanding of God's love for the children and in the celebratory nature of the Sacrament. It differed significantly, however, in the adults' more future-oriented, ecclesiastical concerns and the children's emphasis on their new recognition and individual status in both their local parish and their family. All the children interviewed after their First Communion talked of Jesus, taste, anxiety, and family. Not surprisingly, their opinions about each topic differed, though not, as I was surprised to discover, in ways that significantly correlated with race or ethnicity.[6] When I began my work with these two parishes, I thought that by comparing three groups of children—Euro-American, Latino, and African American—I might be able to isolate the effects of race on their interpretations. Just as the children could not articulate what linked their parish with other Catholic parishes, they also could not articulate the ethnic and other differences that made their parishes unique. The continuities among the interpretations of all the children were much more noticeable than were the differences that might correlate to ethnicity or race. After having searched the communicants' interviews for comments that set the children of different races apart from each other, I found little that differentiated the three groups in how they thought about the Sacrament. I came to believe that perhaps in the context of these Faith Formation classes and in our discussions of First Communion, the children's excitement at finally getting to taste the body of Christ overshadowed their thoughts about how this Mass coincided with or diverged from the Masses they attended each week or, perhaps, only occasionally.

Though racial and ethnic differences certainly played a significant role in how the adults constructed the family celebrations, the clothes they bought the children, and the liturgies the catechists designed, the children did not see such constructions in terms of race or ethnicity. Instead, the communicants' interpretations focused most intently on the knowledge they were learning or would learn on First Communion Saturday. Through this common focus on First Communion events, age and the common status of all the children as ritual participants were greater factors than the often-used interpretive categories of race, class, and gender.

As they stood at the altar and crossed themselves, placed the Host in their mouths, and put the chalice to their lips, the young communicants felt a powerful sense of transition from exclusion to parish membership. The children's expression of the importance of their gestures during this transition differed in many ways from the recollection of the events by the adults around them, who tended to view these ritual gestures as much less significant in their memories of their own First Communion. For instance, the parents and teachers at Holy Cross and Blessed Sacrament never mentioned to me their childhood experiences in learning to make the sign of the cross. Yet, the children constantly rehearsed the gestures and discussed them repeatedly in our conversations leading up to their First Communion. Perhaps Ryan, Ferris, and their classmates whom I encountered in the mall years after the event may have forgotten what it was like to be unable to perform these motions, like their parents have. Perhaps the adults do not remember the concomitant sense of exclusion they felt in their parish before First Communion.

Because the children in my study will continue to interpret and reinterpret the ritual of their First Communion through their life experiences, their initial perceptions of this event cannot be retrieved later in their original vividness or with all their original meanings. Having received the Sacrament thousands of times since their First Communion, the uniqueness of that first experience tends to blend in with later receptions in adult memories, unless something unusual happened. The parties and celebrations, as unique events, tend to be remembered in more detail than the reception of the Eucharist, which is repeated often. Psychologists have shown that "memory is best for events that violate our expectations," which may explain why many adult reminiscences of the Eucharist center on being yelled at by nuns, disappointed by the effects of the Sacrament, and choking on the Host.[7] For the children, however, the newness of much of the liturgy, its gestures, its tastes, and its symbols meant that a good amount of the ritual stood out as exceptional, at least until future participation in the Sacrament overlaid this one. The tendency to turn regular events into general scripts may explain, in large part, why most adults described their childhood religious experiences using primarily abstract reasoning and prescribed doctrine, whereas the children mediated their understanding of religion through their senses (taste, sight, and touch) as well as their emotions (excitement, anxiety, and joy).

Although I worked with only a small group of Catholic children, it would not be surprising if Protestant, Muslim, Buddhist, and Jewish children are also oriented much more toward the sensory aspects of religion than many scholars of religion realize. If this is true, then attending closely to children's responses might prompt scholars of religion to reconsider the (still) reigning assumption that Protestants emphasize spirit over matter, while sacramentality—the tendency to celebrate the presence of the sacred in the profane—belongs only to the sensual Catholic imagination.[8] Are children to be excluded from this generalization? Could it be that children associated with all faiths have much in common in their interpretations of religion in general and in their understanding of the tenets of their particular faith and traditions? Knowledge of official doctrine often dominates adult interpretations, whereas most young children are likely to feel less constrained by dogma. Not surprisingly, my interviews showed that none of the seven-, eight-, and nine-year-old children in my study could define "Catholicism" doctrinally. Perhaps this is why they felt free to discuss the full range of their experiences rather than only those that fit within the bounds of "Catholicism" as the adults imagined it.

The depth of each child's previous relationship with his or her parish and his or her level of interest in receiving the Eucharist seemed to be the greatest indicator of the extent to which First Communion would lead that child to see himself or herself as a member of that parish and important to Jesus after First Communion. Unlike the children who attended Faith Formation classes and Masses regularly before this sacramental year, some communicants had little or no connection to the parish before their First Communion.

These children did not seem to expect to have a relationship with the parish after receiving the Eucharist. Their only experience with their parish was occasional attendance at Faith Formation classes so that they could receive the Sacrament. Although they were excited to have a special day and taste the bread, they seemed to have learned little about the parish or the Catholic Church, and they had few expectations for the event. This sense of belonging to the parish was vastly diminished with these children. In most cases, these communicants, like many of their classmates, did not return to Faith Formation class after they had received the Sacrament. Like their parents, however, they may return to the Church to have their own children baptized and to have them receive First Communion.

Understanding children's interpretations of their religious experiences may also allow scholars to better understand how adults reach their definitions of Catholicism and First Communion, or Judaism and Seders, or Hinduism and Diwali. How does what practitioners learn as children affect what they believe as adults? Analyzing the child's perception of ritual would provide an important point of comparison with the adult experience and might well open up new lines of inquiry that could otherwise be missed. In addition, comparing the memories that adults have of religious events experienced in their youth with contemporary childhood experiences may also be a fertile ground for exploration. This expansion of the field opens up many fascinating and challenging possibilities.

Although this study looked specifically at seven- through ten-year-olds, the religious experiences of older adults are also greatly underrepresented in scholarship. And while some studies at least consider children, or adults' perceptions of them, few deal systematically or seriously with "senior citizens." Just as with children, scholarship should also focus on the interpretations by the elderly of their then present religious practices and beliefs. It is possible that much of this work has not been done because no rites of passage are designed specifically for the elderly. However, scholars need to add the interpretations of older participants, as well as those of the very young, if they want to understand religious ritual in all its complexity. Minimally, scholars need to include *age* in their demographic profiles, not just class, race, and gender.

Children in American Religion

Revisionist narratives of U.S. religious history began with works such as Jon Butler's *Awash in a Sea of Faith*, David D. Hall's *Lived Religion in America*, and Thomas A. Tweed's *Retelling U.S. Religious History*.[9] These works ask how U.S. religion might look if it were told using a "Catholic" rather than the standard Protestant model; if "lived religion" were a central interpretive category; or if women replaced men at the center of the story. In a similar way, research on children's religious lives does more than simply enrich our understanding of particular practices. In choosing to study the actors in this ritual—both younger and older—I challenge the usual interpretation of initiation rites. While preparing for First Communion with the families and teachers, it became clear to me that the term "First Communion" does not refer only to the act of receiving the bread and wine or to the liturgies in which this occurs.

In this book I offer more than a unique perspective on a specific Catholic ritual. As a volume on children's interpretations of religious ritual, it also has wider implications for the study of religion, especially American religion. Here, I address five of them. First, given the difference between the traditional perception of the ritual of First Communion and the many interpretations that I found at Blessed Sacrament and Holy Cross, this work enriches our understanding of rites of passage generally, including the importance of the sensual and emotional experiences as well as the intellectual impact of religious doctrine. Of particular import is the significance of examining a ritual from a perspective broader than a limited focus on the actual event itself. Second, working with children who are coming to religious indoctrination for the first time allows scholars to analyze afresh how practitioners learn ritual and develop their religious beliefs and practices. Third, attending to the interaction between children's and adults' interpretations of the Sacrament emphasizes the need for scholars to broaden the cast of characters found in their narratives. They must move beyond ageless—or perhaps imagined middle-aged—subjects, acknowledge all their subjects' ages, and discuss the consequences of this demographic in their work. Simultaneously, scholars also need to broaden the spectrum of consultants whom we study, and including that information in our work may also allow us to make important discoveries through comparing the interpretations of practitioners from both the same and different faiths at various ages. Fourth, adding age as a category of interpretive analysis means more than expanding the number of participants; it also provides an opportunity to analyze new sources that offer insights about children, youth, and older adults.[10] Studying children, for instance, might mean that scholars consider new social environments and the affects of those environments on the religious realm, for instance, both public and private schools, and the playground. In this book, I have made the case for using interviews and drawings to work with children in contemporary congregations; however, the use of material culture—from clothing to Sunday school projects, to pageant scripts and costumes—seems to be a promising source for the study of children's religious lives. Fifth, these new voices may also nudge scholars to reconsider some basic themes in the study of American religion, including the structure of congregations and the significance and impact of voluntaryism.

In this book I have made many claims about children in American religion and in American culture more generally. These claims are based on my belief that scholars should consider children in all situations, not only those children currently popular with journalists and social scientists: overstressed whites, poor minorities, or those with a terminal or a mental illness. As Robert Coles termed them, these young people are "children of crisis."[11] By working with healthy white, Latino, and African American children, I hope to have shown the significance of *all* children's voices. Children are important participants in congregations, and understanding children's perceptions of their religious lives is essential to making general claims about religious groups and their practices. If this is so, as I believe, then centering children reminds us of the significance of age as an analytic category, encourages us to turn to other methods and sources, and prompts us to reconsider some influential organizing themes and categories. At the very least, I hope this book will show that we have not understood a ritual until we have decoded its meanings for participants of all ages.

Structured Interview Questions for Parents and Catechists

1. What's your birth date?
2. Where were you born?
3. How long have you lived in North Carolina?
4. How long have you been attending Holy Cross/Blessed Sacrament?
5. Which Mass do you attend?
6. Are you involved in any parish organizations?
7. What year did you receive your First Communion?
8. In which parish? In what city?
9. What do you remember about it?
10. How was your First Communion different from your child's?
11. How was it similar?
12. How do you think he/she felt about participating in the Sacrament as he/she was preparing for it?
13. How do you think he/she feels about receiving the Sacrament now?
14. What aspects of the First Communion class do you feel were most effective? Why?
15. What would you change about the classes if you taught them?
16. What did you want your child to learn from First Communion?
17. How did you feel about the attire?
18. What did your child wear?
19. Why did you pick that suit/dress rather than another one?
20. What did you wear for your First Communion?
21. Did anyone else wear it before or after? Do you have any pictures?
22. Overall, how would you describe your child's First Communion?
23. Is there something I forgot to ask that you think is important for me to know?
24. Would you like me to send you copies anytime I use any information from this interview in print?

Child's Assent Forms

The Sensual and the Local: An Ethnographic Study of Children's Perceptions of First Communion

My name is Susan Bales. I am a graduate student in the religious studies program at the University of North Carolina at Chapel Hill. I am inviting you to participate in a project to help me understand how it feels, and what it means, to be having your First Communion. If you choose to be a part of this study, I will be attending your CCD classes so that I can learn what you are learning about receiving the sacrament. If you decide to talk to me about First Communion, I will ask you questions about what having your First Communion means, why it is important, and what you expect it to be like. I will also ask you to draw me a picture to help me understand how you see First Communion. These interviews will be tape recorded. You will be given a fake name so that no one will know what you said.

You may ask me questions about my research at any time or have your parents call me so that we can talk about it.

_____   _____
(Signature of child)   (Date)

_____   _____
(Signature of researcher)   (Date)

Lo sensual y lo local: Un estudio etnográfico de las percepciones infantiles sobre la Primera Comunión

Me llamo Susan Bales y soy una estudiante de doctorado en el Departamento de Estudios de Religión de la Universidad de Carolina del Norte en Chapel Hill. Quiero invitarte a participar en un proyecto que me ayudará a entender cómo te sientes al estar a punto de recibir tu Primera Comunión y qué es lo que esto significa para ti. Si estas de acuerdo en participar en este estudio, asistiré a tus clases de Primera Comunión para aprender lo que estas aprendiendo en ellas sobre recibir este Sacramento. Si decides hablar conmigo sobre la Primera Comunión, te haré preguntas sobre qué significa para ti recibir la Primera Comunión, por qué es importante, y cómo esperas que sea. También te pediré que me hagas un dibujo que me ayudará a comprender cómo entiendes la Primera Comunión. Grabaré estas entrevistas en un cassette y te asignaré un nombre falso para que nadie sepa lo que me cuentes.

Puedes hacerme preguntas sobre mi proyecto de investigación en cualquier momento, o puedes pedir a tus padres que me llamen por teléfono.

_____   _____

(Firma del niño)   (Fecha)

_____   _____

(Firma del investigador)   (Fecha)

notes

INTRODUCTION

1 All names have been changed except those of the most recognizable members of the community: the priests and the catechists.

2 Bryan T. Froehle and Mary L. Gautier, *Catholicism USA: A Portrait of the Catholic Church in the United States* (Maryknoll, N.Y.: Orbis Books, 2000), 76.

3 A note on terminology: Throughout the book I try to describe my consultants using their actual nationalities whenever possible; Virginia, for instance, is Mexican, not Hispanic. However, many of the children, who had grown up in the United States, had parents from two different Latin American countries, which made finding a succinct descriptor impossible. These children are designated "Latino." Whenever possible I use the term "Latino" over "Hispanic" because it includes those of African and Amerindian descent as well as those of Spanish descent. In quoted material and when discussing the work of the Hispanic Ministry, however, I have retained the use of "Hispanic." Similarly, I generally use the term "white" for Euro-Americans except when I am discussing Latino and Euro-American interaction and "Anglo" seems more appropriate. For more on the use of "Latino," see Anthony M. Stevens-Arroyo's introduction to *Old Masks, New Faces: Religion and Latino Identities*, ed. Anthony M. Stevens-Arroyo and Gilbert R. Cadena, Program for the Analysis of Religion among Latinos no. 2 (New York: Binder Center for Western Hemispheric Studies, 1995), 10–11. The designations "African American" and "Anglo and Latino" refer to the parishes' identities rather than to their actual ethnic makeup. I will discuss these identities in more detail in Chapter 1.

4 Arnold Van Gennep, *Rites of Passage*, trans. Monika B. Vizedom and Gabrielle L. Caffee (Chicago: University of Chicago Press, 1960), 3.

5 Although performance theory informs my work, I will use its vocabulary only to the extent that it reflects my consultant's own categories. For more on performance theory, see Catherine Bell, *Ritual Theory, Ritual Practice* (New York: Oxford University Press, 1992), and her *Ritual: Perspectives and Dimensions* (New York: Oxford University Press, 1997); Ronald L. Grimes, *Ritual Criticism: Case Studies in Its Practice, Essays on Its Theory* (Columbia: University of South Carolina Press, 1990); Richard Schechner, *Essays in Performance Theory, 1970–1976* (New York: Drama Books Specialists, 1977); Richard Schechner and Willa Appel, eds., *By Means of Performance: Intercultural Studies of Theater and Ritual* (Cambridge: Cambridge University Press, 1990); Stanley Jeyaraja Tambiah, "A Performative Approach to Ritual," in *Culture, Thought, and Social Action: An Anthropological Perspective* (Cambridge: Harvard University Press, 1985); Victor Turner, *From Ritual to Theater: The Human Seriousness of Play*, Performance Studies Series (New York: Performing Arts Journal Publications, 1982); and John J. MacAloon, ed., *Rite, Drama, Festival, Spectacle: Rehearsals toward a Theory of Cultural Performance* (Philadelphia: Institute for the Study of Human Issues, 1984).

6 Bell, *Ritual*, 74.

7 Victor Turner, *The Ritual Process: Structure and Anti-Structure* (Chicago: Aldine Publishing Co., 1969). Turner is far from alone here. Studies of initiation rituals follow Van Gennep's lead and focus on ritual structure rather than the participant's interpretations. For more examples, see Van Gennep, *Rites of Passage*; Regis A. Duffy, *On Becoming a Catholic: The Challenge of Christian Initiation* (San Francisco: Harper and Row, 1984); Mircea Eliade, *Rites and Symbols of Initiation: The Mysteries of Birth and Rebirth*, trans. Willard R. Trask (New York: Harper and Row, 1965); Louise Carus Mahdi, Steven Foster, and Meredith Little, eds., *Betwixt and Between: Patterns of Masculine and Feminine Initiation* (La Salle, Ill.: Open Court, 1987); Yehudi A. Cohen, *The Transition from Childhood to Adolescence: Cross-Cultural Studies of Initiation Ceremonies, Legal Systems, and Incest Taboos* (Chicago: Aldine Publishing Co., 1964); Charlotte Johnson Frisbie, *Kinaaldá: A Study of the Navaho Girl's Puberty Ceremony* (Middletown, Conn.: Wesleyan University

Press, 1967); Jean Sybil La Fontaine, *Initiation* (New York: Viking Penguin, 1985).

8 Bell, *Ritual*, 73.

9 Mark I. West, *Children, Culture, and Controversy* (Hamden, Conn.: Archon Books, 1988), 3. For more on Locke's childrearing prescriptions, see John Locke, *Some Thoughts Concerning Education* (Cambridge: Cambridge University Press, 1880), and Philip J. Greven, *The Protestant Temperament: Patterns of Child-Rearing, Religious Experience, and the Self in Early America* (New York: Knopf, 1977).

10 William Wordsworth, "Imitations of Immorality from Recollections of Early Childhood," in *Wordsworth: Poetical Works*, ed. Thomas Hutchinson, revised by Ernest De Selincourt (New York: Oxford University Press, 1936), 460.

11 James R. Kincaid, *Erotic Innocence: The Culture of Child Molesting* (Durham, N.C.: Duke University Press, 1998), 53.

12 The abstraction of stages and other developmental models, as Robert Coles emphasizes, precludes researchers from recognizing individual experience. See Coles, *The Spiritual Life of Children* (Boston: Houghton Mifflin, 1990), 39. For more on the intersection between social and psychological developmental theories, see Chris Jenks, *Childhood* (New York: Routledge, 1996), 36–43.

13 Alan Prout and Allison James, "A New Paradigm for the Sociology of Childhood? Provenance, Promise and Problems," in *Constructing and Reconstructing Childhood: Contemporary Issues in the Sociological Study of Childhood*, ed. Allison James and Alan Prout (New York: Falmer Press, 1990), 11.

14 Jenks, *Childhood*, 47.

15 For more on Piaget's theory of child development, see Jean Piaget, *Judgment and Reasoning in the Child*, trans. M. Warden (New York: Harcourt and Brace, 1928); Jean Piaget and B. Inhelder, *The Psychology of the Child*, trans. H. Weaver (New York: Basic Books, 1969). For current discussions and critiques of Piaget, see Laura E. Berk, *Child Development* (Boston: Allyn and Bacon, 1989); Robbie Case, *Intellectual Development: Birth to Adulthood* (Orlando: Academic Press, 1985); and Margaret E. Gredler, *Learning and Instruction: Theory into Practice*, 3d ed. (Upper Saddle River, N.J.: Merrill, 1997).

16 On the socially constructed character of childhood, see Philippe Ariès, *Centuries of Childhood: A Social History of Family Life*, trans. Robert Baldick (New York: Vintage Books, 1962); Allison James, Chris Jenks, and Alan Prout, *Theorizing Childhood* (New York: Teachers College Press, 1998); Chris Jenks, *Childhood*; Henry Jenkins, "Introduction: Childhood Innocence and Other Modern Myths," in *The Children's Culture Reader*, ed. Henry Jenkins (New York: New York University Press, 1998); Karin Calvert, *Children in the House: The Material Culture of Early Childhood, 1600–1900* (Boston: Northeastern University Press, 1992); Diana Kelly-Byrne, *A Child's Play Life: An Ethnographic Study* (New York: Teachers College Press, 1989); Ashis Nandy, *Traditions, Tyranny and Utopia: Essays in the Politics of Awareness* (Delhi: Oxford University Press, 1987); West, *Children, Culture, and Controversy*; James R. Kincaid, *Child-Loving: The Erotic Child and Victorian Culture* (New York: Routledge, 1992); Jens Qvortrup and M. Christoffersen, *Childhood as a Social Phenomenon*, National Report from Denmark (Vienna: European Cultural Centre, 1990); Jacqueline Rose, *The Case of Peter Pan: The Impossibility of Children's Fiction* (London: Macmillan, 1984); James and Prout, *Constructing and Reconstructing Childhood*; and Berry Mayall, ed., *Children's Childhoods: Observed and Experienced* (London: Falmer Press, 1994).

17 For an in-depth study of the idea that adults must speak for children and its consequences, see Priscilla Alderson, "Researching Children's Rights to Integrity," in Mayall, *Children's Childhoods*. Just as children's capabilities are continually underestimated, adults' abilities are often overestimated. It should be remembered that adults also cannot possibly understand all the implications that their involvement in a particular study might have. Therefore the same care should be taken in working with adults as in working with children.

18 For more on how viewing adults as *the* meaning makers affects scholarship, see Lawrence A. Hirschfeld, "Why Anthropologists Don't Like Children," *American Anthropologist* 104, no. 2 (2002): 611–27.

19 For more on the consequences of society's focus on youth-at-risk, see Mike A. Males, *Framing Youth: Ten Myths about the Next Gen-*

eration (Monroe, Maine: Common Courage Press, 1998). Kincaid, *Erotic Innocence*.

20 Coles, *Spiritual Life of Children*, 25.

21 Calvert, *Children in the House*, 3.

22 Alderson, "Researching Children's Rights to Integrity," 56.

23 As anthropologist Myra Bluebond-Langner highlights in *The Private Worlds of Dying Children* (Princeton, N.J.: Princeton University Press, 1978), young people sometimes fit this paradigm, knowing little about the world (or acting as if they do) because they think that is what adults expect. Her study goes on to suggest, however—and many childhood studies scholars emphasize—that children act in ways which resist this stereotype by formulating and acting on their own interpretations of the world around them. For more on children actively creating their own worlds, see Kelly-Byrne, *Child's Play Life*.

24 Ann Oakley, "Women and Children First and Last: Parallels and Differences between Children's and Women's Studies," in Mayall, *Children's Childhoods*, 23.

25 The quotation is from Coles, *Spiritual Life of Children*, xvii–xviii. See also Robert Coles, *Children of Crisis: A Study of Courage and Fear*, vol. 1 of Children of Crisis Series (Boston: Little, Brown, 1967); Coles, *Migrants, Sharecroppers, Mountaineers*, vol. 2 of Children of Crisis Series (Boston: Little, Brown, 1971); Coles, *The South Goes North*, vol. 3 of Children of Crisis Series (Boston: Little, Brown, 1971); *Eskimos, Chicanos, Indians*, vol. 4 of Children of Crisis Series (Boston: Little, Brown, 1977); Coles, *The Privileged Ones: The Well-Off and Rich in America*, vol. 5 of Children of Crisis Series (Boston: Little, Brown, 1977); and Coles, *The Moral Life of Children* (Boston: Atlantic Monthly Press, 1986), and *The Political Life of Children* (Boston: Atlantic Monthly Press, 1986).

26 John Cooper, *The Child in Jewish History* (Northvale, N.J.: Jason Aronson, 1996), and Marcia J. Bunge, ed., *The Child in Christian Thought* (Grand Rapids, Mich.: W. B. Eerdmans, 2001). For more on religion and children, particularly from theology, see Bonnie Miller-McLemore, *Let the Children Come: Reimagining Childhood from a Christian Perspective* (San Francisco: Jossey-Bass, 2003); John Logan, "Insider-Outsider: Sacramental Theology through

the Eyes of Children and Young People," in *The Candles Are Still Burning: Directions in Sacrament and Spirituality*, ed. Mary Grey, Andrée Heaton, and Danny Sullivan (Collegeville, Minn.: Liturgical Press, 1995), 160–68; and Maureen Junker-Kenny and Norbet Mette, eds., *Little Children Suffer* (Maryknoll, N.Y.: Orbis Books, 1996). For more on historical, anthropological, and psychological studies of children's religious experience, see Philip J. Greven, *Spare the Child: The Religious Roots of Punishment and the Psychological Impact of Physical Abuse* (New York: Alfred Knopf, 1991); Jon Pahl, *Youth Ministry in Modern America: 1930 to the Present* (Peabody, Mass.: Hendrickson Publishers, 2000); Karl Sven Rosengren, Carl N. Johnson, and Paul L. Harris, eds., *Imagining the Impossible: Magical, Scientific, and Religious Thinking in Children* (New York: Cambridge University Press, 2000); Robert Mark Bauman, "The Inner Light: Children's Lived Experience in the Quaker Practice of Meeting for Worship" (Ph.D. diss., University of Maryland, College Park, 2001); and Susan J. Palmer and Charlotte Hardman, eds., *Children in New Religions* (New Brunswick, N.J.: Rutgers University Press, 1999). See also Kincaid, *Erotic Innocence*, 256. For more on the problems associated with memory and its relationship with the actual event, see M. A. Conway, D. C. Rubin, H. Spinnler, and W. A. Wagner, eds., *Theoretical Perspectives on Autobiographical Memory* (Boston: Kluwer Academic Publishers, 1992); Janice Haaken, *Pillar of Salt: Gender, Memory, and the Perils of Looking Back* (New Brunswick, N.J.: Rutgers University Press, 1998); John Kotre, *White Gloves: How We Create Ourselves through Memory* (New York: Free Press, 1995), and Robert S. Siegler, *Children's Thinking*, 2d ed. (Englewood Cliffs, N.J.: Prentice-Hall, 1991). For more on memory, see Harold Rosen, *Speaking from Memory: The Study of Autobiographical Discourse* (Stoke-on-Trent, Staffordshire: Trentham Books, 1998).

27 Kincaid, *Erotic Innocence*, 256.

28 Ronald L. Grimes, *Marrying and Burying: Rites of Passage in a Man's Life* (Boulder, Colo.: Westview Press, 1995), 25.

29 Oakley, "Women and Children First and Last," 28.

30 Kincaid, *Child-Loving*, 62.

31 Grimes, *Ritual Criticism*, 38.

1 My method for studying congregations has been shaped by Nancy Tatom Ammerman, *Congregations and Community* (New Brunswick, N.J.: Rutgers University Press, 1997); Nancy Tatom Ammerman, Jackson W. Carroll, Carl S. Dudley, and William McKinney, eds., *Studying Congregations: A New Handbook* (Nashville: Abingdon Press, 1998); Gary Dorsey, *Congregation: The Journey Back to Church* (Cleveland: Pilgrim Press, 1998); Carl S. Dudley, Jackson W. Carroll, and James P. Wind, eds., *Carriers of Faith: Lessons from Congregational Studies* (Louisville: John Knox Press, 1991); James Hopewell, *Congregation: Stories and Structures*, ed. Barbara Wheeler (Philadelphia: Fortress Press, 1987); and R. Stephen Warner, *New Wine in Old Wineskin: Evangelicals and Liberals in a Small-Town Church* (Berkeley: University of California Press, 1988).

2 Along with illustrating that the children belonged to Jesus, this multicolored flock, all standing around their savior, may have been an effort to illustrate the parishioners' perceptions of their parish as welcoming people of all backgrounds into its African American home.

3 This is a direct quote from the banner. All other Bible verses come from *The New Oxford Annotated Bible*, ed. Bruce M. Metzger and Ronald E. Murphy (New York: Oxford University Press, 1991).

4 Fieldnotes, Holy Cross Catholic Church, Durham, N.C., 3 May 1997.

5 The prayers of petition, which focused on the congregation, marked a notable shift from the children's usual concerns. At the First Communion retreat and during class, their prayers centered on helping the poor, protecting the soldiers, and stopping violence, robbery, and drug dealing. These more typical prayers seemed to reflect the parish's concern with social justice, as well as its location in Durham, which at the time had the highest murder rate in North Carolina.

6 The sense of belonging that this hand-holding and gestures of encouragement gave the children could not equal the feelings of belonging that they would tell me about during our post-Communion conversations, as I discuss in Chapters 3 and 4.

7 For an overview of African American Catholic institutional history, see Cyprian Davis, O.S.B., *The History of Black Catholics in*

the United States (New York: Crossroad, 1990). For discussions of the early Church in the South, see Randall M. Miller and Jon L. Wakelyn, eds., *Catholics in the Old South: Essays on Church and Society* (Macon, Ga.: Mercer University Press, 1983). For more on the Catholic Church's discussion about slavery and segregation, see William A. Osborne, *"The Segregated Covenant": Race Relations and American Catholics* (New York: Herder and Herder, 1967); John T. Gillard, *Colored Catholics in the United States* (Baltimore: Josephite Press, 1941); John T. McGreevy, *Parish Boundaries: The Catholic Encounter with Race in the Twentieth-Century Urban North* (Chicago: University of Chicago Press, 1996); and Edward D. Reynolds, S.J., *Jesuits for the Negro* (New York: American Press, 1949). For more on contemporary African American Catholicism, see National Conference of Black Catholic Bishops, *Plenty of Good Room: The Spirit and the Truth of African American Catholic Worship* (Washington, D.C.: United States Catholic Conference, 1990); Dorothy Ann Blatnica, V.S.C., *At the Altar of Their God: African American Catholics in Cleveland, 1922–1961* (New York: Garland Publishing, 1995); and Nessa Theresa Baskerville Johnson, *A Special Pilgrimage: A History of Black Catholics in Richmond* (Richmond, Va.: Diocese of Richmond, 1978). For more on African American religion more broadly, see Lawrence W. Levine, *Black Culture and Black Consciousness: Afro-American Folk Thought from Slavery to Freedom* (New York: Oxford University Press, 1977); C. Eric Lincoln and Lawrence H. Mamiya, *The Black Church in the African American Experience* (Durham, N.C.: Duke University Press, 1990); Albert J. Raboteau, *Slave Religion: "The Invisible Institution" in the Antebellum South* (New York: Oxford University Press, 1978), and *Fire in the Bones: Reflections on African American Religious History* (Boston: Beacon Press, 1995); and Gayraud S. Wilmore, *Black Religion and Black Radicalism: An Interpretation of the Religious History of the African American People*, 6th ed. (Maryknoll, N.Y.: Orbis Books, 1991).

8 Jualynne E. Dodson and Cheryl Townsend Gilkes, "'There's Nothing Like Church Food': Food and the U.S. Afro-Christian Tradition; Re-Membering Community and Feeding the Embodied S/spirit(s)," *Journal of the American Academy of Religion* 63 (Fall 1995): 521.

9 Fieldnotes, First Communion Mass, Holy Cross Catholic Church, Durham, N.C., 2 May 1997.

10 Unlike at Holy Cross, no flashbulbs accompanied this procession because Father Briant Cullinane, pastor of Blessed Sacrament Catholic Church, prohibited the parents from taking pictures during the liturgy.

11 Fieldnotes, Blessed Sacrament First Communion, 5 May 2001.

12 "Shout to the Lord" music and lyrics by Darlene Zschech.

13 Melissa, eight-year-old Latina American, interviewed by the author, Blessed Sacrament Catholic Church, Burlington, N.C., 8 April 2001.

14 During the church tour, Father Briant told one Mexican boy that the church no longer allowed lit candles in the sanctuary because the large numbers of candles being used were a fire hazard and had caused some damage to the right-side wall of the sanctuary.

15 José, interviewed by the author, Blessed Sacrament Catholic Church, Burlington, N.C., 27 October 2001.

16 Ibid.

17 For an overview of Hispanic Catholicism, see Ana María Díaz-Stevens, *Oxcart Catholicism on Fifth Avenue: The Impact of the Puerto Rican Migration upon the Archdiocese of New York* (Notre Dame: University of Notre Dame Press, 1993), and Jay P. Dolan and Allan Figueroa Deck, S.J., eds., *Hispanic Catholic Culture in the U.S.: Issues and Concerns* (Notre Dame: University of Notre Dame Press, 1994).

18 Helen Rose Ebaugh and Janet Saltzman Chafetz, eds., *Religion and the New Immigrants: Continuities and Adaptations in Immigrant Congregations* (Walnut Creek, Calif.: AltaMira Press, 2000), 385.

19 Dorothy C. Bass, "Congregations and the Bearing of Tradition," in *America Congregations*, vol. 2, *New Perspectives in the Study of Congregations*, ed. James P. Wind and James W. Lewis (Chicago: University of Chicago Press, 1994), 177.

20 Elizabeth, eight-year-old white girl, interviewed by the author, Blessed Sacrament Catholic Church, Burlington, N.C., 4 November 2001; Alison, eight-year-old white girl, interviewed by the author, Blessed Sacrament Catholic Church, Burlington, N.C., 30 September 2001.

21 Maureen Fan, "Triangle Takes Valley's Lead: Burgeoning Raleigh-

Durham Faces Familiar Challenges." *San Jose Mercury News*, 8 July 2001, 1A.

22 Father John Heffernan, forty-seven, interviewed by the author, Immaculate Conception, Durham, N.C., 17 January 1999.

23 Jon W. Anderson, "An Ethnographic Overview of Cultural Differences of Bible Belt Catholics," in *The Culture of Bible Belt Catholics*, ed. Jon W. Anderson and William B. Friend (New York: Paulist Press, 1995), 11.

24 Quoted in Sam Boykin, "Growing up Catholic in the South: Bob Jones Controversy Reopens Old Wounds," *Raleigh Spectator*, 12–18 April 2000, 11.

25 Gerald L. Lewis, "The Diocese of Raleigh: An Overview," <http://www.dioceseofraleigh.org/html/history1.html>.

26 Ibid.; Jay P. Dolan, *The American Catholic Experience: A History from Colonial Times to the Present* (Notre Dame: University of Notre Dame Press, 1992), 128.

27 The Archdiocese of Baltimore believed that by 1868, there were seven hundred Catholics in the more than fifty thousand square miles of North Carolina. See <http://www.archbalt.org/content_asp?id=74>.

28 In 1999, for example, 15.3 percent of southerners self-identified as Catholic in comparison with 1990, when most of the South was less than 4 percent Catholic. Here I am using "South" as the Gallup Poll defines it: the eleven former Confederate states (South Carolina, Mississippi, Florida, Alabama, Georgia, Louisiana, Texas, Virginia, Arkansas, North Carolina, Tennessee), plus Texas and Oklahoma. The developments that I discuss here do not include areas of Texas and Florida that have historically had substantial Latino populations.

29 The Research Triangle Park is a light industrial center that is located between Raleigh, Durham, and Chapel Hill, which has come to be called the Triangle.

30 Most of the African Americans at Holy Cross had family in the area or in Louisiana, while the Latinos came primarily from Mexico, as I stated earlier.

31 Brian, nine-year-old white boy, interviewed by the author, Blessed Sacrament Catholic Church, Burlington, N.C., 11 May 2001.

32 Ms. Mary Key, forty-five-year-old white woman, interviewed by the

author, Blessed Sacrament Catholic Church, Burlington, N.C., 27 February 2001.

33 Britney, seven-year-old white girl, interviewed by the author, Blessed Sacrament Catholic Church, Burlington, N.C., 18 March 2001.

34 "Diocesan Study Confirms Sky High Hispanic Numbers, Challenges to Ministry," *NC Catholic Online* at <http://www.nccatholic.org/news.php?artID=404>, 2 July 2002.

35 Richard Stradling, "A Different Vibe," *News and Observer*, 24 May 2002, A1.

36 Vikki Cheng, "Durham Is 'All-Minority,'" *News and Observer*, 5 April 2001, sec. A, pp. 1, 20. The city of Durham's non-Hispanic white population decreased from 51 percent in 1990 to 42 percent in 2000. Over that same decade, the total population of Durham County grew from 181,835 to 223,314, with the majority of those newcomers being Hispanics (an increase of 6.53 percent) and Asians (1.47 percent) who moved to the city looking for jobs and a low cost of living. Frank Medlin, "Population by Race and Ethnicity, 1990–2000," *News and Observer*, 20A.

37 Maureen Fan, "Triangle Takes Valley's Lead." The Greensboro nonprofit group Faith in Action, whose numbers Governor Jim Hunt's Office of Hispanic/Latino Affairs used in their reporting, estimated that North Carolina's Latino population rose from 76,745 in 1990 to 315,000 in 1998. While their starting number matched that of the Census Bureau, Faith in Action counted 200,000 more Latinos in the area. Mike Fuchs, "Alamance County's Hispanic Community Center in Burlington Helps Growing Number of Spanish Speakers Overcome Cultural and Language Barriers," *Greensboro News Record*, 10 January 2000, B1.

38 Virginia, seven-year-old Mexican girl, interviewed by the author, Blessed Sacrament Catholic Church, Burlington, N.C., 8 April 2001.

39 For more information on the Catholic Church's role in the lives of earlier European migrants, see Jay P. Dolan, *The Immigrant Church: New York's Irish and German Catholics, 1815–1865* (Baltimore: Johns Hopkins University Press, 1975), and Dolores Liptak, R.S.M., *Immigrants and Their Church* (New York: Macmillan, 1989).

40 The Jesuits sent Reverend Risacher to found a mission parish for

African American Catholics in response to Pope Pius XII's Encyclical Letter to the Church of the United States, written 1 November 1939. Pope Pius XII stated: "We confess that we feel a special paternal affection, which is certainly inspired of Heaven, for the Negro people dwelling among you. . . . We therefore invoke an abundance of heavenly blessings and pray fruitful success for those whose generous zeal is devoted to their welfare." For more on the reasons for Rev. Risacher's mission, see Rev. John A. Risacher, S.J., "The Beginnings of the Jesuit Mission for the Negroes in Durham, N.C., December 1939–December 1943," unpublished manuscript, 1.

41 Anne Duncan, "The History of Holy Cross Catholic Church in Durham, North Carolina" (1989), unpublished manuscript. As an African American parish under white leadership, the parishioners have had a great deal of control over the "shape of [their] worship" and their nonliturgical activities. Thus, although the official parish history, like most others, chronicles the pastors' tenures and changes in membership, the parishioners of Holy Cross tell a slightly different story. When I talked to them, in their living rooms, vacant rooms in the church's Activity Center, and local bagel shops, they focused on the more informal and timeless aspects of parish life. The institutional history fades into the background as the parishioners highlight lay interactions and decisions. As one parishioner said, "We just think we know better what needs to be done, and we got folks who can make it happen." Richard, sixty-six-year-old African American man, interviewed by the author, Holy Cross Catholic Church, Durham, N.C., 2 April 1999.

42 As white investors and workers flocked to the area for jobs in the tobacco industry in the 1870s, the creation of the first African American–owned bank in 1898 and the insurance company North Carolina Mutual Provident Society (which became North Carolina Mutual Life) attracted black businessmen to Durham's Hayti district with the promise of jobs and loans. William Kenneth Boyd, *The Story of Durham: City of the New South* (Durham, N.C.: Duke University Press, 1925), 281, 57. For more on the history of Durham, see James G. Leyburn, *The Way We Lived: Durham, 1900–1920* (Elliston, Va.: Northcross House, 1989), and Betsy Holloway,

Heaven for Beginners: Recollections of a Southern Town (Orlando, Fla.: Persimmon Press, 1986).

43 Jim Wise, "Symbols of Hayti's Grand Past Re-emerge, but the Community's Legacy Depends on People Working to Preserve Its History," *Durham (N.C.) Herald Sun*, 4 November 2001, C1. As Wise explains, areas inhabited by freed blacks were often designated "Hayti," a corruption of Haiti, in the Reconstruction South. This designation continues to be used in Durham for the neighborhood east of the former Bull Durham tobacco factory. For more on the Hayti district, see Nayo Barbara Malcolm Watkins, *Hayti Lived Before* (Durham, N.C.: N. Watkins/Bodacious Consulting Organization, 1998).

44 Patrick Byker, "Not a Great Conspiracy," *Durham (N.C.) Herald Sun*, 28 January 2001, A13.

45 Anne Duncan, "Supplement to History of Holy Cross Church," unpublished manuscript, 1989, 9. These parish membership numbers represent those families that had officially joined the parish. Since many Latinos were not official members, the reported numbers are likely to be low.

46 Ms. McLean, forty-three-year-old white woman, interviewed by the author, 30 March 1999, Durham, N.C.

47 Ms. King, thirty-one-year-old white woman, interviewed by the author, 31 March 1999, Durham, N.C.

48 *Holy Cross Catholic Church Bulletin*, 21 March 1999, 4.

49 Mr. Green, twenty-six-year-old African American man, interviewed by the author, Durham, N.C., 19 February 1998.

50 "Durham Church's Decision Angers Hispanic Parishioners," *Greensboro News Record*, 15 October 1996, B2; Michael Kammie, "Catholic Church to Drop Bilingual Service," *Durham (N.C.) Herald Sun*, 14 October 1996, 1A–2A.

51 Each Mass at Holy Cross has its own character. The 11:15 A.M. Mass, directly after Faith Formation classes, has many children and a fledgling choir. Saturday's 5:00 P.M. Mass is small, quiet, and meditative. There is no choir, and parishioners sing traditional Catholic hymns. Although there are two other Masses, the Sunday 9:00 A.M. Mass gospel choir sings at holiday Masses and public events.

52 The preceding parish history relies heavily on Right Rev. Francis K. O'Brien, Pastor, "History: Church of the Blessed Sacrament (June 1960)," *History of Churches in Burlington and Alamance Counties* (Burlington–Alamance County Chamber of Commerce, 1963), and the unpublished outline, "The Life of the Church," from the Blessed Sacrament Catholic Church's Parish Directory, 1998.

53 Blessed Sacrament Mission Statement, *Blessed Sacrament Catholic Church Bulletin*, 2.

54 Father Briant Cullinane, O.F.M. Conv., seventy-one-year-old white man, interviewed by the author, Blessed Sacrament Catholic Church, Burlington, N.C., 12 October 2001.

55 *Blessed Sacrament Weekly Bulletin*, 14 July 2002.

56 Ms. Mary Key, 21 February 2001.

57 Director of Diocese of Raleigh Diocese Media Center, telephone conversation with author, April 1999.

58 Ronald L. Grimes, *Ritual Criticism: Case Studies in Its Practice, Essays on Its Theory* (Columbia: University of South Carolina Press, 1990), 37–38.

59 Of course, the children live in multiple worlds, of which their congregation is only one. Many other aspects of the children's lives, such as school, family, and friends, may have affected the children's interpretations of the Sacrament. Given the constraints of my research, however, I only had access to the congregations and what the adults and children told me about their family lives.

CHAPTER TWO

1 My approach to fieldwork has been shaped by many works, including Karen McCarthy Brown, *Mama Lola: A Vodou Priestess in Brooklyn* (Berkeley: University of California Press, 1991); James Clifford, "Notes on (Field)notes," in *Fieldnotes: The Makings of Anthropology*, ed. Roger Sanjek (Ithaca: Cornell University Press, 1990), 47–70; Carolyn Fluehr-Lobban, ed., *Ethics and the Profession of Anthropology: Dialogue for a New Era* (Philadelphia: University of Pennsylvania Press, 1991); R. Marie Griffith, *God's Daughters: Evangelical Women and the Power of Submission* (Berkeley: University of California Press, 1997); Glenn Hinson, *Fire in My Bones: Transcendence and the Holy Spirit in African American Gospel* (Philadelphia: University of Pennsylvania Press, 2000); Diana Kelley-Byrne, *A Child's*

Play Life: An Ethnographic Study (New York: Teachers College Press, 1989); Robert A. Orsi, *The Madonna of 115th Street: Faith and Community in Italian Harlem, 1880–1950* (New Haven, Conn.: Yale University Press, 1985); Paul Stoller, *The Taste of Ethnographic Things: The Senses in Anthropology* (Philadelphia: University of Pennsylvania Press, 1989); James L. Peacock and Ruel W. Tyson Jr., *Pilgrims of Paradox: Calvinism and Experience among the Primitive Baptists of the Blue Ridge* (Washington, D.C.: Smithsonian Institution Press, 1989); James V. Spickard, J. Shawn Landres, and Meredith B. McGuire, *Personal Knowledge and Beyond: Reshaping the Ethnography of Religion* (New York: New York University Press, 2002); and Ruel W. Tyson Jr., James L. Peacock, and Daniel W. Patterson, eds., *Diversities of Gifts: Field Studies in Southern Religion* (Urbana: University of Illinois Press).

2 Allison James and Alan Prout, preface to *Constructing and Reconstructing Childhood: Contemporary Issues in the Sociological Study of Childhood*, edited by Allison James and Alan Prout (London: Falmer Press, 1997), xiv. For more on research methods when working with children, see Pia Christensen and Allison James, *Research with Children: Perspectives and Practices* (London: Falmer Press, 2000), and M. Elizabeth Graue and Daniel J. Walsh, *Studying Children in Context: Theories, Methods, and Ethics* (Thousand Oaks, Calif.: Sage Publications, 1998).

3 Robert A. Orsi, "Mapping the Ground of Children's Religion: A Beginning," unpublished manuscript, 2001, 38.

4 For more on the situatedness of all ethnographic writing, see John Camaroff and Jean Camaroff, *Ethnography and the Historical Imagination* (Boulder, Colo.: Westview Press, 1992), 8–9. For more on the situatedness of all authors, see Thomas A. Tweed, ed., introduction to *Retelling U.S. Religious History* (Berkeley, Calif.: University of California Press, 1997), and Thomas A. Tweed, "Between the Living and the Dead: Fieldwork, History, and the Interpreter's Position," in *Personal Knowledge and Beyond: Reshaping the Ethnography of Religion*, ed. James V. Spickard, J. Shawn Landres, and Meredith B. McGuire (New York: New York University Press, 2002), 63–74. See also Donna Haraway, *Simians, Cyborgs, and Women: The Reinvention of Nature* (New York: Routledge, 1991).

5 I recognize that the children's perceptions of First Communion

are shaped by their lives both inside and outside the parish. I lacked the time or resources for extended homestays with a number of members of each First Communion class to investigate the specific ways in which their life at school, at home, and on the playground affected their interpretations of this event. Therefore, I chose to concentrate on the parish as the primary place where the children would learn about, and ultimately experience, the Eucharist. In so doing, I hoped that my conversations with the children and their parents about their daily lives would shed light on some of the most significant non-church factors that helped shape their understanding of the Sacrament.

6 Father Briant Cullinane, O.F.M. Conv., seventy-one-year-old white man, interviewed by the author, Blessed Sacrament Catholic Church, Burlington, N.C., 12 October 2001.

7 Mr. Dwyer, thirty-nine-year-old Anglo man, interviewed by the author, Blessed Sacrament Catholic Church, Burlington, N.C., 12 November 2001.

8 Since I did not do an extended homestay with any of the communicants, this kind of information from the parents and the children provided the primary source through which I could glean some information about what the children learned at home. The adults and I sat down together in structured interviews, all but one of which was in English. For a copy of the list of questions, see Appendix A.

9 Robert Coles, *The Spiritual Life of Children* (Boston: Houghton Mifflin, 1990), 15.

10 Given more time, these relationships most certainly would have developed even more, and our comfort levels with each other would have become even greater. Unfortunately, however, First Communion preparation and Mass occur within a limited time frame of seven months. As I would soon find out, most children were not involved in Faith Formation classes before this important sacramental year, and most would cease being involved in the classes when the term ended in the spring. Thus, extending my interaction with the classes as a whole was impossible.

11 This exchange with Christy, eight-year-old Brazilian American, occurred 17 December 2000, Blessed Sacrament Catholic Church, Burlington, N.C.

12 Conversation with Jennifer, fieldnotes, Holy Cross Catholic Church, Durham, N.C., 19 January 1997; interaction with Stephanie's father from fieldnotes, Blessed Sacrament Catholic Church, Burlington, N.C., 21 January 2000; Britney, eight-year-old white girl, interviewed by the author, Blessed Sacrament Catholic Church, Burlington, N.C., 2 December 2001.

13 Fieldnotes, Blessed Sacrament Faith Formation class, Burlington, N.C., 5 November 2000.

14 Ferris, eight-year-old African American boy, interviewed by the author, Holy Cross Catholic Church, Durham, N.C., 8 February 1998.

15 Melissa, eight-year-old Latina American girl, interviewed by the author, Blessed Sacrament Catholic Church, Burlington, N.C., 8 April 2001.

16 Katie, seven-year-old white girl, interviewed by the author, Holy Cross Catholic Church, Durham, N.C., 18 March 2001.

17 While it seems that the potential negative repercussions of talking about how one feels about First Communion might be few, this is not always the case with ethnographic projects. Many discussions about lessening the impact of consultants' participation in ethnographic studies helped to inform my own work with the children, their parents, priests, and catechists to ensure that I protected them from as many repercussions as possible. Keeping all the participants anonymous, other than those people who are immediately recognizable (the priests and the catechists), was the first step I took to lessen this impact. For more on the ethics of doing ethnography, see Ruth Behar, "Writing in My Father's Name: A Diary of *Translated Woman*'s First Year," in *Women Writing Culture*, ed. Ruth Behar and Deborah A. Gordon (Berkeley: University of California Press, 1995), 65–82; William Graves III and Mark A. Shields, "Rethinking Moral Responsibility in Fieldwork: The Situated Negotiation of Research in Anthropology and Sociology," in *Ethics and the Profession of Anthropology: Dialogue for a New Era*, ed. Carolyn Fluehr-Lobban (Philadelphia: University of Pennsylvania Press, 1991), 132–51; "Appendix I: American Anthropology Association, Revised Principles of Professional Responsibility, 1990," in *Ethics and the Profession of Anthropology*, ed. Carolyn Fluehr-Lobban (Philadelphia: University of Pennsylvania Press, 1991), 274–79.

18 Priscilla Alderson, "Researching Children's Rights to Integrity," in *Children's Childhoods: Observed and Experienced*, ed. Berry Mayall (London: Falmer Press, 1994), 60.

19 In response to the requests that I not include their children, I did not interview the children of these two parents, and their classroom responses do not appear in my discussion.

20 Anthropologist Myra Bluebond-Langer found a similar response in her study of children, a response that seems to have as much to do with the adults' understanding of children as with the legal standards about consent and permission. In hospitals, schools, and churches, parents speak for children by consenting to the children's participation in research studies and, in the case of hospitals, surgery. While children may be consulted by their parents and doctors, it is a parent's or guardian's name that appears on the bottom line. This legal process seems both to affect and to reflect children's relative invisibility in research. Minors, especially young children, appear in the written reports as objects of study, readily accepting what is happening to them (even if the reality of specific research situations is something quite different), rather than as people to be consulted and informed. See Bluebond-Langner, *The Private Worlds of Dying Children* (Princeton, N.J.: Princeton University Press, 1978).

21 In this discussion I emphasized that I would be recording this conversation so as to ensure that I would write down their words correctly. Although most children seemed to ignore the microphone, some communicants seemed intimidated by its presence. It also seemed that the microphone's presence made other children feel special. In all three groups, some children simply wanted to play with the microphone, pretending they were rock stars. In these cases, the children and I agreed that they could have fun with the microphone after we talked. Agreeing to this arrangement, Dean immediately grabbed the microphone after our interview and began singing, "I feel good . . ." Dean, seven-year-old white boy, from Blessed Sacrament Catholic Church, interviewed by the author, O'Charlie's Restaurant, Burlington, N.C., 25 February 2001.

22 See Appendix B. Although I had assent forms in both English and

Spanish, all the children asked for the English form, just as all but one of them asked that the interviews be conducted in English.

23 None of the parents in this study inquired about what their children had said. Many of the children, however, showed their mothers or fathers their drawings, and a couple had the parents listen to part of our recorded conversation. Three of the interviews also took place with the child and his or her parent together. In all these cases, the parent let the child give his or her opinions about the Sacrament without interruption, although one mother did try to encourage her son to give the "right" answer to the meaning of the body and blood.

24 Elizabeth, eight-year-old white girl, interviewed by the author, Blessed Sacrament Catholic Church, Burlington, N.C., 4 November 2001.

25 Since the Blessed Sacrament First Communion class was split into two rooms, I decided it would take me twice as long to get to know the children because I alternated between the rooms each Sunday.

26 Although this sample size is small, I feel that the degree of continuity among the interviews and drawings attests to some common understandings. Although many researchers have similar pressures, the tremendous attrition rate after the children receive the Sacrament (approximately 40 percent for Holy Cross's 1997 First Communion class, 75 percent for the Latino portion of Blessed Sacrament's 2001 class, and 30 percent for the white portion) made it especially difficult to find consultants after First Communion. Adding to the difficulties was the sporadic attendance of many children, who were still on the official roll a year after they first received the Sacrament.

27 Coles uses drawings as sources in all of his work, but he discusses his methodology most fully in *Children of Crisis: A Study of Courage and Fear* (Boston: Little, Brown, 1967), and *Their Eyes Meeting the World: The Drawings and Paintings of Children*, ed. Margaret Sartor (Boston: Houghton Mifflin, 1992). Coles, however, was not the first psychiatrist to use children's drawings. Anna Freud pioneered the use of children's drawings in psychoanalysis in the late nineteenth century. For more on Anna Freud's method and other early uses of children's artwork, see Anna Freud, *Introduction to the Technic*

of Child Analysis (New York: Nervous and Mental Disease Publishing Co., 1928), and Melanie Klein, *The Psycho-Analysis of Children*, trans. Alix Strachey (London: Hogarth Press, 1949).

28 Paul, eight-year-old African American boy, from Holy Cross Catholic Church, interviewed by the author, at his home, Chapel Hill, N.C., 14 December 1997; Christopher, eight-year-old Anglo, interviewed by the author, Blessed Sacrament Catholic Church, Burlington, North Carolina, 1 April 2001.

29 I felt that the children's range of possibilities would have been limited if I had included play, because any dolls and toys that I might have brought to the discussion would have inevitably influenced their stories much more.

30 Linda Whitney Peterson and Milton Edward Hardin, *Children in Distress: A Guide for Screening Children's Art* (New York: W. W. Norton, 1997), 15. For more on children and art, see Coles, *Their Eyes Meeting the World*; Jacqueline J. Goodnow, *Children Drawing* (Cambridge: Harvard University Press, 1977); Joseph H. Di Leo, M.D., *Young Children and Their Drawings* (New York: Brunner/Mazel Publishing, 1970); and Dr. Myra F. Levick, with Diana S. Wheeler, *Mommy, Daddy, Look What I'm Saying: What Children Are Telling You through Their Art* (New York: M. Evans and Co., 1986).

31 Christy, eight-year-old Latina, interviewed by the author, Blessed Sacrament Catholic Church, Burlington, N.C., 1 April 2001.

32 Maureen, seven-year-old white girl, interviewed by the author, Holy Cross Catholic Church, Durham, N.C., 13 April 1997 and 18 February 1998; Melissa, eight-year-old Latina American girl, interviewed by the author, Blessed Sacrament Catholic Church, Burlington, N.C., 8 April 2001.

33 Christopher, 1 April 2001.

CHAPTER THREE

1 The preceding events were taken from my fieldnotes, Holy Cross Faith Formation class, Durham, North Carolina, 6 April 1997. This particular class at Holy Cross was somewhat atypical of the classes I attended. Most classes at both parishes had a higher attendance rate, a more formal tone, and, especially at Blessed Sacrament, an art project.

2 Melissa, nine-year-old Latina American, interviewed by the au-

thor, Blessed Sacrament Catholic Church, Burlington, N.C., 2 December 2001.

3 Marie Joseph Nicholas, O.P., *What Is the Eucharist?*, trans. R. F. Trevett (New York: Hawthorne Book Publishers, 1960), 38.

4 Ibid., 35.

5 *Catechism of the Catholic Church* (London: Geoffrey Chapman, 1994), 298.

6 Ms. Mary Key, forty-five-year-old white woman, interviewed by the author, Blessed Sacrament Catholic Church, Burlington, N.C., 27 February 2001.

7 Thomas Pègues, *Catechism of the "Summa Theologica" of Saint Thomas Aquinas, for the Use of the Faithful*, trans. Ælred Whitacre (London: Burns, Oates & Washbourne, 1922).

8 C. Vollert, "Transubstantiation," in *New Catholic Encyclopedia* (New York: McGraw Hill, 1967), 14:259.

9 This discussion by Father Barry occurred during the First Communion retreat, 26 April 1997.

10 Michael, eight-year-old African American boy, interviewed by the author, Holy Cross Catholic Church, Durham, N.C., 27 April 1997.

11 This concern about the children spitting out the Eucharist seems to be less of a worry for the adults involved in First Communion liturgies. However, it is a great concern of the communicants themselves. Pope Pius X, *Quam Singulari: Decree of the Sacred Congregation of Discipline of the Sacraments on First Communion*, 8 August 1910, Papal Encyclicals Online, <http://www.geocities.com/papalencyclicals/Pius10/p10quam.htm>.

12 Ibid.

13 "A New Approach to First Communion," *U.S. Catholic* 34 (November 1968): 42.

14 Pius X, *Quam Singulari*.

15 Much of the concern about age of reception and the exact age of reason was intertwined with his concern about age of First Confession. For instance, upon instituting *Quam Singulari*, the Diocese of Fort Wayne, Indiana, released a statement that explained: "Even though a more thorough and accurate sacramental confession should precede First Holy Communion, which does not happen everywhere, yet the loss of first innocence is always to be deplored and might have been avoided by receiving Holy Eucharist

in the more tender years." Archbishop S. G. Messmer, "First Holy Communion of Children," 1911, Francis P. Clark Printed Material, 73/2553, University of Notre Dame Archives, Notre Dame, Ind.

16 Britney, eight-year-old white girl, interviewed by the author, Blessed Sacrament Catholic Church, Burlington, N.C., 2 December 2001.

17 Bishop Joseph Gossman, "Diocesan Guidelines 3.3.3 Sacrament of the Eucharist," unpublished, January 1994.

18 Cara, eight-year-old African American girl, interviewed by the author, Holy Cross Catholic Church, Durham, N.C., 15 February 1998.

19 Ms. Ann Fabuel, forty-nine-year-old white woman, interviewed by the author, Blessed Sacrament Catholic Church, Burlington, N.C., 17 December 2000. The Second Vatican Council stated that "parents are to be acknowledged as their [child's] primary and principal educators." "The Declaration on Christian Education," *Gravissimum Educationis*, in *Trent to Vatican II*, vol. 2 of *Decrees of the Ecumenical Councils*, ed. Norman P. Tanner (London: Sheed & Ward; Washington, D.C.: Georgetown University Press, 1990), 961.

20 Ms. Fister, interviewed by the author, Blessed Sacrament Catholic Church, Burlington, N.C., 5 November 2000.

21 Ms. Lauffer, forty-five-year-old white woman, interviewed by the author, Holy Cross Catholic Church, Durham, N.C., 8 February 1997.

22 Fieldnotes, Holy Cross Faith Formation class, 22 January 1997.

23 Ms. Hernandez, Mexican women, interviewed by the author, Blessed Sacrament Catholic Church, 29 April 2001.

24 Britney, 18 March 2001.

25 Ibid.

26 Data calculated by comparing attendance from First Communion class to the rosters from the following year from Blessed Sacrament and Holy Cross Faith Formation classes. The rate of return dropped even further in the second and third years following First Communion. This continued attrition may have been the result of families moving out of the dioceses or of their decreased interest in their child's faith development for the years in between First Communion and Confirmation.

27 Created by Castellino de Castelli in 1536 and disbanded by the

Vatican in 1971, Pope Pius X mandated that all countries implement Confraternity of Christian Doctrine (CCD) programs in 1905. See Mary Charles Bryce, O.S.B., "The Confraternity of Christian Doctrine in the United States," in *Renewing the Sunday School and the CCD*, ed. D. Campbell Wyckoff (Birmingham, Ala.: Religious Education Press, 1986), 27, and Jay P. Dolan, *The American Catholic Experience: A History from the Colonial Times to the Present* (Notre Dame: University of Notre Dame Press, 1992), 391. For more on the history of CCD, see Pope Pius X, *Acerbo Nimis: Encyclical Letter of Pope Pius X on Teaching Christian Doctrine, April 15, 1905* (Washington, D.C.: Confraternity of Christian Doctrine, 1946), and Mary Charles Bryce, O.S.B., "The Evolution of Catechesis from the Catholic Reformation to the Present," in *A Faithful Church: Issues in the History of Catechesis*, ed. John H. Westerhoff III and O. C. Edwards Jr. (Wilton, Conn.: Morehouse-Barlow Co., 1981).

28 Janet Welsh, "Baltimore Catechism," in *Encyclopedia of Catholicism* (New York: Harper Collins, 1995), 129.

29 Ms. Hernandez, 29 April 2001.

30 In his book *My First Communion: What Very Young Children Need to Know of Their First Holy Communion* (New York: Edward O'Toole Co., 1941), 3 (General Collection, Printed Material, 1700s-, #4617–18, University of Notre Dame Archives, Notre Dame, Ind.), the Most Reverend Louis LaRavoire Morrow, D.D., addressed catechists, imploring them, "Therefore, in teaching him [the communicant] his religion, let us not starve him on the dry husks of technical definitions. Let us feed his child heart by speaking in the simplest of words, by telling the truths of religion in narrative form, by making of the catechism lesson a very personal affair between him and Jesus. It is not so important that the child memorize theological terms; it is very important that he learn to love God" (3).

31 Timothy Walch, *Parish School: American Catholic Parochial Education from Colonial Times to the Present* (New York: Crossroad Publishing Co., 1996), 119. For more on John Dewey's educational philosophy, see John Dewey, *Democracy and Education: An Introduction to the Philosophy of Education* (New York: Macmillan, 1916). Secondary sources include John Blewett, *John Dewey: His Thought*

and Influence (New York: Fordham University Press, 1960), and Steve Fishman, "Dewey's Educational Philosophy: Reconciling Nested Dualisms," in *John Dewey and the Challenge of Classroom Practice*, ed. Stephen M. Fishman and Lucille McCarthy (New York: Teacher's College Press, 1998), 16–29.

32 Quoted in ibid., 121.

33 Declared by Pope Paul VI, *Gravissimum Educationis*, 28 October 1965, translated under the title "Declaration on Christian Education," in Tanner, *Decrees*, 959–68.

34 Ms. Key, 27 February 2001.

35 Fieldnotes, Holy Cross Catholic Church, Durham, N.C., 27 April 1997.

36 *Trends in the Catechesis of Children in the United States: A Report of the Specialists in Elementary and Family Centered Religious Education* (Department of Education, United States Conference, 1976), John F. Dearden Manuscripts, CDRD 11/01, University of Notre Dame Archives, Notre Dame, Ind.

37 For more on the Church's attitude toward Reconciliation, see Vatican II's Constitution on Sacred Liturgy, *Sacrosanctum Concilium*, in Tanner, *Decrees*, 820–43. For secondary scholarship, see James Dallen, *The Reconciling Community: The Rite of Penance* (New York: Pueblo Publishing Co., 1986).

38 *Trends in the Catechesis of Children.*

39 Sofia Cavalletti, *The Religious Potential of the Child: The Description of an Experience with Children from Ages Three to Six*, trans. Patricia M. Coulter and Julie M. Coulter (New York: Paulist Press, 1983). For more of Cavalletti's writing on Montessori, see "The 'Maria Montessori' School of Religion," in *The Church and the Child*, ed. E. M. Standing (St. Paul, Minn.: Catechetical Guild, 1965), 124–32. For Maria Montessori's writings on religion, see Standing, *Church and the Child*, pt. 1, 3–61.

40 For more on Maria Montessori and her method, see E. M. Standing, *Maria Montessori: Her Life and Work* (Fresno, Calif.: Academy Library Guild, 1957); Carol Garhart Mooney, *Theories of Childhood: An Introduction to Dewey, Montessori, Erickson, Piaget, and Vygotsky* (St. Paul, Minn.: Redleaf Press, 2000); Elizabeth G. Hainstock, *The Essential Montessori: An Introduction to the Woman, the Writings,*

the *Method, and the Movement* (New York: New American Library, 1986); and E. M. Standing, *The Montessori Revolution in Education*, 2d paperback ed. (New York: Schocken Books, 1966).

41 Cavalletti, *Religious Potential of the Child*, 45.

42 *The Catechesis of the Good Shepherd: An Introduction* (Association for the Catechesis of the Good Shepherd).

43 "Holy Cross Catholic Church First Sacraments Handbook, 1996–1997," unpublished; emphasis added.

44 Britney, 2 December 2001.

45 Fieldnotes, Blessed Sacrament Faith Formation, Burlington, N.C., 11 March 2001.

46 Ibid., 22 April 2001.

47 Maureen, seven-year-old white girl, interviewed by the author, Holy Cross Catholic Church, Durham, N.C., 13 April 1997.

48 Fieldnotes, Holy Cross Faith Formation, Durham, N.C., 11 March 1997.

49 Ibid., 6 April 1997.

50 Fieldnotes, Friendship retreat, 26 April 1997.

51 Ms. Fabuel, 17 December 2000.

52 *Coming to Jesus* (New York: William H. Sadlier, 1999).

53 Ms. Richards, forty-four-year-old white woman, interviewed by the author, Blessed Sacrament Catholic Church, Burlington, N.C., 18 March 2001.

54 Along with behavior problems, the catechists at Blessed Sacrament also worked to keep both the Spanish-speaking and English-speaking children interested. Even with the efforts to integrate the children by having translators and supplementary classes, the teachers also had to find a way to handle the "language barrier with the Spanish children and the fact that they [had] already had class and . . . [were] a little tired through the whole class." Ibid.

55 Morrow, *My First Communion*, 1.

56 Lily, nine-year-old Mexican girl, interviewed by the author, Blessed Sacrament Catholic Church, Burlington, N.C., 1 April 2001.

57 Ms. Carla Wright-Jukes, thirty-six-year-old African American woman, interviewed by the author, Holy Cross Catholic Church, Durham, N.C., 17 February 1997.

58 Samantha, nine-year-old white girl, interviewed by the author,

Blessed Sacrament Catholic Church, Burlington, N.C., 22 October 2001.

59 Justin, eight-year-old African American boy, interviewed by the author, Holy Cross Catholic Church, Durham, N.C., 27 April 1997.

60 Kim, eight-year-old Latina, interviewed by the author, Blessed Sacrament Catholic Church, Burlington, N.C., 1 April 2001.

61 Paris, eight-year-old African American girl, interviewed by the author, Holy Cross Catholic Church, Durham, N.C., 27 April 1997.

62 Although I sensed growing anticipation in most of the children's voices, perhaps more of them did not talk about these feelings because our conversations occurred within a context in which anticipation was assumed.

63 Dean, seven-year-old white boy, from Blessed Sacrament Catholic Church, interviewed by the author, O'Charlie's Restaurant, Burlington, N.C., 25 February 2001.

64 Roxanna, eight-year-old Mexican girl, interviewed by the author, Blessed Sacrament Catholic Church, Burlington, N.C., 22 April 2001. Although she asked to do the interview in English and she spoke English during the entire conversation, Roxanna said this commonly used seven-word phrase (which translated is "the body of Christ and the blood of Christ") in Spanish. Perhaps she felt more comfortable using Spanish for this phrase because she heard it repeated each weekend during the Spanish Mass. Her parents may have also said it when they talked with her about her upcoming First Communion. Thus, most likely Roxanna heard this phrase many more times in Spanish than in English.

65 Cara, 15 February 1998.

66 Ferris, eight-year-old African American boy, interviewed by the author, Holy Cross Catholic Church, Durham, N.C., 8 February 1998.

67 Gossman, "Diocesan Guidelines."

68 Although I found little written about the intersection of taste and religion, the fall 1995 issue of the *Journal of the American Academy of Religion* dealt entirely with religion and food in different traditions. See also Constance Classen, *Worlds of Sense: Exploring the Senses in History and across Cultures* (New York: Routledge, 1993), and Jane Fajans, "The Transformative Value of Food: A Review Essay," in *Food and Foodways* 3 (1988): 143–66. For a discussion of the importance of food in Protestantism, see Daniel Sack, *White-*

bread Protestantism: Food and Religion in American Religion (New York: St. Martin's Press, 2000).

69 Ryan, nine-year-old African American boy, interviewed by the author, Holy Cross Catholic Church, Durham, N.C., 1 February 1998. Although many of the white, Latino, and African American children mentioned taste in their interviews, it might have been more emphasized by those at Holy Cross because of the central role that food plays in African American church communities. Scholars Jualynne E. Dodson and Cheryl Townsend Gilkes found that "the sense of solidarity that communities of African Americans feel is nurtured in a variety of settings where food is shared" (Dodson and Gilkes, "'There's Nothing Like Church Food': Food and the U.S. Afro-Christian Tradition; Re-Membering Community and Feeding the Embodied S/spirit[s]," *Journal of the American Academy of Religion* 63 [Fall 1995]: 522).

70 Elizabeth, eight-year-old white girl, interviewed by the author, Blessed Sacrament Catholic Church, Burlington, N.C., 4 November 2001.

71 Britney, 18 March 2001.

72 Paris, 27 April 1997.

73 Melissa, 8 April 2001.

74 Fieldnotes, First Communion Rehearsal, Holy Cross Catholic Church, Durham, N.C., 2 May 1997.

75 Elizabeth, 4 November 2001; Dean, 25 February 2001.

76 Maureen, 13 April 1997. Maureen's reference to grape juice seems to emphasize the influence of the surrounding Protestant churches that do use juice instead of wine for communion.

77 Hunter, eight-year-old African American boy, interviewed by the author, Holy Cross Catholic Church, Durham, N.C., 15 February 1998.

78 Ms. Lauffer, 8 February 1998.

79 Cara, 15 February 1998.

80 Katie, eight-year-old Mexican American girl, interviewed by the author, Blessed Sacrament Catholic Church, Burlington, N.C., 18 March 2001.

81 Ryan, 1 February 1998.

82 Father David Barry, interviewed by the author, Holy Cross Catholic Church, Durham, N.C., 22 January 1998.

83 Fieldnotes from Holy Cross's Second Grade Faith Formation lesson, 13 April 1997.

84 Michael, 27 April 1997. During the interview and the time I spent with the children in class, they all knew that I had not had a First Communion. As they explained what the Sacrament meant to them and what it was like to receive it, the children often expressed some sympathy for me. Melissa said, for instance, that "if you came to Blessed Sacrament they would let you have a First Communion," while Katie explained that First Communion was important to her because if she hadn't had it, "then I would be like you." Melissa, 2 December 2001; Katie, 18 March 2001.

85 Paul, seven-year-old African American boy, from Holy Cross Catholic Church, interviewed by the author, at his home, Chapel Hill, N.C., 14 December 1997.

86 Hunter, 15 February 1998.

87 Maureen, Britney, and Ferris did draw themselves standing before the altar with their backs to the congregation; however, only Maureen colored the priest's arms outstretched before her. These children did not freeze the moment at which they were about to receive the Eucharist; instead, their pictures seemed to focus on the congregation or the altar.

88 I discuss the implications of these drawings further in Chapter 4; here I am focusing solely on what they might reveal about the children's understanding of themselves as agents.

89 Mr. John Dwyer, thirty-nine-year-old white man, interviewed by the author, Blessed Sacrament Catholic Church, Burlington, N.C., 12 November 2001.

90 Father David Barry, 18 February 1997.

91 Father Briant Cullinane, O.F.M. Conv., seventy-one-year-old white man, interviewed by the author, Blessed Sacrament Catholic Church, Burlington, N.C., 12 October 2001.

92 Father Barry, 18 February 1997.

93 Ms. Fabuel, 17 December 2000.

94 Ms. Richards, 18 March 2001.

95 The preceding paragraph came from my fieldnotes, Holy Cross Faith Formation class, 4 March 1997.

96 Hunter, 15 February 1998.

97 Paris, 13 April 1997.

98 Fieldnotes, Blessed Sacrament Catholic Church, Burlington, N.C., 28 January 2001.

99 Father Briant, 12 October 2001.

100 The above events were recorded during the Saturday, 26 April 1997, Holy Cross First Communion "Friendship" retreat.

101 Only one or two fathers ever showed up to the meetings at Holy Cross and Blessed Sacrament. At Blessed Sacrament, those fathers who did attend the meetings had non-Catholic spouses.

102 Along with the difference in where the adults and children stood in relationship to First Communion (one group the audience and the other the actors), eating the bread and drinking the wine may have provided some communicants with a means to experience as well as to discuss the deeper doctrinal implications of the Eucharist that they could not yet articulate in a way that would have been immediately understandable to adults, who expected an explanation closer to the official church doctrine.

103 Ferris, 8 February 1998.

104 One exception was Michael, who drew "the place for the First and Second Readings" as part of his First Communion picture. Michael's inclusion of this "place," however, may have simply reflected his effort to show me that he had been paying attention in class and that he knew what the different areas of the church were for, especially since the lectern was not central to the action of his picture.

105 Maureen, 13 April 1997.

106 While it could be argued that the children incorporated the objects because they saw them in church each week, I believe that many of the children decided to include more detail in their pictures (not simply the bread and the wine) as they learned more about the Church and about the objects used in the Mass. Such detail revealed increased attention to and the importance of these ritual items. I interviewed Dean and Katie, for instance, many months before First Communion, and they included almost no detail in their pictures. However, all but one of Holy Cross's communicants, each of whom I interviewed much closer to First Communion than the children at Blessed Sacrament, included the altar in their picture. The vast majority of the children at both parishes, interviewed within five weeks of their First Communion or less,

included the altar, chalice, or the liturgical colors in their drawings not only because it was essential to their First Communion experience but also because they seemed to feel that it showed their
knowledge of the Church.

107 This trend excludes those children who rarely attended Faith Formation classes and Mass. These children, such as Kim and Christy,
included only generic religious things such as a Bible in their drawings, with no clear discussion of First Communion.

108 Zdzislaw Mach, *Symbols, Conflict, and Identity: Essays in Political
Anthropology* (New York: State University of New York Press, 1993),
25.

109 Paris, 27 April 1997.

110 Brian, eight-year-old white boy, interviewed by the author, Blessed
Sacrament Catholic Church, Burlington, N.C., 11 May 2001.

111 Elizabeth, eight-year-old white girl, interviewed by the author,
Blessed Sacrament Catholic Church, Burlington, N.C., 4 November 2001.

112 Alison, eight-year-old white girl, interviewed by the author, Blessed
Sacrament Catholic Church, Burlington, N.C., 30 September 2001.

113 Ferris, 8 February 1998.

114 Fieldnotes, Faith Formation class, Blessed Sacrament Catholic
Church, Burlington, N.C., 21 January 2001.

115 Britney, 2 December 2001.

116 Ms. Fabuel, 17 December 2000.

117 Maureen, 18 February 1998.

118 Ms. Cement, forty-four-year-old African American woman, from
Holy Cross Catholic Church, interviewed by the author, at her
home, Chapel Hill, N.C., 14 December 1997.

119 Ms. Hernandez, 29 April 2001.

CHAPTER FOUR

1 Fieldnotes, Blessed Sacrament Catholic Church, 11 February 2001.

2 Ms. Mary Key, forty-five-year-old white woman, interviewed by the
author, Blessed Sacrament Catholic Church, Burlington, N.C., 27
February 2001.

3 Bishop Joseph Gossman, "Diocesan Guidelines 3.3.3 Sacrament of
the Eucharist," unpublished, January 1994.

4 Christopher, seven-year-old white boy, interviewed by the author,

Blessed Sacrament Catholic Church, Burlington, N.C., 1 April 2001.

5 Ryan, nine-year-old African American boy, interviewed by the author, Holy Cross Catholic Church, Durham, N.C., 1 February 1998.

6 Paris, eight-year-old African American girl, interviewed by the author, Holy Cross Catholic Church, Durham, N.C., 27 April 1997.

7 Ms. Patricia Matterson, fifty-four-year-old Panamanian woman, interviewed by the author, Blessed Sacrament Catholic Church, Burlington, N.C., 28 January 2001.

8 Fieldnotes, Blessed Sacrament Catholic Church, 24 September 2000.

9 Britney, eight-year-old white girl, interviewed by the author, Blessed Sacrament Catholic Church, Burlington, N.C., 2 December 2001.

10 Ms. Wright-Jukes, thirty-six-year-old African American woman, interviewed by the author, Holy Cross Catholic Church, Durham, N.C., 16 February 1997. Unlike earlier generations that might have been taught to fear God and his judgment, both parishes worked hard to help the children understand that the church was a safe, judgment-free space. They were very concerned that the children not feel alone and isolated. The catechists, parents, and priests wanted the children to know that if they needed a safe place to go and someone to talk to, they could always come to the church and talk to the priest, who would not judge them, break their confidence, or punish them.

11 Fieldnotes, "First Communion Class Workshop IV: Presentation of the Lord's Prayer," Holy Cross Catholic Church, 2 February 1997.

12 Father Briant, seventy-one-year-old white man, interviewed by the author, Blessed Sacrament Catholic Church, Burlington, N.C., 12 October 2001.

13 Fieldnotes, Blessed Sacrament Faith Formation classes, 15 October 2000.

14 Ms. Fabuel, fifty-year-old white woman, interviewed by the author, Blessed Sacrament Catholic Church, Burlington, N.C., 22 January 2001.

15 Christy, eight-year-old Latina, interviewed by the author, Blessed Sacrament Catholic Church, Burlington, N.C., 1 April 2001.

16 Like Christy, most of the children highlighted God's love and con-

stant presence verbally in our conversations and in class. Lily, however, made it the center of her First Communion drawing on which she wrote, "God love you." Looking at her drawing, she explained, "I have the cross where God died and the hearts for God's love and the flowers are a gift from God." Lily, nine-year-old Mexican, interviewed by the author, Blessed Sacrament Catholic Church, Burlington, N.C., 1 April 2001.

17 This emphasis on Jesus as friend seems to differ vastly from the image offered to older Catholics when they were children, the image of Jesus as heavenly judge. Though I can find no scholarly work that addresses the changes in Catholics' understanding of Jesus' character, the historical and cultural context of these parishes may influence the catechists' decision to emphasize Jesus as loving friend in a few significant ways. Stephen Prothero, *American Jesus: How the Son of God Became a National Icon* (New York: Farrar, Straus, and Giroux, 2003).

18 Fieldnotes, "Friendship" First Communion retreat.

19 Emphasis added.

20 Hunter, eight-year-old African American boy, interviewed by the author, Holy Cross Catholic Church, Durham, N.C., 15 February 1998.

21 Maureen, seven-year-old white girl, interviewed by the author, Holy Cross Catholic Church, Durham, N.C., 13 April 1997.

22 John J. MacAloon, "Introduction: Cultural Performance, Cultural Theory," in *Rite, Drama, Festival, Spectacle: Rehearsals toward a Theory of Cultural Performance*, ed. John J. MacAloon (Philadelphia: Institute for the Study of Human Issues, 1984), 10.

23 Lily, 1 April 2001.

24 Catherine Bell, *Ritual: Perspectives and Dimensions* (New York: Oxford University Press, 1997), 80.

25 Ruel W. Tyson Jr., James L. Peacock, and Daniel W. Patterson, eds., *Diversities of Gifts: Field Studies in Southern Religion* (Urbana: University of Illinois Press, 1988), 5.

26 Britney, 2 December 2001.

27 Kim, fieldnotes, Blessed Sacrament Catholic Church, Burlington, N.C., 11 May 2001.

28 Holy Cross even included a short tutorial on genuflecting and its meaning in its First Communion Handbook for 1997 to assist

those parents who might have been away from the Church for some time.

29 Paul Connerton, *How Societies Remember* (Cambridge, England: Cambridge University Press, 1989), 95.

30 Maureen, 18 February 1998.

31 Barbara G. Myerhoff, "A Death in Due Time: Construction of Self and Culture in Ritual Drama," in MacAloon, *Rite, Drama, Festival, Spectacle*, 155; emphasis added.

32 In our first conversation, Melissa told me some of the forty to fifty people she was going to invite and the room in which they were going to celebrate. Melissa, eight-year-old Latina American, interviewed by the author, Blessed Sacrament Catholic Church, Burlington, N.C., 8 April 2001.

33 Ibid., 2 December 2001.

34 Fieldnotes, First Communion, Blessed Sacrament, 12 May 2001.

35 Elizabeth, eight-year-old white girl, interviewed by the author, Blessed Sacrament Catholic Church, Burlington, N.C., 4 November 2001.

36 Cara, eight-year-old African American girl, interviewed by the author, Holy Cross Catholic Church, Durham, N.C., 15 February 1998.

37 Maureen, 18 February 1998.

38 The two chairs in the balcony of the first drawing represent the place where Maureen and her mother sat each Sunday with the eleven o'clock choir. As one viewer of the post-Communion drawing pointed out, perhaps the bird's-eye view that Maureen offers in this drawing is her view, or her mother's view, of the altar each week from the balcony. Similarly, Britney also decreases the emphasis on herself in her post-Communion drawing. Before Communion she depicts herself facing the congregation in larger-than-life fashion; after First Communion she draws the viewer's attention to the priest by letting the viewer see only her back. Unlike Maureen, however, her inclusion of the audience seems to have remained the same.

39 Maureen, 18 February 1998.

40 Ibid.

41 José, nine-year-old Mexican, interviewed by the author, Blessed Sacrament Catholic Church, Burlington, N.C., 27 October 2001.

42 Hunter, 15 February 1998.

43 Alison, eight-year-old white girl, interviewed by the author, Blessed Sacrament Catholic Church, Burlington, N.C., 30 September 2001.

44 Maureen, 18 February 1998.

45 Ruel W. Tyson Jr., "Introduction—Method and Spirit: Studying Diversity of Gestures in Religion," in *Diversities of Gifts: Field Studies in Southern Religion*, ed. Ruel W. Tyson Jr., James L. Peacock, and Daniel W. Patterson (Urbana: University of Illinois Press, 1988), 3.

46 Ryan, 1 February 1998.

47 Paul, eight-year-old African American boy, from Holy Cross Catholic Church, interviewed by the author, at his home, Chapel Hill, N.C., 14 December 1997.

48 Living in the Protestant Bible Belt, many of the children had parents who had converted to Catholicism either as children, especially in the case of many adults at Holy Cross, or when they married. Other communicants had close family members who attended Baptist and Methodist churches. One child at Blessed Sacrament alternated between attending Blessed Sacrament and a local United Church of Christ church, although she came to Faith Formation classes at Blessed Sacrament each week so she would be prepared for her First Communion. A child at Holy Cross also went to synagogue one week a month with her mother's partner. Through these family connections, then, many children had intimate understandings of other churches and religions that allowed them to notice differences in practice. This understanding, however, did not lead to a sense that there were core beliefs and practices that united their parish with others.

49 Ryan, 1 February 1998. While Ryan was the only child who expressed knowledge of a non-Judeo-Christian religion in the interview, most children had some experience with Baptists. For instance, "Baptists," said Ferris, "serve real bread that we eat everyday for toast. They serve that . . . instead of those round things" (Ferris, eight-year-old African American boy, interviewed by the author, Holy Cross Catholic Church, Durham, N.C., 8 February 1998). Likewise, Elizabeth, from Blessed Sacrament, who had attended a Baptist church, told me: "Some churches serve grape juice. That's the only difference" (4 November 2001). Most often, however, those children who attempted to respond to my inquiry

offered something akin to Ryan's answer that he was Catholic "because Mommy just said I was Catholic" (1 February 1998) or Britney's "I don't know what non-Catholic feels like" (18 March 2001). Part of this disinterest in differentiating their faith from that of others may be because the children did not discuss their religion with their friends, either Catholic or non-Catholic; they apparently did not even discuss important events like First Communion. The children appeared unconcerned with their Catholic identity, which seemed to have little meaning to them, focusing instead on the changes occurring in two kinds of important relationships, their relationship within their parish and that with Jesus.

50 Dean, seven-year-old white boy, interviewed by the author, O'Charlie's Restaurant, Burlington, N.C., 25 February 2001.

51 Maureen, 13 April 1997.

52 Ferris, 8 February 1998.

53 José, 27 October 2001.

54 Since children from Blessed Sacrament's English Masses were not allowed to be altar servers until they were in the fifth grade, the children did not talk about their increased responsibilities during Mass.

55 Hunter, 15 February 1998.

56 Britney, 2 December 2001.

57 The adults' goals for the children often overlapped, especially when the catechists had children in the First Communion class. Parents also expressed a desire for the Sacrament to deepen their children's relationship with Jesus, and the catechists talked of their hope that First Communion would be a special day, working hard to that end. Perhaps because each assumed that the other would handle a certain aspect of the First Communion process, each group had a distinctive emphasis—a particular element of the sacramental experience that they sought to pass on to the children.

58 Ms. Anne Fister, interviewed by the author, Blessed Sacrament Catholic Church, Burlington, N.C., 5 November 2000.

59 Ms. Minerva Jeffries, interviewed by the author, Blessed Sacrament Catholic Church, Burlington, N.C., 23 September 2001. Ms. Fabuel later wrote of her catechetical preparation in an e-mail,

stating: "It is mainly the calling from God. And as we all know, when he calls—we can answer or not." E-mail to author received 8 May 2002.

60 Mr. Jones, forty-two-year-old white man, from Blessed Sacrament Catholic Church, interviewed by the author, Franklin Street Pizza and Pasta, Chapel Hill, N.C., 19 March 2001.

61 Ms. Fabuel, 17 December 2000.

62 Melissa, eight-year-old Nicaraguan American, interviewed by the author, Blessed Sacrament Catholic Church, Burlington, N.C., 8 April 2001.

63 Virginia, seven-year-old Mexican, interviewed by the author, Blessed Sacrament Catholic Church, Burlington, N.C., 8 April 2001.

64 José, eight-year-old Mexican boy, interviewed by the author, Blessed Sacrament Catholic Church, Burlington, N.C., 29 April 2001; Roxanna, eight-year-old Mexican girl, Blessed Sacrament Catholic Church, Burlington, N.C., 22 April 2001; Elizabeth, 4 November 2001.

65 Alison, 30 September 2001.

66 Mr. Jones, 19 March 2001.

67 Paul, 14 December 1997.

68 Hunter, 15 February 1998.

69 Ms. Fister, 5 November 2000.

70 Paris, 27 April 1997.

71 Maureen, 18 February 1998.

72 Ms. Fister, 5 November 2000.

73 Ibid.

74 Britney, 18 March 2001.

75 Virginia, 8 April 2001.

76 Lily, 1 April 2001.

77 Ferris, 8 February 1998.

78 Christy, 1 March 2001.

79 Gary Wray McDonough, *Black and Catholic in Savannah, Georgia* (Knoxville: University of Tennessee Press, 1993), 268.

80 Martha Manning, *Chasing Grace: Reflections of a Catholic Girl Grown Up* (New York: HarperSanFrancisco, 1996), 170.

81 Kathleen Hage, "The Communion Dress," *Commonweal*, 8 May 1998, 31.

82 "Needy Girls of Europe Will Have American First Communion Dresses," in *North Carolina Catholic*, 13 July 1954, 3.

83 Ibid.

84 Penny Storm, *Functions of Dress: Tool of Culture and the Individual* (Englewood Cliffs, N.J.: Prentice-Hall, 1987), 241. For more on religion and dress, see Linda B. Arthur, ed. *Religion, Dress and the Body* (Oxford: Berg, 1999); Ysamur Flores-Peña and Roberta J. Evanchuk, *Santería Garments and Altars: Speaking without a Voice* (Jackson: University of Mississippi Press, 1994); Barbara Shreier, *Becoming an American Woman: Clothing and the Jewish Immigrant Experience, 1880–1920* (Chicago: Chicago Historical Society, 1995); and Stephen Scott, *Why Do They Dress That Way?* (Intercourse, Pa.: Good Books, 1986). For information on the study of clothing more generally, see Anne Hollander, *Seeing through Clothes* (New York: Viking Press, 1978); Aileen Ribeiro, *Dress and Morality* (New York: Holmes and Meier, 1986); Arthur Asa Berger, *Reading Matter: Multi-disciplinary Perspectives on Material Culture* (New Brunswick, N.J.: Transaction Publishers, 1991); Alison Lurie, *The Language of Clothes* (New York: Random House, 1981); and Grant McCracken, "Clothing as Language: An Object Lesson in the Study of the Expressive Properties of Material Culture," in *Material Anthropology: Contemporary Approaches to the Study of Material Culture*, ed. Barrie Reynolds and Margaret A. Stott (Lanham, Md.: University Press of America, 1987).

85 Maureen did not want to wear a dress or veil. Her mother told Ms. Wright-Jukes that Maureen wanted to wear pants and a red bow tie instead of a white dress. Ms. Wright-Jukes suggested that she wear a white bow and the white pants that her mother had mentioned in an earlier conversation. Ms. Wright-Jukes ended the conversation by saying that Maureen should wear what makes her comfortable, as after all it is her First Communion. On First Communion Sunday, Maureen wore a white dress that she and her mother bought on a special trip to Washington, D.C., and a white headband with silk flowers on it. Fieldnotes, Holy Cross Catholic Church, 9 February 1997.

86 Ms. Mary Key, quoted in 15 March 2000 parents' meeting fieldnotes, Blessed Sacrament Catholic Church, Burlington, N.C.

87 Virginia, 8 April 2001.

88 Hunter, 15 February 1998; Eric, nine-year-old white boy, interviewed by the author, Blessed Sacrament Catholic Church, Burlington, N.C., 11 May 2001.

89 Ferris, 8 February 1998.

90 Ryan, 1 February 1998.

91 Ms. Cement, forty-four-year-old African American woman, from Holy Cross Catholic Church, interviewed by the author, at her home, Chapel Hill, N.C., 14 December 1997.

92 Father David Barry, interviewed by the author, Holy Cross Catholic Church, Durham, N.C., 18 February 1997.

93 Alison, eight-year-old white girl, interviewed by the author, Blessed Sacrament Church, Burlington, N.C., 30 September 2001.

94 Maureen, 21 February 1998.

95 Cara, 15 February 1998.

96 Paris, 27 April 1997.

97 Ms. Wright-Jukes, 16 February 1997.

98 Hannah, ten-year-old African American girl, interviewed by the author, Holy Cross Catholic Church, Durham, N.C., 1 February 1998.

99 Dean, 25 February 2001.

100 Ms. Wright-Jukes, 16 February 1997.

101 Victor Turner, *The Ritual Process: Structure and Anti-Structure* (Chicago: Aldine Co., 1968), 103.

CONCLUSION

1 Ruel W. Tyson Jr., introduction to *Pilgrims of Paradox: Calvinism and Experience among the Primitive Baptists of the Blue Ridge*, ed. James L. Peacock and Ruel W. Tyson Jr. (Washington, D.C.: Smithsonian Institution Press, 1989), 4.

2 I borrow the term "parallel congregations" from Paul David Numrich, *Old Wisdom in the New World: Americanization in Two Immigrant Theravada Buddhist Temples* (Knoxville: University of Tennessee Press, 1996), xxii.

3 Barbara Pegg, director of religious education, fifty-one, interviewed by the author, Immaculate Conception Catholic Church, Durham, N.C., 27 January 1998.

4 Fieldnotes, First Communion Workshop, Blessed Sacrament Catholic Church, Burlington, N.C., 7 April 2001.

5 Ms. Key, forty-five-year-old white woman, interviewed by the au-

thor, Blessed Sacrament Catholic Church, Burlington, N.C., 13 February 2001.

6 The greatest difference among the children was their personalities, particularly whether they were shy and, of course, whether they were willing to be interviewed. The number of children that fell into each category seemed to be about the same across racial and parish lines. These variations in personality had a major impact on this study. The loquacious children offered much more material for analysis than did the shy children. Thus, the talkative and confident communicants' perceptions appear in this study more than those of the more introverted interviewees. And there was a final group of children with whom I did not talk, and therefore their feelings and interpretations remain outside the reach of this analysis, except for my general observations of their body language at First Communion and their classroom responses and behavior.

7 John F. Kihlstrom, "Memory, Autobiography, History," <http://ist -socrates.berkeley.edu/~kihldtrm/rmpaoo.htm>. A shorter version of this article appeared in *Proteus: A Journal of Ideas on the Subject of Memory* 19, no. 2 (Fall 2002).

8 For more on the sacramental imagination, see Andrew Greeley's *The Catholic Myth: The Behaviors and Beliefs of American Catholics* (New York: Scribner, 1990).

9 Jon Butler, *Awash in a Sea of Faith: Christianizing the American People* (Cambridge: Harvard University Press, 1990); David D. Hall, ed., *Lived Religion in America: Toward a History of Practice* (Princeton, N.J.: Princeton University Press, 1997); Thomas A. Tweed, ed., *Retelling U.S. Religious History* (Berkeley: University of California Press, 1997).

10 I have suggested the use of ethnography as a helpful method for analyzing children's interpretations. Although fieldwork offers great promise for researchers who work with contemporary populations, historians cannot interview young Victorian children or ask them to draw pictures. There are, of course, other means to gain *some* insights into the religious worlds of these children. Scholars, for instance, might begin to analyze toys, art projects, and workbooks of past generations for the ways that children used them rather than how adults hoped that they would be used. One

example of a missed opportunity for this kind of examination appears in historian Karin Calvert's excellent volume *Children in the House: The Material Culture of Early Childhood, 1600–1900* (Boston: Northeastern University Press, 1992). As Calvert discusses how she uses the modifications that adults make to children's toys to examine how adults interpret childhood, she highlights one needlepoint in particular. On the back of it, its young creator had stitched: "Patty Polk did this and hated every stitch she did in it. She loves to read much more" (5). Scholars interested in children need to take seriously the messages and clues children have left behind in artifacts. Patty, it seems, wanted to tell someone, or perhaps remind herself, of her own values and preferences, regardless of who was forcing her to do what. And, most important, Polly was recording her feelings at the time of the event, not attempting to recall them through the distortion of subsequent years. Thus, if scholars look at the marks that children have left behind in books and houses, on tables and toys, we can learn more about the lives of children. Although I would caution researchers to be careful not to make too much of these sources without having the children to help interpret them, these new discoveries gleaned through material culture could then be read alongside the texts that children have left for us. Such artifacts—from toys and art projects to diaries and school essays—might provide historians with compelling sources for reconstructing children's lives.

11 See Robert Coles's Children of Crisis Series.

bibliography

Alderson, Priscilla. "Researching Children's Rights to Integrity." In *Children's Childhoods: Observed and Experienced*, edited by Berry Mayall, 33–44. London: Falmer Press, 1994.

Ammerman, Nancy Tatom. *Congregations and Community*. New Brunswick, N.J.: Rutgers University Press, 1997.

Ammerman, Nancy Tatom, Jackson W. Carroll, Carl S. Dudley, and William McKinney, eds. *Studying Congregations: A New Handbook*. Nashville: Abingdon Press, 1998.

Anderson, Jon W., and William B. Friend, eds. *The Culture of Bible Belt Catholics*. New York: Paulist Press, 1995.

Ariès, Philippe. *Centuries of Childhood: A Social History of Family Life*. Translated by Robert Baldick. New York: Vintage Books, 1962.

Arthur, Linda B., ed. *Religion, Dress and the Body*. Oxford: Berg, 1999.

Bass, Dorothy C. "Congregations and the Bearing of Tradition." In *New Perspectives in the Study of Congregations*. Vol. 2 of *American Congregations*, edited by James P. Wind and James W. Lewis, 169–91. Chicago: University of Chicago Press, 1994.

Bauman, Robert Mark. "The Inner Light: Children's Lived Experience in the Quaker Practice of Meeting for Worship." Ph.D. diss., University of Maryland, College Park, 2001.

Behar, Ruth, "Writing in My Father's Name: A Diary of *Translated Woman*'s First Year," in *Women Writing Culture*, edited by Ruth Behar and Deborah A. Gordon, 65–82 (Berkeley: University of California Press, 1995);

Bell, Catherine. *Ritual: Perspectives and Dimensions*. New York: Oxford University Press, 1997.

———. *Ritual Theory, Ritual Practice*. New York: Oxford University Press, 1992.

Berger, Arthur Asa. *Reading Matter: Multidisciplinary Perspectives on Material Culture*. New Brunswick, N.J.: Transaction Publishers, 1991.

Berk, Laura E. *Child Development* (Boston: Allyn and Bacon, 1989).

Berube, Maurice R. *Eminent Educators: Studies in Intellectual Influence*. Westport, Conn.: Greenwood Press, 2000.

Blatnica, Dorothy Ann, V.S.C. *At the Altar of Their God: African American Catholics in Cleveland, 1922–1961*. New York: Garland Publishing, 1995.

Blessed Sacrament Catholic Church Bulletin.

Blewett, John. *John Dewey: His Thought and Influence*. New York: Fordham University Press, 1960.

Bluebond-Langner, Myra. *The Private Worlds of Dying Children*. Princeton, N.J.: Princeton University Press, 1978.

Boyd, William Kenneth. *The Story of Durham: City of the New South*. Durham, N.C.: Duke University Press, 1925.

Boykin, Sam. "Growing Up Catholic in the South: Bob Jones Controversy Reopens Old Wounds." *Raleigh Spectator*, 12–18 April 2000, 12–14.

Brown, Karen McCarthy. *Mama Lola: A Vodou Priestess in Brooklyn*. Berkeley: University of California Press, 1991.

Bryce, Mary Charles, O.S.B. "The Confraternity of Christian Doctrine in the United States." In *Renewing the Sunday School and the CCD*, edited by D. Campbell Wyckoff. Birmingham, Ala.: Religious Education, 1986.

———. "The Evolution of Catechesis from the Catholic Reformation to the Present." In *A Faithful Church: Issues in the History of Catechesis*, edited by John H. Westerhoff III and O. C. Edwards Jr., 204–35. Wilton, Conn.: Morehouse-Barlow Co., 1981.

Bunge, Marcia J., ed. *The Child in Christian Thought*. Grand Rapids, Mich.: W. B. Eerdmans, 2001.

Butler, Jon. *Awash in a Sea of Faith: Christianizing the American People*. Cambridge, Mass.: Harvard University Press, 1990.

Byker, Patrick. "Not a Great Conspiracy." *Durham (N.C.) Herald Sun*, 28 January 2001, A13.

Calvert, Karin. *Children in the House: The Material Culture of Early Childhood, 1600–1900*. Boston: Northeastern University Press, 1992.

Camaroff, John, and Jean Camaroff. *Ethnography and the Historical Imagination*. Boulder, Colo.: Westview Press, 1992.

Carey, Patrick W. *The Roman Catholics in America*. Westport Conn.: Praeger, 1996.

Case, Robbie. *Intellectual Development: Birth to Adulthood*. Orlando: Academic Press, 1985.

Catechism of the Catholic Church. London: Geoffrey Chapman, 1994.

The Catechesis of the Good Shepherd: An Introduction. Association for the Catechesis of the Good Shepherd.

Cavalletti, Sofia. *The Religious Potential of the Child: The Description of an Experience with Children from Ages Three to Six*. Translated by Patricia M. Coulter and Julie M. Coulter. New York: Paulist Press, 1983.

Cheng, Vikki. "Durham Is 'All-Minority.'" *News and Observer*, 5 April 2001, sec. A, pp. 1, 20.

Christensen, Pia, and Allison James. *Research with Children: Perspectives and Practices*. London: Falmer Press, 2000.

Classen, Constance. *Worlds of Sense: Exploring the Senses in History and across Cultures*. New York: Routledge, 1993.

Clifford, James. "Notes on (Field)notes." In *Fieldnotes: The Makings of Anthropology*, edited by Roger Sanjek, 47–70 (Ithaca: Cornell University Press, 1990).

Cohen, Yehudi A. *The Transition from Childhood to Adolescence: Cross-Cultural Studies of Initiation Ceremonies, Legal Systems, and Incest Taboos*. Chicago: Aldine Publishing Co., 1964.

Coles, Robert. *Children of Crisis: A Study of Courage and Fear*. Vol. 1 of Children of Crisis Series. Boston: Little, Brown, 1967.

———. *Eskimos, Chicanos, Indians*. Vol. 4 of Children of Crisis Series. Boston: Little, Brown, 1977.

———. *Migrants, Sharecroppers, Mountaineers*. Vol. 2 of Children of Crisis Series. Boston: Little, Brown, 1971.

———. *The Moral Life of Children* (Boston: Atlantic Monthly Press, 1986).

———. *The Political Life of Children* (Boston: Atlantic Monthly Press, 1986).

———. *The Privileged Ones: The Well-Off and Rich in America*. Vol. 5 in Children of Crisis Series. Boston: Little, Brown, 1977.

———. *The South Goes North*. Vol. 3 of Children of Crisis Series. Boston: Little, Brown, 1971.

———. *The Spiritual Life of Children*. Boston: Houghton Mifflin, 1990.

———. *Their Eyes Meeting the World: The Drawings and Paintings of Children*. Edited by Margaret Sartor. Boston: Houghton Mifflin, 1992.

Coming to Jesus. New York: William H. Sadlier, 1999.

Connerton, Paul. *How Societies Remember*. Cambridge, England: Cambridge University Press, 1989.

Conway, M. A., D. C. Rubin, H. Spinnler, and W. A. Wagner, eds. *Theoretical Perspectives on Autobiographical Memory*. Boston: Kluwer Academic Publishers, 1992.

Cooper, John. *The Child in Jewish History*. Northvale, N.J.: Jason Aronson, 1996.

Dallen, James. *The Reconciling Community: The Rite of Penance*. New York: Pueblo Publishing Co., 1986.

Davis, Cyprian, O.S.B. *The History of Black Catholics in the United States*. New York: Crossroad, 1990.

Decrees of the Ecumenical Councils. Vol. 2, *Trent to Vatican II*. London: Sheed & Ward; Washington, D.C.: Georgetown University Press, 1990.

Dewey, John. *Democracy and Education: An Introduction to the Philosophy of Education*. New York: Macmillan, 1916.

———. "My Pedagogical Creed." Reprinted in *Dewey on Education: Appraisals*. Edited by Reginald D. Archambault. New York: Random House, 1966.

Díaz-Stevens, Ana María. *Oxcart Catholicism on Fifth Avenue: The Impact of the Puerto Rican Migration upon the Archdiocese of New York*. Notre Dame: University of Notre Dame Press, 1993.

Di Leo, Joseph H., M.D. *Young Children and Their Drawings*. New York: Brunner/Mazel Publishing, 1970.

"Diocesan Study Confirms Sky High Hispanic Numbers, Challenges to Ministry." *NC Catholic Online* <http://www.nccatholic.org/news.php?artID=404>. 2 July 2002.

Dodson, Jualynne E., and Cheryl Townsend Gilkes. "'There's Nothing Like Church Food': Food and the U.S. Afro-Christian Tradition; Re-Membering Community and Feeding the Embodied S/spirit(s)." *Journal of the American Academy of Religion* 63 (Fall 1995): 519–38.

Dolan, Jay P. *The American Catholic Experience: A History from Colonial Times to the Present*. Notre Dame: University of Notre Dame Press, 1992.

————. *The Immigrant Church: New York's Irish and German Catholics, 1815–1865*. Baltimore: Johns Hopkins University Press, 1975.

Dolan, Jay P., and Allan Figueroa Deck, S.J., eds. *Hispanic Catholic Culture in the U.S.: Issues and Concerns*. Notre Dame: University of Notre Dame Press, 1994.

Dorsey, Gary. *Congregation: The Journey Back to Church*. Cleveland: Pilgrim Press, 1998.

Dudley, Carl S., Jackson W. Carroll, and James P. Wind, eds. *Carriers of Faith: Lessons from Congregational Studies*. Louisville: John Knox Press, 1991.

Duffy, Regis A. *On Becoming a Catholic: The Challenge of Christian Initiation*. San Francisco: Harper and Row, 1984.

Duncan, Anne. "The History of Holy Cross Catholic Church in Durham, North Carolina." Unpublished manuscript, 1989.

————. "Supplement to History of Holy Cross Church." Unpublished manuscript, 1989.

"Durham Church's Decision Angers Hispanic Parishioners." *Greensboro News Record*, 15 October 1996, B2.

Ebaugh, Helen Rose, and Janet Saltzman Chafetz, eds. *Religion and the New Immigrants: Continuities and Adaptations in Immigrant Congregations*. Walnut Creek, Calif.: AltaMira Press, 2000.

Eliade, Mircea. *Rites and Symbols of Initiation: The Mysteries of Birth and Rebirth*. Translated by Willard R. Trask. New York: Harper and Row, 1965.

Fajans, Jane. "The Transformative Value of Food: A Review Essay." *Food and Foodways* 3 (1988): 143–66.

Fan, Maureen. "Triangle Takes Valley's Lead: Burgeoning Raleigh-Durham Faces Familiar Challenges." *San Jose Mercury News*, 8 July 2001.

Fishman, Steve. "Dewey's Educational Philosophy: Reconciling Nested Dualisms." In *John Dewey and the Challenge of Classroom Practice*, edited by Stephen M. Fishman and Lucille McCarthy, 16–29. New York: Teacher's College Press, 1998.

Fitzpatrick, Joseph P. *One Church, Many Cultures: Challenge of Diversity*. Kansas City, Mo.: Sheed & Ward, 1987.

Flores-Peña, Ysamur, and Roberta J. Evanchuk. *Santería Garments and Altars: Speaking without a Voice*. Jackson: University of Mississippi Press, 1994.

Fluehr-Lobban, Carolyn, ed. *Ethics and the Profession of Anthropology: Dialogue for a New Era*. Philadelphia: University of Pennsylvania Press, 1991.

Fowler, James W. *Stages of Faith: The Psychology of Human Development and the Quest for Meaning*. San Francisco: Harper and Row, 1981.

Freud, Anna. *Introduction to the Technic of Child Analysis*. New York: Nervous and Mental Disease Publishing Co., 1928.

Frisbie, Charlotte Johnson. *Kinaaldá: A Study of the Navaho Girl's Puberty Ceremony*. Middletown, Conn.: Wesleyan University Press, 1967.

Froehle, Bryan T., and Mary L. Gautier. *Catholicism USA: A Portrait of the Catholic Church in the United States*. Maryknoll, N.Y.: Orbis Books, 2000.

Fuchs, Mike. "Alamance County's Hispanic Community Center in Burlington Helps Growing Number of Spanish Speakers Overcome Cultural and Language Barriers." *Greensboro News Record*, 10 January 2000, B1.

Gillard, John T. *Colored Catholics in the United States*. Baltimore: Josephite Press, 1941.

Goodnow, Jacqueline J. *Children Drawing*. Cambridge: Harvard University Press, 1977.

Gossman, Bishop Joseph. "Diocesan Guideline 3.3.3 Sacrament of the Eucharist." Unpublished, January 1994.

Graue, M. Elizabeth, and Daniel J. Walsh. *Studying Children in Context: Theories, Methods, and Ethics*. Thousand Oaks, Calif.: Sage Publications, 1998.

Gredler, Margaret E. *Learning and Instruction: Theory into Practice*. 3d ed. Upper Saddle River, N.J.: Merrill, 1997.

Greeley, Andrew M. *The Catholic Myth: The Behaviors and Beliefs of American Catholics*. New York: Scribner, 1990.

Greven, Philip J. *The Protestant Temperament: Patterns of Child-*

Rearing, Religious Experience, and the Self in Early America. New
York: Knopf, 1977.

———. *Spare the Child: The Religious Roots of Punishment and the
Psychological Impact of Physical Abuse.* New York: Alfred Knopf,
1991.

Griffith, R. Marie. *God's Daughters: Evangelical Women and the Power
of Submission.* Berkeley: University of California Press, 1997.

Grimes, Ronald L. *Marrying and Burying: Rites of Passage in a Man's
Life.* Boulder, Colo.: Westview Press, 1995.

———. "Re-inventing Ritual." *Soundings* 75 (Spring 1992): 21–41.

———. *Ritual Criticism: Case Studies in Its Practice, Essays on Its
Theory.* Columbia: University of South Carolina Press, 1990.

Haaken, Janice. *Pillar of Salt: Gender, Memory, and the Perils of
Looking Back.* New Brunswick, N.J.: Rutgers University Press,
1998.

Hage, Kathleen. "The Communion Dress." *Commonweal,* 8 May
1998.

Hainstock, Elizabeth G. *The Essential Montessori: An Introduction to
the Woman, the Writings, the Method, and the Movement.* New
York: New American Library, 1986.

Hall, David D., ed. *Lived Religion in America: Toward a History of
Practice.* Princeton, N.J.: Princeton University Press, 1997.

Haraway, Donna. *Simians, Cyborgs, and Women: The Reinvention of
Nature.* New York: Routledge, 1991.

Hinson, Glenn. *Fire in My Bones: Transcendence and the Holy Spirit in
African American Gospel.* Philadelphia: University of Pennsylvania
Press, 2000.

Hirschfeld, Lawrence A. "Why Anthropologists Don't Like
Children." *American Anthropologist* 104, no. 2 (2002): 611–27.

Hollander, Anne. *Seeing through Clothes.* New York: Viking Press,
1978.

Holloway, Betsy. *Heaven for Beginners: Recollections of a Southern
Town.* Orlando, Fla.: Persimmon Press, 1986.

Holy Cross Catholic Church Bulletin. 21 March 1999.

"Holy Cross Catholic Church First Sacraments Handbook, 1996–
1997." Durham, N.C.

Hopewell, James. *Congregation: Stories and Structures.* Edited by
Barbara Wheeler. Philadelphia: Fortress Press, 1987.

James, Allison, Chris Jenks, and Alan Prout. *Theorizing Childhood.* New York: Teachers College Press, 1998.

James, Allison, and Alan Prout. Preface to *Constructing and Reconstructing Childhood: Contemporary Issues in the Sociological Study of Childhood,* edited by Allison James and Alan Prout. London: Falmer Press, 1997.

Jenkins, Henry, ed. *The Children's Culture Reader.* New York: New York University Press, 1998.

Jenks, Chris. *Childhood.* New York: Routledge, 1996.

Johnson, Nessa Theresa Baskerville. *A Special Pilgrimage: A History of Black Catholics in Richmond.* Richmond, Va.: Diocese of Richmond, 1978.

Jones, Arthur. "Hispanic 'Catholics Ignored.'" *National Catholic Reporter* 36 (11 February 2000).

Junker-Kenny, Maureen, and Norbet Mette, eds. *Little Children Suffer.* Maryknoll, N.Y.: Orbis Books, 1996.

Kammie, Michael. "Catholic Church to Drop Bilingual Service." *Durham (N.C.) Herald Sun,* 14 October 1996, 1A–2A.

Kelly-Byrne, Diana. *A Child's Play Life: An Ethnographic Study.* New York: Teachers College Press, 1989.

Kihlstrom, John F. "Memory, Autobiography, History." <http://istsocrates.berkley.edu/~kihldtrm/rmpa00.htm>.

Kincaid, James R. *Child-Loving: The Erotic Child and Victorian Culture.* New York: Routledge, 1992.

———. *Erotic Innocence: The Culture of Child Molesting.* Durham, N.C.: Duke University Press, 1998.

Klein, Melanie. *The Psycho-Analysis of Children.* Translated by Alix Strachey. London: Hogarth Press, 1949.

Kotre, John. *White Gloves: How We Create Ourselves through Memory.* New York: Free Press, 1995.

Kuhn, Annette. *Family Secrets: Acts of Memory and Imagination.* New York: Verso, 1995.

La Fontaine, Jean Sybil. *Initiation.* New York: Viking Penguin, 1985.

Lawless, Elaine. "Negotiating Interpreting Differences." *Journal of American Folklore* 105 (1992): 313.

Levick, Dr. Myra F., with Diana S. Wheeler, *Mommy, Daddy, Look What I'm Saying: What Children Are Telling You through Their Art* (New York: M. Evans and Co., 1986.

Levine, Lawrence W. *Black Culture and Black Consciousness: Afro-American Folk Thought from Slavery to Freedom*. New York: Oxford University Press, 1977.

Lewis, Gerald. "The Diocese of Raleigh: An Overview," <http://www.dioceseofraleigh.org/html/history1.html>.

Leyburn, James G. *The Way We Lived: Durham, 1900–1920*. Elliston, Va.: Northcross House, 1989.

"The Life of the Church." From the Blessed Sacrament Catholic Church's Parish Directory, 1998. Unpublished.

Lincoln, C. Eric, and Lawrence H. Mamiya. *The Black Church in the African American Experience*. Durham, N.C.: Duke University Press, 1990.

Liptak, Dolores, R.S.M. *Immigrants and Their Church*. New York: Macmillan, 1989.

Locke, John. *Some Thoughts concerning Education*. Cambridge: Cambridge University Press, 1880.

Logan, John. "Insider-Outsider: Sacramental Theology through the Eyes of Children and Young People." In *The Candles Are Still Burning: Directions in Sacrament and Spirituality*, edited by Mary Grey, Andrée Heaton, and Danny Sullivan, 160–68. Collegeville, Minn.: Liturgical Press, 1995.

Lurie, Alison. *The Language of Clothes*. New York: Random House, 1981.

MacAloon, John J., ed. *Rite, Drama, Festival, Spectacle: Rehearsals toward a Theory of Cultural Performance*. Philadelphia: Institute for the Study of Human Issues, 1984.

Mach, Zdzislaw. *Symbols, Conflict, and Identity: Essays in Political Anthropology*. New York: State University of New York Press, 1993.

MacSweeny, Margaret Phyllis. "First Communion." *Literary Digest*, June 28, 1930, 38.

Mahdi, Louise Carus, Steven Foster, and Meredith Little, eds. *Betwixt and Between: Patterns of Masculine and Feminine Initiation*. La Salle, Ill.: Open Court, 1987.

Males, Mike A. *Framing Youth: Ten Myths about the Next Generation*. Monroe, Maine: Common Courage Press, 1998.

Manning, Martha. *Chasing Grace: Reflections of a Catholic Girl Grown Up*. New York: HarperSanFrancisco, 19.

Mayall, Berry, ed. *Children's Childhoods: Observed and Experienced.* London: Falmer Press, 1994.

McCracken, Grant. "Clothing as Language: An Object Lesson in the Study of the Expressive Properties of Material Culture." In *Material Anthropology: Contemporary Approaches to the Study of Material Culture*, edited by Barrie Reynolds and Margaret A. Stott, 103–28. Lanham, Md.: University Press of America, 1987.

McDonough, Gary Wray. *Black and Catholic in Savannah, Georgia.* Knoxville: University of Tennessee Press, 1993.

McGreevy, John T. *Parish Boundaries: The Catholic Encounter with Race in the Twentieth-Century Urban North.* Chicago: University of Chicago Press, 1996.

Medlin, Frank. "Population by Race and Ethnicity, 1990–2000," *News and Observer*, 20A.

Miller, Randall M., and Jon L. Wakelyn, eds. *Catholics in the Old South: Essays in Church and Culture.* Macon, Ga.: Mercer University Press, 1983.

Miller-McLemore, Bonnie. *Let the Children Come: Reimagining Childhood from a Christian Perspective.* San Francisco: Jossey-Bass, 2003.

Mooney, Carol Garhart. *Theories of Childhood: An Introduction to Dewey, Montessori, Erickson, Piaget, and Vygotsky.* St. Paul, Minn.: Redleaf Press, 2000.

Morrow, Louis LaRaviore, D.D. *My First Communion: What Very Young Children Need to Know of Their First Holy Communion.* New York: Edward O'Toole Co., 1941. General Collection, Printed Material, 1700s–, #4617–18, University of Notre Dame Archives, Notre Dame, Ind.

Myerhoff, Barbara G. "A Death in Due Time: Construction of Self and Culture in Ritual Drama." In *Rite, Drama, Festival, Spectacle: Rehearsals toward a Theory of Cultural Performance*, edited by John J. MacAloon, 149–78. Philadelphia: Institute for the Study of Human Issues, 1984.

Nandy, Ashis. "Reconstructing Childhood: A Critique of the Ideology of Adulthood." In *Traditions, Tyranny and Utopias: Essays in the Politics of Awareness*, 56–76. Delhi: Oxford University Press, 1987.

National Conference of Black Catholic Bishops. *Plenty of Good*

Room: The Spirit and the Truth of African American Catholic Worship. Washington, D.C.: United States Catholic Conference, 1990.

"Needy Girls of Europe Will Have American First Communion Dresses." *North Carolina Catholic*, 13 July 1954.

"A New Approach to First Communion." *U.S. Catholic* 34 (November 1968): 42–46.

Nicholas, Marie Joseph, O.P. *What Is the Eucharist?*. Translated by R. F. Trevett. New York: Hawthorne Books, 1960.

Numrich, Paul David. *Old Wisdom in the New World: Americanization in Two Immigrant Theravada Buddhist Temples*. Knoxville: University of Tennessee Press, 1996.

Oakley, Ann. "Women and Children First and Last: Parallels and Differences between Children's and Women's Studies." In *Children's Childhoods: Observed and Experienced*, edited by Berry Mayall, 13–32. London: Falmer Press, 1994.

O'Brien, Right Rev. Francis K. Pastor. "History: Church of the Blessed Sacrament (June 1960)." In *History of Churches in Burlington and Alamance Counties*. Burlington–Alamance County Chamber of Commerce, 1963.

Orsi, Robert A. *The Madonna of 115th Street: Faith and Community in Italian Harlem, 1880–1950*. New Haven, Conn.: Yale University Press, 1985.

———. "Mapping the Ground of Children's Religion: A Beginning," unpublished manuscript, 2001.

Osborne, William A. *"The Segregated Covenant": Race Relations and American Catholics*. New York: Herder and Herder, 1967.

Pahl, Jon. *Youth Ministry in Modern America: 1930 to the Present*. Peabody, Mass.: Hendrickson Publishers, 2000.

Palmer, Susan J., and Charlotte E. Hardman. *Children in New Religions*. New Brunswick, N.J.: Rutgers University Press, 1999.

Peacock, James L., and Ruel W. Tyson Jr. *Pilgrims of Paradox: Calvinism and Experience among the Primitive Baptists of the Blue Ridge*. Washington, D.C.: Smithsonian Institution Press, 1989.

Pègues, Thomas. *Catechism of the "Summa Theologica" of Saint Thomas Aquinas, for the Use of the Faithful*. Translated by Ælred Whitacre. London: Burns, Oates & Washbourne, 1922.

Peterson, Linda Whitney, and Milton Edward Hardin. *Children in*

Distress: A Guide for Screening Children's Art. New York: W. W. Norton, 1997.

Piaget, Jean. *Judgment and Reasoning in the Child*. Translated by M. Warden. New York: Harcourt and Brace, 1928.

Piaget, Jean, and B. Inhelder. *The Psychology of the Child*. Translated by H. Weaver. New York: Basic Books, 1969.

Pius X, Pope. *Acerbo Nimis: Encyclical Letter of Pope Pius X on Teaching Christian Doctrine, April 15, 1905*. Washington, D.C.: Confraternity of Christian Doctrine, 1946.

———. *Quam Singulari: Decree of the Sacred Congregation of Discipline of the Sacraments on First Communion*. 8 August 1910. Papal Encyclicals On-Line, <http://www.geocities.com/papalencyclicals/Pius10/p10quam.htm>.

Prothero, Stephen. *American Jesus: How the Son of God became a National Icon*. New York: Farrar, Straus, and Giroux, 2003.

Prout, Alan, and Allison James. "A New Paradigm for the Sociology of Childhood? Provenance, Promise and Problems." In *Constructing and Reconstructing Childhood: Contemporary Issues in the Sociological Study of Childhood*, edited by Allison James and Alan Prout. New York: Falmer Press, 1990.

Qvortrup, Jens, ed. *Childhood Matters: Social Theory, Practice and Politics*. Aldershot: Avebury, 1994.

Qvortrup, Jens, and M. Christoffersen. *Childhood as a Social Phenomenon*. National Report from Denmark. Vienna: European Cultural Centre, 1990.

Raboteau, Albert J. *Fire in the Bones: Reflections on African American Religious History*. Boston: Beacon Press, 1995.

———. *Slave Religion: "The Invisible Institution" in the Antebellum South*. New York: Oxford University Press, 1978.

Reynolds, Edward D., S.J. *Jesuits for the Negro*. New York: American Press, 1949.

Ribeiro, Aileen. *Dress and Morality*. New York: Holmes and Meier, 1986.

Risacher, Rev. John A., S.J. "The Beginnings of a Jesuit Mission for the Negroes of Durham, North Carolina," December 1939–December 1943. Unpublished manuscript.

Rose, Jacqueline. *The Case of Peter Pan: The Impossibility of Children's Fiction*. London: Macmillan, 1984.

Rosen, Harold. *Speaking from Memory: The Study of Autobiographical Discourse*. Stoke-on-Trent, Staffordshire: Trentham Books, 1998.

Rosengren, Karl Sven, Carl N. Johnson, and Paul L. Harris, eds. *Imagining the Impossible: Magical, Scientific, and Religious Thinking in Children*. New York: Cambridge University Press, 2000.

Sack, Daniel. *Whitebread Protestantism: Food and Religion in American Religion*. New York: St. Martin's Press, 2000.

Schechner, Richard. *Essays in Performance Theory, 1970–1976*. New York: Drama Books Specialists, 1977.

Schechner, Richard, and Willa Appel, eds. *By Means of Performance: Intercultural Studies of Theater and Ritual*. Cambridge: Cambridge University Press, 1990.

Scott, Stephen. *Why Do They Dress That Way?* Intercourse, Pa.: Good Books, 1986.

Shreier, Barbara. *Becoming an American Woman: Clothing and the Jewish Immigrant Experience, 1880–1920*. Chicago: Chicago Historical Society, 1995.

Smith, Jonathan Z. *To Take Place*. Chicago: University of Chicago Press, 1987.

Standing, E. M. *Maria Montessori: Her Life and Work*. Fresno, Calif.: Academy Library Guild, 1957.

———. *The Montessori Revolution in Education*. 2d paperback ed. New York: Schocken Books, 1966.

———, ed. *The Church and the Child*. St. Paul, Minn.: Catechetical Guild, 1965.

Stevens-Arroyo, Anthony M. Introduction to *Old Masks, New Faces: Religion and Latino Identities*, edited by Anthony M. Stevens Arroyo and Gilbert R. Cadena. Program for the Analysis of Religion among Latinos no. 2. New York: Binder Center for Western Hemispheric Studies, 1995.

Stoller, Paul. *The Taste of Ethnographic Things: The Senses in Anthropology*. Philadelphia: University of Pennsylvania Press, 1989.

Storm, Penny. *Functions of Dress: Tool of Culture and the Individual*. Englewood Cliffs, N.J.: Prentice-Hall, 1987.

Stradling, Richard. "A Different Vibe." *News and Observer*, 24 May 2002, A1.

Tambiah, Stanley Jeyaraja. "A Performative Approach to Ritual." In *Culture, Thought, and Social Action: An Anthropological Perspective.* Cambridge: Harvard University Press, 1985.

Turner, Victor. *From Ritual to Theater: The Human Seriousness of Play.* Performance Studies Series. New York: Performing Arts Journal Publications, 1982.

———. *The Ritual Process: Structure and Anti-Structure.* Chicago: Aldine Publishing Co., 1969.

Tweed, Thomas A. "Between the Living and the Dead: Fieldwork, History, and the Interpreter's Position." In *Personal Knowledge and Beyond: Reshaping the Ethnography of Religion*, edited by James V. Spickard, J. Shawn Landres, and Meredith B. McGuire, 63–74. New York: New York University Press, 2002.

———. *Our Lady of the Exile: Diasporic Religion at a Cuban Catholic Shrine in Miami.* New York: Oxford University Press, 1997.

———, ed. *Retelling U.S. Religious History.* Berkeley: University of California Press, 1997.

Tyson, Ruel W., Jr., James L. Peacock, and Daniel W. Patterson, eds. *Diversities of Gifts: Field Studies in Southern Religion.* Urbana: University of Illinois Press, 1988.

Van Gennep, Arnold. *Rites of Passage.* Translated by Monika B. Vizedom and Gabrielle L. Caffee. Chicago: University of Chicago Press, 1960.

Vecchione, Patrice. "First Communion." In *Catholic Girls*, edited by Amber Coverdale and Patrice Vecchione, 14–16. New York: Plume Books, 1992.

Vollert, C. "Transubstantiation." In *New Catholic Encyclopedia*, 14:259. New York: McGraw Hill, 1967.

Walch, Timothy. *Parish School: American Catholic Parochial Education from Colonial Times to the Present.* New York: Crossroad Publishing Co., 1996.

Warner, R. Stephen. *New Wine in Old Wineskin: Evangelicals and Liberals in a Small-Town Church.* Berkeley: University of California Press, 1988.

Watkins, Nayo Barbara Malcolm. *Hayti Lived Before.* Durham, N.C.: N. Watkins/Bodacious Consulting Organization, 1998.

Welsh, Janer. "Baltimore Catechism." In *Encyclopedia of Catholicism.* New York: Harper Collins, 1995.

West, Mark I. *Children, Culture and Controversy*. Hamden, Conn.:
   Archon Books, 1988.

Wilmore, Gayraud S. *Black Religion and Black Radicalism: An
   Interpretation of the Religious History of the African American
   People*. 6th ed. Maryknoll, N.Y.: Orbis Books, 1991.

Wind, James P., and James W. Lewis, eds. *American Congregations*.
   Vol. 2, *New Perspectives in the Study of Congregations*. Chicago:
   University of Chicago Press, 1994.

Wise, Jim. "Symbols of Hayti's Grand Past Re-emerge, but the
   Community's Legacy Depends on People Working to Preserve Its
   History." *Durham (N.C.) Herald Sun*, 4 November 2001, C1.

Wordsworth, William. "Imitations of Immorality from Recollections
   of Early Childhood." In *Wordsworth: Poetical Works*, edited by
   Thomas Hutchinson, revised by Ernest De Selincourt. New York:
   Oxford University Press, 1936.

index

nity building at Blessed Sacrament Church, 51; and preparation of children for First Communion, 105, 108–9, 121–22; and prohibition of photography during First Communion liturgy, 197 (n. 10). *See also* Blessed Sacrament Catholic Church

Dalton, Ms., 159
Dance, African, 20, 27, 50, 145–46
Dean (communicant), 86, 93–94, 95, 148, 167, 175, 206 (n. 21), 217 (n. 106)
Developmental psychology, 8–9
Dewey, John, 82
Dodson, Jualynne E., 27
Drawings by children: anxiety produced by, 65; reasons for use of, 65; Coles's use of, 65, 207 (n. 27); and fieldwork methodology, 65–68; pre-Communion drawings, 66, 67, 94–98, 115, 117, 140, 141, 144–45, 148–49, 150; of Host and chalice, 67, 102, 108; post-Communion drawings, 103–4, 113–16, 140–43, 145, 148–50, 216 (n. 87); of dress, 113, 162, 163; of altar table, 113–14, 117; of Mass objects and symbols, 113–16, 217–18 (nn. 106–7); of godparents, 141; of speaking before congregation, 143; of candle lighting, 144; par-

ents' viewing of, 207 (n. 23); Anna Freud's use of, 207–8 (n. 27); of lectern for readings, 217 (n. 104); different perspectives in, 221 (n. 38)
Dress: of First Communicants, 23, 25, 26, 35, 37, 157–66; girls' dresses and veils, 25, 157–62, 164–66, 225 (n. 85); and brides of Christ, 26; boys' outfits, 38, 160, 162–64; drawings of, 113, 162, 163; adults versus children on, 157–59, 163–65
Du Bois, W. E. B., 47–48
Durham, N.C.: Asian population of, 45, 199 (n. 36); Hispanic population of, 45, 199 (n. 36); population of, 45, 199 (n. 36); black businesses in, 47–48, 200 (n. 42); Hayti district of, 47–48, 200–201 (nn. 42–43)
Dwyer, Mr., 57, 104–5, 127

Easter candle, 24–25
Eating. *See* Food; Taste
Ebagh, Helen Rose, 40
Education for First Communion. *See* Faith Formation classes
Elderly, 182
Elizabeth (communicant), 41, 64, 99–100, 115, 116, 139, 154, 155, 222 (n. 49)
Emotions. *See* Anxiety and fear; Excitement and anticipation about First Communion

Epistle to the Galatians, 74
Eric (communicant), 160, 163
Ethics of ethnography, 61–64, 205 (n. 17)
Ethnic identity: of Blessed Sacrament Catholic Church, 40–42, 46–47, 50–52, 175–77; of Holy Cross Catholic Church, 40–42, 47–50; and parallel congregations, 175; children's function as ethnic integrators, 175–77
Ethnography: and children's perceptions as sources, 54–55; and in-between status of author during fieldwork, 55–61; impact of race and ethnicity on, 56–57; impact of gender on, 59–60; and consent of minors, 61–64, 186–87, 206–7 (n. 22); ethics of, 61–64, 205 (n. 17); anonymity of children in fieldwork, 64; and recorded conversations with children, 64–65; nervousness of children during interviews and drawing, 65, 67–68; and drawings, 65–68
Eucharist: taste of, 1, 92–103, 139, 167, 170, 174, 215 (n. 69); union with Jesus through, 18, 30, 74, 99, 105–6, 108–9, 123; consecration of, 23, 103–11; children receiving, at First Communion, 23–24, 25, 31, 36; children's responses to tasting wine, 24, 31, 100–101, 139, 167, 170; eating and swallowing of Host, 31, 100, 107, 139, 167; drawings of Host and chalice, 67, 102, 108; history and ritual practice of, 72–76; and transubstantiation, 73–74, 101–2, 105–11, 170–71; in New Testament, 74; wine used alone for, 74; papal encyclical on, 74, 75, 209 (nn. 11, 15); spitting out, as concern, 74, 139, 209 (n. 11); instruction on receiving, 91–119; wine versus grape juice for, 100, 215 (n. 76), 222 (n. 49); and Last Supper, 121–22, 132, 155; as special food, 122–23; Spanish phrase for, 214 (n. 64). *See also* First Communion
Excitement and anticipation about First Communion, 92–95, 104–5, 153–54, 167, 170–71
Ezekiel (communicant), 20

Fabuel, Ann, 28, 29, 76, 77, 86, 105–8, 118, 127–30, 135, 153, 223–24 (n. 59)
Faith Formation classes: discussion and activities during, 69–70, 71, 85–88, 106–10, 121–23, 127–30; at Holy Cross Catholic Church, 69–70, 80, 83, 85, 87–91, 105–7, 109–12, 128–31, 135, 136; adults' goals and expectations for, 69–71, 105–6, 118–19, 125–29, 139–

40, 151–52; on First Communion history and ritual practice, 72–76; requirements for First Communion, 75–76; and parents' role in First Communion preparation, 76, 78–79, 83, 210 (n. 19); and children's inability to interpret their faith, 76–77; teaching of principles, practice, and participation in, 76–91; and agency of children in faith formation, 77–78; attrition rate in, following First Communion, 79–80, 181–82, 207 (n. 26), 210 (n. 26); and Catholic identity, 79–81; on fundamentals of Catholicism, 81–83; motivations of catechists for teaching, 81; drills used in, 83; Cavalletti's principles for, 84–85; on commandments, 85–86; at Blessed Sacrament Catholic Church, 85–88, 107–9, 112, 121–23, 127–30, 135, 175–77, 213 (n. 54); dislike of, by children, 86, 167; instructional materials for, 88–89; boredom and distracting behavior of children during, 89–91, 129, 175; and receiving the Eucharist, 91–118; on transubstantiation, 105–11; role-playing activities in, 109–10, 127–28; on Mass objects and symbols, 111–18; on Jesus' love, 125–33; on ges-

tures, 134–38; for learning ritual, 173–74

Greven, Philip, 12
Grimes, Ronald L., 5, 13, 15, 52

Hage, Kathleen, 158–59
Hall, David D., 183
Hall, G. Stanley, 82
Hannah (sister of Ryan), 166,
  226 (n. 98)
Hernandez, Ms., 119
Hispanics: North Carolina
  population of, 41, 45–46, 199
  (nn. 36–37); and Catholic
  Church in North Carolina,
  45–47; at Holy Cross Catholic
  Church, 48–49; at Blessed
  Sacrament Catholic Church,
  50–52; use of term, 189 (n. 3).
  See also Blessed Sacrament
  Catholic Church; Blessed
  Sacrament First Commu-
  nion Mass; Spanish-speaking
  children
Holy Communion. See Eucharist; First Communion
Holy Cross Catholic Church:
  gospel music at, 22, 25, 27,
  49–50; food at, 26, 27; ethnic
  identity of, 40–42, 47–50;
  membership of, 47, 48–49;
  history of, 47–48, 49, 51, 200
  (n. 40); white parishioners at,
  48; Hispanic parishioners at,
  48–49; parishioners' leadership of, 200 (n. 41); characteristics of different Masses at,
  201 (n. 51). See also Faith Formation classes; Holy Cross
  First Communion Mass

Holy Cross First Communion
  Mass: preparations before,
  19–20; description of, 19–28;
  African welcome dance at,
  20, 27, 50, 145–46; banner
  for, 20–21, 28, 132, 195 (n. 2);
  homily during, 21–22, 28;
  gospel music at, 22, 25, 27;
  prayers of petition at, 22, 195
  (n. 5); Lord's Prayer at, 23, 28;
  Kiss of Peace at, 23, 28, 34;
  children receiving Eucharist
  at, 23–24, 25; godparents at,
  23–25, 140, 141; photography
  in, 24, 25; candle lighting at,
  24–25; celebration after, 26,
  27. See also First Communion; Holy Cross Catholic
  Church
Host. See Eucharist
Hudson, Ms., 24
Hunt, Jim, 199 (n. 37)
Hunter (communicant), 69,
  100–101, 103, 107, 132, 143–
  44, 150, 155, 160
Hymns. See Music

Immaculate Conception Catholic Church, 176
Initiation rituals. See Rites of
  passage
Instruction for First Communion. See Faith Formation
  classes
Interview questions for parents
  and catechists, 185
Interviews of children: Spanish-
  speaking children choose

English during, 57; compared with interviews of adults, 57–58; gender differences in, 59–60; recording of, 64–65, 206 (n. 12); parents' involvement in, 207 (n. 23)

Interviews of parents, 57

James, Allison, 8, 54
Jeffries, Minerva, 29, 31, 107–8, 152
Jennifer (communicant), 59–60
Jesuits, 47, 49, 199–200 (n. 40)
Jesus: union with, through Eucharist, 18, 30, 74, 99, 105–6, 108–9, 123; and brides of Christ, 26; discussion of, in Faith Formation class, 69–70, 87–88, 121–22; sacraments and Christ's presence, 73; humanity of, 84; as friend, 84, 127–28, 130–31, 220 (n. 17); at Last Supper, 121–22, 132, 155; love of, 125–33, 174; as judge, 127, 131; as good shepherd, 131–32, 147
John (communicant), 20
Jones, Mr., 152–53, 155
José (communicant), 36, 39–40, 66, 95, 103, 143, 150, 154, 173
Judaism, 61, 222 (n. 48)
Julie (communicant), 26, 106
Justin (communicant), 93, 94

Katie (communicant), 1, 11–12, 61, 81, 82, 102, 113, 119, 216 (n. 84), 217 (n. 106)

Key, Mary, 32, 44, 51, 73, 82, 85, 160, 176
Kim (communicant), 28, 31, 93, 135–36, 218 (n. 107)
Kincaid, James R., 7, 13, 14
King, Ms., 48
Kiss of Peace, 23, 28, 34

Last Supper, 121–22, 132, 155
Latinos: North Carolina population of, 41, 45–46, 199 (nn. 36–37); and Catholic Church in North Carolina, 45–47; meaning of term, 189 (n. 3). *See also* Blessed Sacrament Catholic Church; Blessed Sacrament First Communion Mass; Hispanics; Spanish-speaking children
Lauffer, Ms., 77, 132
Lily (communicant), 92, 134, 156, 220 (n. 16)
Locke, John, 7
Lord's Prayer, 23, 28, 118, 128–29
Love: of God, 108–9, 128–30, 147, 219–20 (n. 16); of Jesus, 125–33, 174

MacAloon, John J., 134
Mach, Zdzislaw, 112
Manning, Martha, 158
Maria (communicant), 36
Mary. *See* Virgin Mary/Virgin of Guadalupe
Mass: Holy Cross First Communion Mass, 19–28; bilingual

(n. 3); statistics on, in Durham County, N.C., 199 (n. 36)
Williams, Ms., 20, 69–70, 87–88
Wine. *See* Eucharist
Wise, Jim, 201 (n. 43)

Wordsworth, William, 7
Wright-Jukes, Ms., 26, 88–89, 92, 104, 128–29, 132, 165, 225 (n. 85)

Printed in the United States
88208LV00002B/186/A